P9-DVU-260

D0037745

From Fact to Fiction

Edmund Ware Smith

(EDMUND WARE) and ROBESON BAILEY
pseud.

From Fact to Fiction

New York and London

D. APPLETON–CENTURY COMPANY, INC.

447

PRINTED IN THE UNITED STATES OF AMERICA

Foreword

This book is a collaboration between a writer and a teacher of writing. Its plan developed in the seminar room, to which the teacher had invited the writer to talk to students about the composition of stories. For the subject of his talk, the writer chose one of his own stories, described its origin and development, explained the problems it posed and the devices he used to overcome them or to gain certain effects. Then he read the story aloud. In the concluding period of the seminar, the teacher discussed the wider generalities implied in the writer's preface and in the story itself. The method may be likened to a sandwich—a story between two slices of comment.

Students tell us that the method is good. We think, therefore, that the book may be helpful to people who wish to write professional fiction, and that it may offer teachers a fresh and effective means of presenting some of the techniques in the writing of short stories.

We do not believe that emphasis on "formula," as such, is of much use to the beginning writer. On the other hand, we do strongly believe that learning to write stories, like learning any other highly skilled craft, requires close and painstaking attention to technique. The long quotation in Chapter III explains more fully our attitude toward the writing of magazine fiction. Great thoughts and delicate perceptions are not enough unless one learns to fashion something from them.

The colloquial and discursive quality of the comments is a deliberate effect. Most of the chapters were spoken before they were written, and we have tried to keep something of the ease and good humor characteristic of informal discussion. There is no particular significance to the order of chapters; we suggest that the student read the book in its entirety before attempting to use it, chapter by chapter, as an aid in his own work.

The stories themselves were chosen for a variety of reasons, which accounts for their variety of kind. They range from the serious to the hilarious and represent several contrasting points of view, or methods of a writer's approach to his material. Most of them were chosen to illustrate particular problems. One or two appear because the writer or teacher liked them; one or two for amusement value; and one because it is a love story. With the exception of "Weather Prophet," they have all been published in magazines, and four of them, including "Weather Prophet," have been published in books, either in anthologies or in collections of the writer's stories.

For permission to reprint the stories, the writer wishes to thank Whit Burnett; Herbert R. Mayes, editor of *Good Housekeeping;* the editors of *The Saturday Evening Post;* the editor of *Redbook;* the editor of *Esquire; Story;* and The Derrydale Press. For assistance, not to mention collaboration, in the writing of "Mr. Barstow's Infidelity," the writer is grateful to H. W. Baxter.

The teacher wishes to make grateful acknowledgement to the Bread Loaf Writers' Conference in general, and to two of its staff members, Edith Mirrielees and Bernard DeVoto, in particular. Professor Mirrielees' book, *The Story Writer,* is the best of its kind, and it should be found beside the dictionary on the desk of every writer of fiction. The teacher has leaned heavily on that book for many of his comments, especially those under the heading, "Points of View," in Chapter X.

Thanks are also due the editors of Little, Brown & Company for permission to reprint the long quotation in Chapter III from Bernard DeVoto's *Minority Report,* and Alfred A. Knopf, Inc. for permission to reprint the paragraph from Stephen Crane's "The Blue Hotel." Unless otherwise stated, the brief illustrative excerpts in the teacher's comments are from students' papers or were composed by him on the spur of the moment.

EDMUND WARE
ROBESON BAILEY

Northampton, Mass.

Contents

I

II

III

VII

VIII

IX

X

I

THE WRITER COMMENTS

DISTORTION OF FACT

In speaking to students, or to himself, the writer has been tempted to define fiction; and in giving in to the temptation he has debouched a large number of unsatisfactory definitions, but only one which seems helpful. *Fiction is the purposeful distortion of fact into a unit of truth.* On first examination, this definition seems too glib, having somehow an irresponsible sound, as might an instance of spontaneous combustion. One feels an arrogance in a single sentence which purports to call the turn on a subject as complex, mysterious, and generally elusive as fiction. Yet the sentence is illuminating, and it will stand analysis. Of course the distortion of fact must be successful, as well as purposeful, which leaves the definition with a frayed end. But if you distort so as to achieve the unit of truth, perhaps success is implicit.

To me, the process of distortion of fact is the most useful and most revealing of all the processes at a writer's command. It is also notable that you can create a truth with little or no regard to the fact which inspired your story.

Obviously, not all stories have a spring-board in fact, or actual happening, or circumstance. But a great many of them do. The important thing for the writer is not what happened, but what might have happened; and there, precisely, is where distortion works its way. Supposing, for the sake of a time element in a story's framework, you are compelled to alter the unalterable distance from New York to Chicago. You may change a fact as indisputable as geography simply by changing the names of New York and Chicago to something else. Between your own new cities the mileage may be anything you want for the sake of the unit of truth, which is to say your finished story.

Stories, or their ideas, come from your own set of sense perceptions operating either deliberately or spontaneously against the background of your total experience. Since everyone's experience is different from everyone else's, it is impossible for two individuals to see, or feel, the same story in the same way—much less write it in the same words. One can't even imagine a set of identical twins who could do it. Therefore, it follows that in the manner of telling a story, starting from a given original conception, there is variety equal to the number of writers extant.

Assume that you have a story involving three characters. It is possible to tell it from the point of view of any of them and in the first or third person. Each point of view and every writer would change the story. I am not of the belief that there is one best way to tell a story. But there is probably one best way that one particular writer could tell it. All he has to do is find the way, and make himself believe it the best way while he is writing.

Returning to the definition of fiction, there follows a brief example of a story which started from a fact, and through distortion, or because of it gives, I hope, a final flavor of truth in human experience. The story has appeared in various magazines and an anthology, which gives the writer confidence to discuss it—particularly as the case history of one small fact, and what happened to it.

The story has an added interest because it is one of the few which, in the writer's experience, can be traced clearly and simply from fact to final form. There are none of the ramifications that confuse the origins of most stories.

The fact came into being in a cabin on a lake at the head-waters of the St. Croix River near the New Brunswick border. It was in the month of May. A ten-year-old boy and his grandfather were in the cabin making it ready for the arrival of the owner. One night the grandfather died in his sleep of a heart attack, and the ten-year-old boy walked up the lake shore half a mile to break the news to the nearest neighbor and get help. I learned about the fact eight or nine years after it happened. I read about it in the camp diary, date of May 21, and the entry was written by the neighbor.

Tom Chamberlain died in his sleep last night. His grandson George found him and come up the shore to informe me.

(Signed) John Belmore

There is the fact. The distortion follows. But perhaps it is well to say that the fact stayed in the writer's mind several years before anything began happening to it; yet something must have been happening subconsciously, because the story was written one morning in about an hour—a phenomenon which quite likely fans the writer's affection for it.

The distortion begins at once and involves the little boy. A ten-year-old boy finding his grandfather dead is a touching thing, and if one fools with the idea a while, it may become even a moving thing. Presently you want to write about it so that other people may be moved as you are moved, because this is an incident dealing with life and death, about which all people are curious and in which all people are interested and entangled.

How are you going to make other people feel two, or four, or perhaps ten per cent of the emotion you are now feeling about that boy? The question isn't phrased as consciously as that, of course—but it's there just the same, a working part of your compulsion to express something that is big in your mind and growing bigger.

You know it's a good story—if you can tell it right. It's a wonderful and simple story, but you haven't put a line on paper yet, and you have nothing to go on except that entry in the camp diary written by the neighbor.

Then, step by step, but without any particular order, the steps being in experimental directions, you are starting the story's distortions. For the sake of clarity, the writer has arranged the steps in a sequence more orderly than they seemed to take by themselves.

First, make the boy a little older so that he can feel more, be more articulate, and perhaps understand a little more. Ten years old is too young. The idea of death, you suspect, is just scary to age ten—part curiosity, part wonder, part boogy-man, part not wanting to be alone, and in general somewhat divorced from self. When you're ten, death simply doesn't happen to you.

In the space of a second, the boy becomes seventeen. Why seventeen? Because that's old enough so that his voice has changed, and a good deal of his adolescence has been shaken out of him by hard work and by the businesss of living in the wild lands. But seventeen will also preserve a small portion of that adolescence, and you wish to preserve it because, perhaps, it might contribute some of the stuff of poetry, or dreams, or wondering. How do you know that? Because that's the way it was when you were seventeen. Like others of the same age, you were so full of wondering, and hope, and confidence that there were times when you thought you would blow up—and some of that remnant of adolescence is going to make this a better story.

The next step evolved from story-telling's number one axiom: the more important the event to the leading character, the more important the story. Therefore, that death has got to mean something tremendous to the boy. How are you going to make the death important? You answer: by bringing it closer to the boy, closer than his grandfather was or could be. So you take the grandfather, who did the actual dying, advance him by a distance of one generation, and he becomes the boy's father.

Having now a father and son and having a native caution concerning father-and-son stories because they have a tendency to become teary, you must nevertheless make their relationship a close one. This, clearly enough, is stressing the importance of the death, and it is now becoming apparent that the original fact is disappearing, except for the death.

Meanwhile, you have linked the father and son through a mutual dependency of living together in the wilderness, through their work, and their pride in it, and through a mutual trust and a sharing in achievement. You caution yourself once more against sentimentality. This story is bigger than sentimental, even though shot full of sentiment. The sentiment is all right, because without it, you don't have any story at all. In this case, however, proceed slowly and with regard to red lights.

What about the neighbor that came down to relieve the boy's fears and take charge of things? What becomes of the neighbor, anyway? The thing to do with that poor neighbor is to eliminate him entirely. Distort him right out of the original fact, and you are really getting somewhere. Or rather, the boy is. The boy is in a very terrifying predicament. You have made death a great deal more important to him by obliterating the neighbor. Death is in the boy's lap now—his, alone. Just to make it bite harder, you move the boy and his father 'way up-river on a little lake somewhere, and the boy is then right up against a big thing.

The father is dead. You wonder if he should have died in some unpleasant and dramatic way, such as drowning, or cutting his leg with a broad axe and bleeding to death. No! A red light has blinked, warning you away from a field of luscious corn. You halt, and look backward to the fact, and find that you can save another good thing —the fact of the father's dying in his sleep, dying quietly, without any shooting or stabbing. It's good the way it happened, and you decide to leave it alone, with the father lying there dead in his bunk in the cabin, and the boy alone with him, no neighbors near, and it's twenty-eight miles down-river to the nearest town.

The town must have a name, and you name it Privilege—after a hamlet you once saw located on a lumberman's blue-print map. Privilege has stuck in your memory like some other good names for towns—Falls Church, in Virginia; and Short Falls, in New Hampshire; and Steamboat, Nevada; and Wytopitlock, in Maine.

You have to see and feel that twenty-eight miles of river and lake which leads from the cabin to the town of Privilege, and you must name all the rapids and portages so that they will sound true. This is going to be quite a different journey from a half-mile walk up a lake shore to rouse a neighbor. But the original fact has no importance any more. There isn't even any unit of truth in it. The big truth must be found in the boy's journey down to Privilege with his father's body in the canoe. It must be found in the way the boy faces, for the first time, the flat, unknowable fact of death and its brutal, unprecedented machinery.

In all the boy's world, his father was dearest and most alive. There will be the stunning effect of shock, and there will be the strange momentum of the habit of his father's being alive. This momentum becomes suddenly important to the story's unfolding. It is instinctive in the boy to talk to his father and listen for his father's answer. This illusory business will sustain the boy on his long and difficult journey; it will lead directly to the device of the speed of the trip. The boy knows he isn't going to be sustained forever by the echoes of imaginary words from his father's lips, and so their last trip together is the fastest they ever made.

The writer wishes to make another grateful acknowledgement to the fact which produced "Last Trip Together." The fact gave the story its wilderness background, and until this moment the writer never considered any other. At this belated instant, he perceives a wealth of new methods of writing the same story. How would it be if the boy were riding in the express car from Boston to New York accompanying his father's casket? How would it be if the express agent, riding in the car, told the story from his observation of the scene? It could be a very fine thing indeed, what with the expressman unloading crates of chickens at Worcester, trunks for prep-school boys at Hartford, or armloads of bound skis at New Haven, the while he is deeply concerned with the powerful experience going on inside the boy who is riding with his father's body. However, this writer has written the story once, and it was harrowing enough.

THE STORY

Last Trip Together

My old man laid there in his bunk in the cabin, an' the swamp robins never stopped singin'. First off, it hadn't seemed right for nothin' to be singin', but lookin' at it another way, I was glad of them robins goin' it. Maybe they remembered how he always loved their song an' thought he could hear it now. They was everywheres around in the woods by the lake. They made it seem like the old man might wake up pretty quick an' say: "Web—hear them robins? Storm 'fore night. Better load me in the canoe an' start."

It was twenty-eight mile to Privilege, an' I knew I ought to get a move on, but couldn't seem to. There was things of his in the cabin I couldn't bear to touch, things as much a part of the old man as his hands was: his paddle, his hewin' axe, his watch, an' the pen he wrote in the diary with.

Mr. Usher, the New York sportsman that we built the cabin for, he wanted the diary kept regular, an' Father hadn't missed a day till this one. I went over to the table where the diary laid open with his pen in the middle of it. The date was May 21, an' I dipped the pen an' wrote down how it happened:

Jim Rivers and son Web here since the ice cleared hewing sills and peeling spruce for the addition. He complained bein tired, said when we was done work he would lay abed the next morning to seven o'clock. Last nite we was all done, and this morning I couldn't raise him from sleep, as he must of past away durin the nite.

We are leaving 8 a.m. bound for Privilege. Wind southwest, clear, temp. 58°. This entry by his son Web Rivers.

Father was heavy an' didn't handle good. I had to joggle him an' bump him 'round wrappin' him in the tarp, but I wrapped him fine'ly, an' toted him down to the shore, an' laid him on the beach by my canoe.

I walked back to the cabin to close up an' get a few things. I got my tea boiler an' some tea, an' dippers for us to drink out of. I took my old man's paddle to use on the trip down. Seemed like if I used his paddle, he would be helpin' me, like all the other times.

I put everythin' inside the cabin that the porcupines might chew up. After I locked the door, I went down an' took the middle thwart out of my canoe so he could lay out straight. Then I loaded him an' started for the outlet.

It was our last trip together, an' in some ways the best we ever had. I could really be some use to him now, it seemed. All he'd ever showed me an' told me was clear in my head, an' I had to do the talkin' an' thinkin', an' make the decisions for the both of us.

Off Mink Carryin' Place, there come a blustery breeze. "Father," I says, tuggin' at his feet, "you come to the stern a little. She's bow-heavy." After he come back, the canoe handled good in the cross-chop.

His paddle was sure a good one—thinned down at the handle an' throat, an' the blade edged so 'twould knife the water without a sound. Many's the dry doe we'd sneaked onto an' shot in closed time with him paddlin' with this very paddle, still as a cat on a cushion. He was a good woodsman, my old man was, an' he showed me everything I know.

At the outlet where the lake emptied into the Little Mopang River, I went ashore to cut a pole to set down-stream with. "You wait here," I says to him. "I won't be long."

I found a dry spruce, good an' springy, knotted it off smooth, an' we started again. On the quick water, I aimed to show him everything he had learned me. "Take the left channel, the way the water is," he seemed to say, an' he sure must of been proud, the way I handled her on Ellum Stump Rips, an' the Elbows, an' Hell's Gate. I was good that mornin', an' we made a fast run. I never realized how fast till we come to the long dead-water. I unwrapped the tarp then an' took out his watch, an' it was only five minutes past ten. Twelve mile in two hours!

"It's too fast, Web, an' you ain't had no breakfast."

"That's so, Father! I never thought about it. Where'll we boil her this noon?"

"Same place."

"By that rock across Chancery Portage?"

"Yes, sir. That's where. It'll be out of the wind, an' we can see the lake."

We come down lacin' the suds over the last pitch of rips, an' I throwed the pole away. It was all lake or dead-water from there, an' his paddle made the canoe jump. I lugged him across Chancery Portage an' only set him down once when my heart got poundin' so I was scared it wouldn't hold out. But it made me 'shamed to set him down. "You used to lug me across when I was little. So now it's your turn, Father."

"But there ain't no hurry, Web. Take it easy, boy. We got all day."

When I come with him to the shore of the big lake, I looked out an' seen a black cloud in the northwest. I figured he was right about them robins predictin' a storm, so I set him down comfortable agin' a big pine that would shelter him while I went back for the canoe. I had to take a little time puttin' the middle thwart back in, but she carried faster that way. The shower broke while I was on the way over, but I was dry under the canoe, an' I knowed he was all right, sittin' there under the pine. I found him just like I left him.

I took my belt axe, split some kindlin' off a cedar stub, an' before I had a fire goin' the rain quit, an' it come off hot an' muggy. Flies commenced to hatch all along that shore, an' the big trout an' salmon come boilin' up two or three foot out of water. I never see such a sight in my life, but my old man had.

"I seen it like that just once before—on the west shore of Otter Lake," he said. He'd told about it lots.

"Say, Father! If Mr. Usher was here now with his friends an' their fly rods!"

"You want to set that down in the diary, Web. It's them things he likes to read."

The tea water boiled, an' I throwed in half a handful, let her boil up once more, an' set her to one side. I spilled in a little cold water, an' when the tea settled I poured the dippers full. I picked up my dipper, an' put it to my mouth, an' said: "Wow!"

"Hot, ain't it?" he said.

While I was waitin' for it to cool, Father moved. I heard him an' looked, an' he had slid a little way down the tree trunk, like somethin' had disturbed him. I looked all around to see what was wrong an' found my mistake. I had left his paddle layin' in the hot sun.

"Well, it was rainin' when I got the canoe over, an' I never thought," I says, an' shoved the blade in the water so it wouldn't warp.

"You want to keep them things in mind, Web."

After we'd had our tea, I took out the middle thwart again, an' laid him out comfortable full length, an' shoved off for the last eight mile down-lake.

It was a wonderful time durin' that last stretch, best we ever had. Everywheres on the shore of the big lake was places where things had happened to us, an' we got talkin' about 'em an' laughin'.

" 'Member in there back of Caribou Rock, an' us layin' quiet with a hind-quarter of moose, an'—"

"Yes, an' them two wardens in the canoe went by not two rod from us an' never suspicioned."

Pretty quick we rounded Leadmine Point, an' there was an open place in the trees on shore. "That's where we was bark-peelin' two springs ago, an' them jeesely yellow jackets drove us to hell out, 'member?"

"Yes, an' it was right here—no, maybe farther north—where the squall hit that time. 'Member?"

"I never thought we'd make it that time, Father. Never thought we'd get ashore."

We were away out from Leadmine now, an' you could see just where the Injun Village was by the sun on the white cross on their church. I kep' lookin' over there a long time, till he said: "Web, you keep clear of them young squaws, boy, or you'll hate the smell of sweet-grass the rest of your life."

I laughed, an' the sound set two loons to hollerin', an' then I said: "By God, Father! How'd *you* know about that?"

"You just mind what I tell you."

The loons hollered again, so I laid the paddle on the gunwales, wet my hands in the water, an' whistled to them. Then we started again, an' pretty quick the houses in Privilege come into view, dancin' a little in the distance across the water.

I leaned forward an' says: "What time is it?"

"You take my watch an' quit botherin' me."

So I took it out from his pocket an' looked, an' it was only quarter past one. "Say, did you wind her?"

"I wound her last night. She's goin' all right."

"It ain't only quarter past one. I thought it must of stopped."

"No, time don't stop. It's the fastest we ever made it down, Web. It's too fast. You're beat out. Do like I say, now, an' slow down. There ain't no hurry."

My arms shook clear'n to the shoulders, an' my belly felt crawly, but I didn't feel played out to speak of. Still an' all, every time I give a rake with his paddle, I could hear the water sing along her bows, an' I guess we was travelin' fast.

When we got 'way down below Genius Island, I seen a man on the public landin' at Privilege. He begun to walk back up the hill, but turned an' seen our canoe comin', an' stopped in his tracks. We was maybe a quarter-mile or so away, but he stayed there watchin', like he seen somethin' queer.

There was a dog layin' in the sun on the landin', an' he stood up an' shook, an' looked an' looked, with his nose pointed high.

When I looked toward the hill again, the man was comin' back down to the wharf. He met another man, an' they come on down together. Some others come out of the boat-house an' stood; an' two more that was on the dam come over an' stood.

For a minute, I couldn't figure what the trouble was. I says: "Quite a crowd gatherin' there, Father," an' never a sound from the old man, never no sound at all.

Now, with them standin' there an' starin' on the landin', I knew. They stood there like crows around a wing-broke hawk, only they wasn't cacklin'. They was almighty still. I sided in to the landin', an' felt myself get dizzy, an' reached out an' grabbed the edge of the wharf. I got my balance an' looked up into the faces of them devils standin' there. They done it to me. It was *them* made me see where he hadn't talked at all, an' how all the time it was just me answerin' my own self!

FACT AND FICTION

"Truth is stranger than fiction" the saying goes, and people who have never tried to write fiction refuse to believe it. People who have successfully tried to write fiction will tell you that truth is so much stranger than fiction that you cannot use it as fiction.

What do we mean by "truth"? In this context we mean exactly what Mr. Ware means by "fact." We mean things that exist verifiably in nature; we mean actual experience—the things that happen to people from the outside without reference to their conscience, consciousness, or character, such as the inexplicable good or bad fortune that may befall a man, the grotesque coincidences which shape all our lives. And, for the writer, we mean such minor experiences as Mr. Ware's casual discovery of an entry in a camp diary, experiences which in themselves are nothing, but which, under the writer's self-conscious manipulation, may evolve into significances they never possessed as mere facts, may evolve into other and more important kinds of "truths" about human life.

There are, this is to say, two kinds of truths: one kind interests the writer of fiction, and one kind does not. These two kinds may be called *truth of fact* and *truth of representation.* The fiction writer's interest centers wholly in the latter.

Despite Mr. Ware's thorough discussion of this point, I labor it further because I find it about the most important and difficult for the beginning writer to understand. Year after year I criticize scenes and dialogue in students' stories because they seem to me implausible, and year after year I get the same answer: "But that scene *actually happened.* I know. I was there. And that's exactly, word for word, what was said. How can it be implausible?"

Often this is said in triumph, as though it vindicated the writer's story against the carping of an academician. It is sometimes said with a kind of haughty condescension, as though the poor academic, sheltered as he is from life's sterner realities, had never experienced a violent family quarrel or witnessed a fatal accident, and therefore could not be expected to believe conversation or scenes totally out of his area of experience. But protestations about the factual reality of scene or dialogue are never an acceptable defense of implausibility. Truth, to repeat, is stranger than fiction dares be, and life itself often downright implausible.

"Why is this so?" the student asks. Fiction, at least what we call realistic fiction, is supposed to be the reflection and effect of life itself, of all its possibilities, its tragedies, comedies, achievements, failures, accidents, ironies, and so on. We are always being told to observe closely, to learn how people act under various circumstances, and to report these reactions in our stories as realistically as possible. Why, then, is not the simple transcription of experience the core of all fiction?

The answer lies in this dual nature of truth, in the distinction between truth of fact and truth of representation. For humble illustration, take the experience of Sammy, a city boy who is visiting his country cousin, Bill. Bill is showing Sammy about the farm, explaining various bucolic matters to him. "Did you ever see a sheep?" Bill asks. "No," answers Sammy, "but I want to see one very much." "Come on, then," says Bill, and they go into the barn. There in a stall is a large ram, and he happens to be black. "Take a good look at it," Bill says. *"There's your sheep."*

In that last sentence, Bill has told Sammy both a truth and a lie. Indubitably, that black ram *is* a sheep. He is a factual truth, but he is stranger than the generality (that is to say, the fiction) which each one of us carries in his head. The black ram is a representative lie.

Thus it is with most of the facts of human experience: They are of this dual nature. The writer of fiction is constrained to tell us representative truths about human experience in general, not bizarre exceptions to it. These representative truths are rarely self-evident, plausible, or important in the daily happenings which make up the immediate facts of living. For example, when Mr. Ware tells us in his preface that "A ten-year-old boy finding his grandfather dead is a touching thing, and if one fools with the idea a while it may become a moving thing," we agree with him. But we are not moved. The heartbreak, the agony, the pathos of Web Rivers are only words to us until they become embodied in the solidified generality that is Web Rivers in the story. And, to a writer of stories, the important thing about Web Rivers is that he never existed in fact, but only in Mr. Ware's mind and emotions. He is, however, more convincing than the actual grandson George, because his pull on our sympathies is stronger. Web Rivers is the distortion of a factual truth into a representative one. Both Mr. Ware's preface and the story itself, amply demonstrate the necessity for that distortion.

We are tempted to propound an excellent heresy: *Fiction is not life.* It is far more the effect of life, the picture of life, composed out of the raw material of fact and experience, a different thing entirely from mere transcription. You are told to "write about people, places, and experiences you know at first hand," and it is the best advice. But look carefully at the words. It is one thing to write *about* something and quite another merely to report it, to write down what actually happened or was said.

It must be understood that the writer of fiction is much more than a mere recording clerk of fact and circumstance. He is that, yes, but he is also—and more importantly—craftsman and creator, and he must always be doing two things at once. He must make use of the facts and experiences he observes in himself and others, and he must always be changing them, adding and subtracting from them in order to gain the picture of life he seeks to create within the story he is writing. Two or three paragraphs ago we mentioned pictures. The story-writer's work is analogous to that of the landscape-painter, who rarely paints exactly what he sees, but who first composes the picture in his mind, giving it a form and shape that may have been suggested by nature, but that did not exist in nature. He will move the gray barn a quarter-mile down the road and paint it red; he will bring into his picture a clump of trees that is not there, and he will paint them a more brilliant green than ever they could have been in reality. Composition is the inescapable rudiment of art, and in fiction it is something more than simple reporting. It is the arrangement of the elements of fact, imagination, emotion, and theme into a patterned entity.

FOOLING WITH AN IDEA

There are some ambitious beginners who understand much of the foregoing, but who nevertheless believe, persistently or wistfully, that somewhere stories exist ready made, waiting for the sensitive soul to find them and capture them by the simple process of writing them down. "I want to write," a student once explained. "I want to express in stories something of the meaning of living, something of mankind's nobility and depravity, kindness and cruelty. I want to protest against malice, to extol generosity, to point out the weakness and strength of human beings, their anguish and ecstasy, their aspiration, achievement, and failure. I want to point out that life is often tragic and as often comic. Where are the stories that show these things? What experiences must I undergo to perceive them? Under what cabbage leaves in what gardens do I find them?"

Part of the answer is simple: you don't find them. You make 'em up. The problem of perception is more subtle, and perhaps it is never, or at best rarely, completely solved. Mr. Ware touches on the problem when he speaks of ". . . your own set of sense perceptions operating either deliberately or spontaneously against the background of your total experience." But let us, explicitly at least, confine this discussion to the finding of stories; some implicit help on the problem of perception may come from the discussion.

All you can hope to find of a story is the seed of it within the garden of your own experience and observation. You yourself must plant and transplant it, prune and shape it, and so bring it, at the cost of your own labor, to a mature form. Mr. Ware's preface to "Last Trip Together" charts the growth of that particular tale from seed to story. He found no story in that camp diary. It is no exaggeration to say that you will find no stories in life.

This principle of growth, of change and distortion may be expressed in many ways. J. P. Marquand once expressed it at a writer's conference with marvelous succinctness. He had been asked to define the short story.

"I cannot define the short story," he answered. "But I can tell you what it must do. It must start in a situation, advance to a predicament, and end with a wow."

Story ideas are abundant, and every writer of fiction suffers from that abundance wherever he goes. His friends, chance acquaintances, even his enemies, are always sidling up to him and saying in a spirit of secrecy and great generosity: "I got the most wonderful idea for a story. Want you to write it up. Be worth a thousand dollars to you, but that's all right. Now listen and get this. The other day I was . . ." What follows is no story at all, but at rare best a story situation. Usually, the writer hears only an anecdote that may be interesting enough to the teller, because it concerns himself, but can hardly interest a stranger.

Most stories by beginners fail right there: they do not go beyond the presentation of a situation; they fulfil only the first of Marquand's three requirements. They are only situations or curious anecdotes and do not tell us anything about the representative truths of human experience. They are, perhaps, good story ideas, but an idea is not a story. The writer has not fooled with the idea long enough or intelligently enough to discover within it the real story. He has recognized, perhaps, that "A ten-year-old boy finding his grandfather dead is a touching thing"; he has not understood that it must be made a moving thing, and he doesn't know how to make it moving even when he has understood the necessity.

For an example, here is the outline of a story recently handed in for a college course in fiction. A girl is returning from the Far West to her eastern college. In St. Louis she meets a friend, and they go on a shopping expedition between trains. The girl barely catches her connecting train, and after settling herself in her Pullman seat, makes two discoveries: first, she has, through miscounting or loss, exactly fifty-nine cents to take her through a thirty-hour train ride. Second, her section is shared by a cool and very haughty lady, impeccably dressed, surrounded by expensive luggage. The girl is hot. For the first time she notices how shabby is her own luggage. She feels grubby. She needs the attention of a hair-dresser. She needs a manicure. Her clothes are creased and messy. Her lipstick is wrong. The story tells of the growth of an obsession; everybody, the girl feels, has somehow divined her predicament and is amused by it. At meal-time the cool lady sits beside her and orders filet mignon. The girl, toying with a glass of milk, watches the lady savor each mouthful. When she returns to her seat the girl feels that every passenger is laughing at her, gloating over her irritating misfortune. Her embarrassment turns to shame and resentment, and they become focused on the lady, who has grown in the girl's mind to monstrous proportions of snobbishness and malevolence.

And there, with the development of the situation only, the story stops.

It is a good story idea, but it needs to be explored. Some exploration, together with a firm enough knowledge of what the situation shows about human nature in general, may suggest how to carry the story through Marquand's two remaining musts—predicament and wow.

Let's try it one way: first, the problem of theme, of what the story, in an abstract sense, is about. What is its purpose? To show that the girl was foolish to have spent all her money and must now pay for her foolishness? No. That's too obvious, too preachy. We think some more. We review the situation.

There she is with fifty-nine cents. We could make it any other amount, but the fact that she has that much, which is totally inadequate to her needs, makes her situation even more irritating than if she had none at all. There are thirty long hours ahead of her. She must eat three meals (we'll have the train leave just before lunch time). She must smoke (we'll add that she's an inveterate smoker and just out of cigarettes). She must tip the porter. She must buy newspapers and magazines to keep occupied. All these cost money, and she has fifty-nine cents.

Let's fool with the idea of money. In a situation like this you don't think anything of it—if you have enough. The girl hasn't enough. What does lack of money, at times and places where money is expected, do to people? It makes them horribly self-conscious. Makes them want it desperately. How desperately? Enough to steal? Maybe. That would depend on character and circumstance. Shall we drive this privileged, well-brought-up young lady (already we have made, unconsciously, one decision about her character) to the crime of stealing? Shall we have the cool lady get up to go to the end of the car and leave her pocketbook open on the seat? Shall the girl take this bit of carelessness as a deliberate challenge? Shall it be a trap? Shall we have her steal and get caught? What then? Or shall we have her steal, repent when she's in possession of the money, and give it back? No, we haven't got much there; the idea is too trite.

There are, however, possibilities in the idea that people take money too seriously. We could show weakness of character beneath the outward trappings of self-respect. Maybe we have something there.

But we have this unconscious decision about the girl's character to consider. Somehow, we've grown fond of her. We've been in a similar situation, and we feel a little sorry for her. Certainly, she's displaying weakness, letting that snob get under her skin, making up the whole idea that everybody knows her secret, being so self-conscious about it all. But she is displaying human, understandable, and comic weakness.

By devious processes, then, we've come to the decision that we want to keep this particular story light. We are going to make a comment on the frailty of human nature, but on the forgiveable and comic frailty. We want to preserve the idea that money is nice, but that its temporary lack shouldn't produce false ideas about oneself and other people.

We have decided, then, on the story's purpose, its point, always the most important single decision that can be made about a story. A student once asked me in some despair: "Does a story *always* have to have a point?" The answer is invariably: "Yes." Sometimes this truth or point of a story is very subtle, no more than an author's implied ironical comment on a given situation, or simply the depiction of the way certain kinds of people act under certain conditions. Beginners are too fond of trying to write this kind of story because it looks easy. It takes great skill, born of long practice, to write it successfully. *The New Yorker* and other magazines often publish stories which sometimes are confusing to beginners because they "don't get the point." Be sure that a point is there, that the author wished to convey something more than the mere presentation of a situation, something greater, more general, more *truthful* than the facts themselves. Mr. Ware's "Last Trip Together" is a good example here. Its point is at once subtle in that it is not obviously in the form of a fable, and also simple in that, as he tells us, ". . . you want to write about it so that other people may be moved as you are moved . . . your compulsion to express something big in your mind and growing bigger."

To return to our girl on the train. We have fooled with the idea until we have a purpose for writing the story. But we are still short of meeting Marquand's triple requirement. We have left her in the situation of having too little money and bitterly resenting it. To carry her into predicament is the next step, and it is going to take some more fooling with the idea.

Because this story has never been written, it gives us dangerous latitude. But we must sketch it out somehow. We must build toward something that is intolerable and that must therefore be resolved. *The girl must get some money,* or she thinks she must, which at this point in the story is the same thing. How? And, a further moment of fooling with the idea, why? The last question is infinitely more important. Its answer is that she really is desperate (in terms, of course, of the present situation), driven to desperation by her obsession and the focus of that obsession on the lady opposite. The lady must be shown that the girl is not ridiculous, that she is a person of quite as much self-respect, quite as much dignity as the lady herself. That necessity, if it can be written convincingly, is the predicament.

She must have money. How is she going to get it? Well, since this is going to be a fairly light story she cannot steal. (In another story, the theft itself would throw the girl into her predicament.) Stealing is out of tone with the story and the character of this pleasant but foolish girl. So we look back again. She had enough money to see her through from Nogales to Northampton. What happened to it? She spent too much on her shopping spree? Hardly; she is a student at college, and therefore, at least in the popular mind, not that wanting in intelligence. She meant to save at least five dollars, and if she had, we wouldn't have had a story.

Ah, she lost it. Well, yes, people do lose money, but somehow it isn't very convincing; it looks contrived by the writer just to get her into this jam in the first place. She miscounted? What about that? Did she hand a clerk in a store a ten-dollar bill thinking it was a five? Possibly, but again not probably. She got on the train, sure in the knowledge that she had five dollars and some change. She finds the change but not the five dollars. What happened to it? She is so upset by her discovery and the immediate consciousness of the amused lady that she cannot think what became of it. She only knows she hasn't got it.

There is, then, five dollars unaccounted for, and this gives us the chance to resolve the story. She is going to find that five dollars, and the effect of the finding is going to account for the wow. She is going to remember that her time was running out, that her last purchase cost under five dollars, that she handed the clerk a ten-dollar bill, grabbed the change, and ran for the station. She tucked the bill somewhere about her person, and now she finds it.

She has her five dollars now, and what happens? Her obsession evaporates. She goes into dinner and deliberately sits beside her section mate. She orders a half-chicken. She looks belligerently at the lady, only to discover that the latter isn't concerned with her at all. Soon she is chatting gaily with her former enemy and finds her a pleasant companion. And, just to solidify the story's point, you can, if you dare, have her lose the five dollars all over again, this time for good, and it won't make any difference to her because she has learned something from the experience. You could change many things in the story. If you wished to introduce a romantic element, you could change the haughty lady into an apparently supercilious young man (say a Harvard Senior).

Light as it is, that at least is a story of a kind, whereas the mere situation, the presentation of a girl in a slight jam and her self-consciousness about it, are not anything. That happens to have been the factual experience behind this story. A girl *did* get on a train and found she had fifty-nine cents to cover a thirty-hour ride. There *was* a haughty and expensive lady sharing her section. The girl *did* become obsessed with the idea that the lady, and everybody else, had somehow divined her embarrassment. The girl suffered in silence and hunger and no cigarettes for thirty hours, and got off the train loathing everybody in it. And so what? So nothing at all. For that is one isolated girl, whose experience as such amounts to nothing more than thirty hours of slight discomfort, and who cares about it? To some extent you must make this girl everygirl, or at least manygirls, in order that your narrative may be a story, in order that it may show some fact of experience or of belief in some way important or amusing to many people.

LITERARY DAMP-OFF

Stories, like tender plants, are subject to many diseases and have a depressing tendency to die on you. They sprout in the imagination and there surge to the lusty maturity of four-color illustrations in the seed catalogues. In reality, though they begin bravely enough as seedlings, they frequently wilt, shrivel, and expire. This literary damp-off is common to both professionals and beginners, but far more common to beginners. Reasons for it are as various as the temperaments of individual writers, but a couple of general warnings may help the beginner.

First, when a situation and its generated ideas have taken firm hold of you, stick with them. Contrary to popular belief, successful stories are not "tossed off" in odd moments. Mr. Ware tells us that "Last Trip Together" required about an hour for its writing; he also tells us that the fact behind the story stayed in his mind several years before anything began happening to it. In this particular case Mr. Ware was exceptionally lucky, and he admits it when he tells us that his affection for the story rests on the fact that it required so short a time for its writing. A lot of the work was done by the subconscious. No writer, however, can trust his subconscious to work for him; it is more likely to work against him. With only rare exception, successful stories are sweated out self-consciously. (See the preface to "Angler, Beware!") And Mr. Ware has confessed that he spent three weeks on page twenty-one of his ninety-sixth story!

Finish your story, then. Wrench it through to some kind of conclusion, some approximation of Marquand's three stages of development, however stale it has grown to you. Only after you have really slaved over the hateful thing dare you abandon it. To start a hundred stories and finish none is less valuable to you than to start and finish one. In writing, to do is to learn. Don't expect the writing of stories to be a delightful release from the cares of the world; as a vocation it exists right at the center of those cares and nowhere else. A professional summed up the writer's agony and his joy when he said: "I hate to write. But I love having written."

For the second warning, don't talk about the story you are going to write. Nothing more rapidly evaporates the life juices of a story than hot air. Keep your story alive within you until it simply has to escape, and then guide that escape by pen or typewriter only. Especially, don't talk about it to your friends. Your friends are the loveliest, most understanding people in the world. But until you become solidly professional they will always look at you as though you were related to Dr. Johnson's dog. "A woman preaching," Dr. Johnson said, "is like a dog's walking on his hind legs. You don't expect to see it done well; but you are surprised to find it done at all." Dr.

Johnson was certainly wrong about women, and your friends may be as certainly wrong about you. But the rightness or wrongness of their attitude has nothing to do with its effect on you. Their interest in, and admiration for, your imaginative agility are going to be bad both for you and for your story. Almost certainly your friends are not going to be competent critics.

"But where," the beginner wails, "am I going to find a competent critic to discuss my story with me after it is written?"

We hope this book may be a kind of introduction to him. For the beginner is right. He needs that critic, and yet the critic is a shy fellow, hard to get to know. There are other possibilities of introduction to him—college and university extension courses, writers' conferences, professional writers, if you're lucky enough to know one or two really well, and wide familiarity with the fiction of the past and the present.

Who is this critic? In his full and essential usefulness, he is yourself. His processes and his work are integral with and inseparable from those of the creative writer; he is the balance-wheel of all creative impulses. And with beginners he is, to repeat, a shy, reluctant, and extremely reticent person. Encourage him. Help him develop his powers. For, though he will often assassinate your dearest brain-children, he is in the long run, the only person you will ever know whose judgments, whose *criticism,* you can trust and profitably use.

II

THE WRITER COMMENTS

IDEA FOR A STORY

The lachrymal title of this story is the exclusive work of Herbert R. Mayes who, as editor of *Good Housekeeping* magazine, is a tireless originator of story ideas, including this one. I wanted to call the story "A Place to Be Alone," but Mr. Mayes was firm. Besides, as a matter of policy, it is well to reflect that the editor is almost always right.

Over a period of years, Mayes and I have exchanged a great many story ideas. But a story idea is not a story. It is a sensation, a frame of mind, an episode or an experience, a sample of material—the bare bones which might be assembled into an arm or leg of the story, but never the full skeleton. Mr. Mayes believes in offering his writer the smallest and yet clearest hint, in order that the writer may exercise his talent with a full free rein for his own and the magazine's benefit.

This story is first of all an example of coöperation between editor and writer. Secondly, it is part of the answer to the common question, "How do you get stories?" or, "Where do story ideas come from?"

"A Place to Cry" originated in Mayes' observation or belief that every man should have a room of his own, a place to crawl into and brood, a lair which he may litter with incomplete hopes, cigarette ashes, and the shards of newspapers salvaged from his small children.

It was easy to see why the idea would go well in a women's magazine, since women presumably are interested in men and in why men wish to hide at certain times. It was not so easy to fashion a story from Mr. Mayes' nebula, and we both knew it. However, neither of us dreamed that the story would revolve around violent death in a tunnel through rock, and that its two leading characters would be sand-hogs. One would be inclined to doubt such subjects as fitting the policy of *Good Housekeeping*. The fact of the matter is that taboos are rare in any good editorial office. If the story is good enough, it can be about almost anything, and it will be published.

Concerning his original idea for "A Place to Cry," Mr. Mayes told me this much: "The children have their own rooms. The living-room belongs to the whole family. The bedroom belongs to the wife, even though the husband sleeps there. When the husband feels the need to be alone, he ought to have a place of his own."

If Mr. Mayes had any specific plans for the development of the story, he withheld them. I borrowed a pencil from him and wrote "place for man to be alone" in a note-book. Leaving his office, I returned to the Biltmore Hotel, and by accident got out of the elevator at the wrong floor. Over a door in the corridor near the elevator was a dimly lighted sign saying "Meditation Chapel." Maybe this was something in the nature of the room Mr. Mayes had in mind; but it was in a hotel, not a house.

Obviously, the Meditation Chapel was designed for the use of travelers far from home who wished to cogitate, or pray, or grieve, or lay business plans in religious surroundings. As you looked through the door, you saw an altar equipped with candles and a narrow aisle flanked by high-backed, deeply carved chairs sufficient to seat about fifteen meditators. There was an austere vase containing lilies, some crucifixes, and an appropriate amount of gold brocade hanging on the walls.

The place was heavy with stillness, privacy, and the invitation to prayer. Sitting in one of the chairs, you tried earnestly to meditate, but all you could meditate about was how the management had thought up the idea. Alone in the room, you felt that others must have been alone there, too. Who were they? What did they think about? Why did they come here and from where?

The first thing you knew, you were doing some actual meditating. Certainly, here was a place to be alone. And certainly there was a story in this room—or in any other room where a man went to be alone with all his selves, including the one he might wish to hide from other people. So it follows that in this case a story idea came from an editor in unwitting collaboration with chance and the management of the Biltmore Hotel.

"A Place to Cry" was initially planned and developed in the Meditation Chapel on the third floor of the Biltmore. Unquestionably the solemn atmosphere colored the story and even established its tone. Such an influence is pure accident—of the kind which, I believe, colors many stories. What produces the frame of mind that enters so powerfully into the minute selection of the words themselves? The answer may be a bar of music, the shape of a cloud, the scents of spring, or the first snow of winter. In short, the answer may be anything.

I have since returned to this chapel in the hope of assembling the skeletons of other stories or putting the heart in them, but to no avail. It wouldn't work again, perhaps because of a self-consciousness engendered by remembering how well it worked the first time, or perhaps because it is often difficult to meditate in a place deliberately arranged like a trap set for the purpose.

Beginning with the curious sensation induced by the chapel's atmosphere, the story grew into its final form in the writer's mind. The process lasted about half an hour. The story's background turned out to be several light-years distant from its stimulus, as is frequently the case. Diversion tunnels through rock and sand-hogs, and the hazards of subterranean construction appear to have no possible association with a tiny altar in a New York hotel. But the connection is there, by reason of sensation and as a result of some necessary questions that the writer asked himself in building his tale—this one, or any other he may write.

Who is the leading character? He is a man. Is he married? Yes, because he must have a house occupied by his wife, his children, and himself, and at some point in the story, this house must have a room for him, and in this room he will eventually find solace or a particular kind of privacy.

Does he need this solace or this place to be alone? Yes, because that is the original premise. Then why hasn't he asked for it and got it, if he has lived long enough to be married and have children? Perhaps he has always denied needing it. That, the writer feels, might make an interesting basis for a conflict within the man.

What kind of man is he going to be? All you know about him is that he is going to do some crying, even if it's the silent kind. It follows at once that this man must not cry easily, otherwise the emotional conflict is diminished.

What kinds of men do not cry easily? There are a great many kinds.

What kinds among those the writer has known? And in what backgrounds that he knows intimately enough to handle realistically? There are flyers and flying, lumberjacks and lumber camps, horse racing, high steel, and finally the experience of two years underground in tunnel construction.

A lot of things happened underground in the tunnels to some very tough men, and if they did any crying, they did it alone. The reader must realize that it wasn't necessary to choose a tunnel man. The choice was by accident of one writer's experience. There are doubtless innumerable bookkeepers, mechanics, professors, and plumbers who do little if any crying. But the underground background, besides putting the writer at ease with his material, offers opportunities for sudden death, chances for being buried alive, and other tests of human fortitude. Thus, by accident, the story takes its background which automatically provides a leading character who doesn't cry easily.

How can the character's scorn of emotion be made even greater? The greater his scorn, or his control of tears, the greater the moment in the story when he is himself overwhelmed. How has he built up his antipathy, beyond the restraint that a good, tough man might possess? Has he hated someone who has given way to tears? That might help, but it would be stronger if it were someone he loves and admires. Who is this someone who has influenced the leading character, and how does the psychology work? The someone obviously can't be a woman, because women, by chivalry, or act of God, or by story-tellers are awarded a liberal allotment of crying—except when they're really hurt.

So this other person must be: (*a*) a man; and (*b*) someone whom the leading character admires and loves. Assume that the leading character, as a small boy, has heard this magnificent person cry. It has perplexed and to some extent disillusioned him because he had supposed the person to be the bravest man on earth, and he had understood—perhaps erroneously—that the brave shed no tears. But he has eavesdropped upon this person's weeping, and it has so affected him that he is a thousand times against so much as a damp eye.

At this point the story has only its leading character, somewhat conditioned, and a background where the shock of disaster can strike logically and bring the character in conflict against his own emotion.

The emotion is going to make him want to be alone for fear he will give in to it in someone's hearing, as his own hero did so long ago. Where is he going to let go his hold on his emotion when it bowls him over? He is going to do it in a place to cry, a room in his house. The room is going to be provided for him by his wife at the instant in his life when he needs it most, and his wife is going to understand exactly why he needs it. This means: (*a*) that the wife must know all about her husband's aversion to emotional display, (*b*) that she must know of the event which breaks him down, (*c*) that she must have moved the family into a new house in which there is a suitable crying room, and (*d*) that the husband must not have seen the house. The last two items seem improbable at first glance. At second glance they seem not only probable, but so much in keeping with the background that they actually enhance it. For obviously, construction men are constantly on the move, their wives constantly finding new houses.

The wife, then, becomes a strong incidental character, and the two children may also be put to work for the story. They shall be boys, and they—or at least one of them—shall be present when the big moment is about to happen. The presence of the boys will give tremendous emphasis, or reëmphasis, to the early episode which conditioned the father against weeping.

There are two questions of great importance as yet unanswered: First, what happening can be cruel, or frightful, or tragic enough to break down the leading character's resistance? His resistance has been built to a point where it seems unbreakable, and yet the story compels you to break it. How? The event will take place underground in a tunnel, and that's your only lead for the time being. It looks as though there would be a cave-in in the tunnel. It looks as though someone would be obliged to die under a ton of granite—or at least get badly injured. You know exactly what the scene will look and feel like, and it tends to get out of proportion. What happens in the tunnel is not the big thing. The big thing is what happens inside of the leading character. The cave-in is just the detonator.

How about having the leading character himself get that ton of granite in the neck? No. That wouldn't go with the story; because, if the leading character got crippled, he would be crying about something that happened to him, not in him. The accident, therefore, must happen to someone else, and you can't think who it is; the whole story turns to ashes because it is all beginning and no ending.

You go back over your previous planning again and again, until, through the dim and beautiful light of the Biltmore Meditation Chapel, you perceive the identity of your man, and you love him so profoundly for revealing himself before you that you feel like a murderer for dropping rocks on him from the ceiling of the tunnel and crushing him to death.

The second important question is: How are you going to tell the story now that it is formed? Or, rather, who is going to tell it? Are you, or is the leading character? The leading character, or the first person, is tempting, and it has the feeling of rightness. The story seems to have greater depth of feeling when told by its major character. It could be told by his wife, but the story is really his. It is the revelation of a man facing something too big for him, and he has every right to tell it in his own words if he wants to.

But how? He must present his basic conflict in the opening paragraphs with a humility becoming him in the face of tragedy. That is one excellent reason why, at the story's opening, the tragedy has already happened. It is so recent in Rush Atwood's heart and mind that he hasn't seen it clearly in its full reality. But Rush comes up out of the tunnel shaft into the daylight knowing he is licked in his lifelong struggle against the display of emotion, and that is why he is trying desperately to maintain his control till he can get home.

What has happened in the cave-in, and to whom, is withheld from the reader in a logical way, because Rush Atwood, who is telling the story, is withholding it from himself. Since Rush cringes from facing it, the suspense is not only heightened, but its device is made to appear more natural, or less of a trick. Rush has got to wait till he gets home before he takes a straight look at what happened in the tunnel —and so has the reader. This gives Rush a chance to tell his personal history to himself and the reader through reflection and memory, and makes it still more reasonable that the identity of the person who died in the tunnel isn't revealed till the last line in the tale.

THE STORY

A Place to Cry

THIRTY-SIX hours after the cave-in, I came up out of the tunnel into the afternoon sunshine. I had been so long in the underground gloom that it took me several seconds to get my eyes accustomed to the light. The first person I saw clearly was a young doctor standing beside the ambulance at the head of the shaft. He came over to me and said: "Mr. Atwood, don't you think you better take a shot of morphine?"

"No thanks," I said, and stood there rubbing the two-day stubble on my chin.

Three or four of the fellows who had worked on the rescue crew looked at me. I saw in their eyes what I wanted to see: Rush Atwood can take it, their eyes said. Rush Atwood can take it! But the words in their eyes didn't do any good at all, because I was Rush Atwood, and for the first time in my life I knew the words weren't true. The cave-in had taken everything out of me, and put nothing back. I wanted that morphine. I wanted oblivion. But only the man who was killed in the tunnel had earned the right to that.

Dutch Lauer, the safety engineer, opened the door of the compressor house and called: "Rush! Your wife's on the phone again."

The outside phone was in the locker room in the compressor house. The men on the four o'clock shift were changing their clothes, getting ready to go to work. When I came in, they stopped talking, and their eyes told me that lie again: Rush Atwood can take it!

Walking across the room to the phone was like an act that no longer has meaning. I didn't want to see or be seen. I wished I were one of those little animals that crawl into their burrows and curl their tails around their tired bodies, burying their faces in their own fur, hiding from life, and death, and the unanswerables; hiding even from the fact that they are hiding, and therefore no longer brave.

"Hello, Marge," I said into the phone. My hands were steady, and my voice calm in my own ears, and it was like a preposterous kind of cheating.

"Rush," Marge begged, "can't you come home—now that it's all over?"

I remembered that Dutch Lauer had told me she had been on the phone almost constantly since the trouble started. It must have been terrible for Marge to stay away, knowing what she knew, knowing me as no one ever did. She felt what was happening in me as if it were happening in herself, and she told me a long time later that was why she stayed away—that, and the children.

"Yes, I'm coming home," I said.

A quick sound of relief came over the wire, and then she asked: "Are you all right, dear?"

"Yes," I lied. "Did they tell you what happened?"

"Yes, Rush. I know all about it. I know everything—absolutely everything. You won't need to talk about it."

How did Marge know I didn't want to talk about it? How does a woman know so much about a man? Does she live only to learn the truths he has concealed from himself by means of unwitting falsehoods? From the day we met, Marge must have known that something like this would overtake me. She knew I hadn't dared think about it yet.

"How is the new house?" I asked.

That question was a manifestation of the way my mind was

dodging around, evading. I had talked to her on the phone a dozen times about the new house. Marge wanted to be near Boston where the children's schools were better, and she had settled the new house three weeks ago. If you are a construction engineer, you live in a lot of different houses, following jobs around. I hadn't seen this house yet. We had struck bad rock in the tunnel from the start, and I had been on the job steadily. Now, I had a premonition that this was going to be a strange home-coming. I was afraid to go home, afraid that Marge might see too much and love me less for what she saw.

"We're all ready for you," Marge said. "The house is lovely. It—wait a second, dear! Ted wants to speak to you."

I heard my five-year-old say: "Hi, Dad!"

"Hi, Ted," I answered. "How are you?"

"I'm fine. How are you?"

Then Mike, who was a year younger, had his innings. He said exactly what Ted said. They always say that, and it's always important to them. They were getting security from me, as I had got it from the sound of my father's voice, and he from his father's. But who was I, now, to give my sons security? I had just learned that there isn't any. When, and how, would my sons learn?

After I said good-bye to Marge, I nodded to the fellows in the locker room. They were filing out on the way to work, and one or two of them said: "Hullo, Rush," but nothing more. They were mighty quiet and decent.

I opened my locker and changed my wet oilskins for street clothes; but for some reason I decided not to shave till I got home. I was to discover that so trivial a decision as that can bring crazy consequences. I walked out of the locker room, rubbing my two-day beard, my mind jumping off little precipices leading back to the goodness of the past. I guess I needed to think of some clean, simple, happy things.

I got into my car and drove toward the main highway, saying to myself: there are so many clean, simple, happy things. Get your mind onto them, and keep it there. So pretty quick, when

I turned into the main highway and settled down for the drive home, I got hold of something good out of my boyhood. . . .

My father was shaving in the bathroom of a house I can't remember. I could see his back and hear the scraping of his old-fashioned razor, and the muscles of his arms were magnificent. So were the faces he made when he shaved his chin and jaws. I stood beside him, worshiping, hungering to be like him, to be as strong and laughing as he, and as wonderfully made. In the memory, he looked down at me and said: "Pete's sake, Rush! Can't you leave me alone? You've watched me shave often enough."

"Will I have whiskers, Father?"

"Sure you will!" He smiled and brushed some lather on my face, and the soap smelled clean. "That'll make 'em grow, Rush!"

"I get awful tired waiting for 'em, Father!"

Then Father called to my mother, who was downstairs getting breakfast. His big voice boomed out joyously in the house: "Mina! Who stole the key to the bathroom?"

"I did," I said. "So I could come in here and be with you."

He made a funny face at himself in the mirror and to his reflection said: "Nick, your last stronghold is gone!"

"What's a stronghold, Father?"

"Place to be alone."

"But I don't ever want to be alone."

"Ah," he said, and suddenly stooped and kissed the top of my head. . . .

That memory lasted me all the way to Worcester, and it made me happy. It seemed so tender, so reassuring, so remote from what had happened in the tunnel during the past thirty-six hours. And yet that memory trapped me in another one which must have been lying in wait, buried in the deepest part of me ever since I was six or seven years old. The association was the word "alone," or "place to be alone"—my father's words.

This other memory was not a happy one. It troubled me, and

as I drove through the five o'clock traffic of Worcester, I could feel the memory steering me along into the present. I wasn't ready to look at the present. I wasn't sure, yet, that I could stand looking at it. The cave-in, and the man dying underground, and all that it meant seemed to be sliding toward me like the prow of a great, dark ship coming through the fog—blurred, but looming inevitably nearer. . . .

One winter afternoon while I was playing in the street, I looked up and saw my father coming home. It was not time for him to come, but there he was, striding along, his eyes straight ahead.

"Hi, Father!" I cried, overjoyed.

He didn't turn, or wave, or answer me. He walked up the steps into the house, and I followed at his heels, yearning for his attention. He went right upstairs to the bedroom where he and Mother slept. He closed the door, and I stood in the hall, hurt, puzzled, and uncertain. Then I heard the sound that frightened me so I must have spent twenty years trying to forget. My father was crying! I couldn't believe it. I was shocked and terrified; and I was ashamed.

I was wandering around in the upstairs hall when the front door banged. It was my mother. She must have heard Father the instant she came in, because she rushed upstairs without dropping the bundles she had brought from the market. She was white as a ghost, her face all tense and hurt.

"Rush!" she gasped. "Go away! Go downstairs!"

"Gosh, Ma—Dad's crying. We got to help him!"

"He's helping himself. Go away, Rush—quickly."

"But—Ma—he's all alone!"

"That's what he wants."

"Why, Ma? Why?"

"So he can talk to himself, and let himself go, and put himself together again."

"But why is he crying so?"

Mother was pushing me along the hall away from the bedroom door. She leaned over me, and I remember the smell of hot baker's bread from one of the bundles she held.

"How do I know why he's crying," she asked softly, "when he probably doesn't know himself? He's tired—dead, dead tired. He's worked like a dog. He ought to have a decent place of his own to let go in."

I was sick with disillusionment. I knew that it was cowardly to cry, but that my father was crying. I couldn't reconcile these things with my adoration for him.

Mother came downstairs with me, and we went out into the kitchen and closed the door. I went straight to a cupboard and got out a hammer, and when I was sure Mother was watching, I brought the hammer down hard on my thumb. The pain made my whole arm quiver. I looked up at Mother, gnawing my lips, and I said: "I'm not going to cry—never in my whole life!"

She came over quickly and kneeled down, enfolding me in her arms as if to shield me from all the brutal warfare of existence. I closed my eyes against her, glad of the darkness and of her warmth. I was too young to understand what she meant when she said: "Rush, dear, it isn't the same kind of hurt."

Thinking so intensely of that time long gone, I didn't realize I had driven through the city of Worcester till I noticed a sign on the big cement turnpike reading: Boston 39. In less than an hour I would be home. I would be facing Marge and the children. I shut my jaws so tight my teeth ached, and I said inwardly: They won't see anything! They won't see anything! Don't let them see!

The electric clock on the dash panel of the car said half past five. The early spring day was soft and tranquil, and for a while I let myself look only at the land and sky. I thought: There's a time when you know that spring is near, when the earth is gentle, and the snow lies dying in the ditches, and you feel that a moment for which you have lived is at hand.

Where had I known that feeling before? When had this fleeting sense of fulfilment poured into me, giving me faith in the goodness and validity of life? The times with Marge came crowding into my heart, and they kept at arm's length the prow of the great, black ship that was moving in to crush me. But the ship was invisible now. I was on the open road home, and the sleepy hills were touched with an omen of green. I thought of Marge, and of the nights I had held her in my arms, and of one night in particular. . . .

Six years ago. We had been married only a few months. I was twenty-two, invincible, and proud. But on this night I was specially proud. I had just been through my first bad trouble underground, and I couldn't wait to tell Marge I had been brave. Walking high and fast, callous in the excitement of myself, I came home to lay my triumph at Marge's feet. I went in by the kitchen door of that first little cottage we lived in. Marge was waiting for me there. It was very late. She was wearing her night dress and a silk kimono and slippers, and when she came toward me the sound of her slippers made me tremble.

I began to spill out what had happened, who had been hurt and how, and I kept repeating a compliment the heading-boss had handed me on some minor feat of rescue work. Marge stood near me, staring, her lips parted in a strange half-smile. I could feel her eyes looking far into me, and my voice ran thin on the subject of myself. I said: "What do you see, when you look at me that way?"

"You," she answered.

"What do you mean?"

"The man I love."

I caught her in my arms, and drew a long breath against her hair, and kissed her till my lips hurt. What did Marge learn about me from a look, a voice too wildly pitched, a kiss too hungry and distraught? Did she see and feel the little boy who wouldn't cry because he'd heard his father crying?

I couldn't sleep that night. In the dark I was living over the turmoil of the day. I didn't want Marge to know it. I tried to breathe evenly and lie very still beside her in our bed. Outside in the grass there was a cricket, singing and singing, and a shaft of moonlight grew in the night and leaned into the room. Marge's voice seemed to come out of nowhere: "Do you want to talk?" she said.

I made a pretense of waking up. "Did you say something, Marge?"

"Do you want to talk—about anything?"

"No—too sleepy."

"Do you want a drink of something?"

"No."

"You're—you're sure, Rush? There's nothing you want?"

"Not a thing."

She was dead quiet for a long time, and I could almost feel her longing to help me, wondering how she could help me. If I'd only had sense enough to understand! She knew I was in the middle of a bad time, even if I didn't. The cricket sang and sang in the grass outside, and the shaft of moonlight moved its patient path. And out of nowhere again came Marge's voice: "Don't you want me, darling?"

"Yes."

Now, nearing home in the sunset, driving along as if nothing had happened, driving through those nice towns west of Boston, I saw how impossible it was to keep the black, iron ship away much longer. It was close. The mist veils hiding it had thinned. Every thought designed to blur the present, had ended somehow by bringing it into sharper focus.

Again, fast out of childhood, that one unhappy memory of my father thrust at me. So cunningly concealed till now, it had conditioned a part of my behavior for more than twenty years. I began to examine some of that behavior with a kind of precarious calm. . . .

There was a house we lived in for two years on the outskirts of a city. My father lived with us there for a time. That was just after my mother died, and Marge was wonderful to him. He was wonderful to Marge, too—and to all of us. I was studying engineering at night-school, and when Father was in the house, the children never bothered me at all. I could study anywhere, any time.

Our boys were two and three, and they worshiped Father. He brought them toy steam-shovels, dump trucks that really dumped, Bucyrus-Erie diggers, and all the fabulous machinery of construction. He'd explain in clear, simple language what each machine was for and how it worked, and Ted and Mike caught on. Father played with them by the hour, and when bedtime came, he'd ride them upstairs on his back.

Marge and I marveled at his way with children. There was something deep and vast about him that they understood. Marge said he knew himself and through himself all others. I can see him now: on all fours in the sand-box in the yard, his brown neck arched, and his dark mane of hair falling over his forehead, his hands moving slowly in the sand as he and the children worked out some problem. Once, when the kids got impatient, I remember his saying: "You want to take a job slow, boys. Always have respect for the earth, especially when you're moving it."

The way he spoke and the way his grandsons listened, you'd think it was poetry. The children will remember that year. After Father left, something happened that makes me remember it, too.

The only chance I had to study for my night classes was between four o'clock and supper time, when I got off the job. And that was the only chance Ted and Mike had to play with me. One afternoon when I was trying to study calculus, they clustered around me, yelling for attention. I was tense with fatigue. I jumped up. I wanted to run away, and there was no place to run. I said something harsh. Marge overheard me and came into the living-room, her eyes bright with that quick, aware-look. She didn't say anything then—just hustled the boys into the kitchen.

That night, when I came home from classes, Marge said: "You're going to have a place of your own, dear. I'm going to fix up your father's room for you."

I felt cold all over, as if she had discovered something degraded in me. Did I hear, in that instant, the echo of my father's crying?

"Just what do you mean?" I asked.

"I think you need a hole you can crawl into."

"Like hell!" I snapped. "I work in holes all day."

Marge smiled. She had heard the defensive resentment in my voice, and it started her thinking. "Rush, dear, you don't understand. The living-room is the family's. The bedroom is more or less mine. The boys have their rooms, but you haven't any place that's just yours."

"I don't need one! I've got nothing to hide!"

"But everyone, no matter who he is, wants a place of his own."

"Not I! I'm different!"

"But, Rush! Your father always wanted a place like that."

"How do you know that?"

"He told me so, dear."

"Then I'm different from my father! Do you hear?"

Marge looked at me exactly the way she had looked that first night when I came home with trouble in my eyes, that night the cricket sang in the grass, and the moonpath moved along the bedroom floor.

"No, Rush," she said slowly, "you're not different from your father. You're like him!"

It was the finest thing that anyone ever said about me, and I didn't know it! I didn't know it! . . .

I didn't even know it now! Driving on the turnpike, so close to home, and the dark just coming, the old resentment caught me. I found our street in that town near Boston, and I turned into it, saying: Don't let them see! Don't let them know!

It seemed that all my thoughts and all my memories had added up to a kind of cheerful half-bitterness, an almost savage resolve to act as if nothing too big for me to stand had happened.

I found the house without any difficulty. Marge must have been watching for me. She opened the front door just as I drew up to the curb. She stood under the porch light, looking out at me, her eyes shadowy. She was wearing a white working dress that always reminded me of a nurse's uniform. Ted and Mike squeezed past her and rushed down the steps into my arms. They squirmed against me, competing for hugs, and I gave them three apiece. They felt warm and alive. They didn't know anything had happened. I thought: You'll never hear your father cry! The thought caught me so unaware that I had a horrible feeling I had spoken aloud. But I hadn't.

"Marge!" I said, going inside, "this is some house!"

She didn't say anything. She held out her arms, and her face was haggard. I kissed her and hung onto her for a moment. Then I said: "Did my beard scratch?"

"I don't mind. You know I don't."

"I ought to shave."

"Wait till after supper, Rush."

"All right."

It was all so commonplace and casual, but each knew what the other was thinking and trying not to think. Marge showed me around the new house. I saw all the old things in their new setting: the lamps, the books, the chairs, the rugs, and the pictures. I thought how many times Marge had moved these things, and I said: "You still like being the wife of a construction engineer?"

She blanched, lifted her hand to her mouth, and bit her knuckles. She thought I was referring to what had happened in the tunnel.

"I—I just meant moving so often, Marge," I said.

"Oh. You know I don't mind that." She sighed and looked at me in a tender, critical way. "You haven't had any sleep, have you?" she asked.

"Not much. Have you?"

"Not much."

We ate supper, and it was almost a happy time. Afterwards, Marge went into the kitchen to wash the dishes. I played with the boys in the living-room. They had a couple of toy tractors with rubber caterpillars, and I put a waste-basket under a rug, making a hill for them to send their tractors over. When they seemed content and absorbed, I went up to the bathroom to shave.

Marge had my home shaving kit in the mirror cabinet, and I got out a new blade, and lathered, and started shaving. My hands were steady as stone, and I knew they were cheating. My eyes looked exactly like my eyes, and it seemed unnatural that they reflected nothing of what they had seen. My mind began drifting, and presently there was no sense of time or location. I had the queer feeling of being in two places at the same instant, and a voice said: "Will I have whiskers, Dad?"

Present and past! My own voice, speaking to my father long ago! But my lips hadn't moved! The voice came again, and I stared straight into the mirror. My lips were tight shut and white.

"Dad, talk to me. When will I get whiskers, to shave?"

I looked down, frightened. Beside me at the wash-bowl stood my oldest son, his lips parted and moist, his eyes luminous with mystery and longing. He had come in so quietly I hadn't heard him. I didn't know how long he had been watching me.

I reached for my shaving brush, and my fingers weren't steady any more, and my heart hammered in my chest. In the mirror my face turned old, gray, and sick. I touched the brush against Ted's cheek, and said: "You'll have whiskers, some day. That'll make 'em grow."

My voice sounded husky, like dry sand sliding off a shovel. I tried to call Marge, and it quit altogether. I tried again, and she heard me, and came running up the stairs. That queer time-confusion got into me again, and I expected to see Marge holding some bundles from the market, and one of the bundles would smell of hot baker's bread. Somehow it seemed that Marge ought to be my mother. But she was Marge, and she was holding a dish towel.

"Ted!" she gasped. "Go away—please. Downstairs."

I heard Ted go, but I didn't see him. I was staring into the mirror, and the glass seemed to part like mist, and out of the mist came the prow of the black, iron ship, and it crushed me. I turned away, my hands over my eyes.

"Marge! Marge—"

"Yes—I'm right here. What is it?"

"I can't stand it! I can't look at it, and I can't see anything else. I've got to go somewhere. I've got to get alone—quick, Marge! Is there a—a place I can go?"

"Yes."

She led me along the upstairs hall to a room at the end, a room she hadn't showed me before. She didn't look at me, because she knew I didn't want her to see me like this. But suddenly I wanted to say something to her, just some little thing to let her know I loved her more than anyone on earth. I said: "Marge—"

She looked at me, then. There was a question in her eyes, and I answered it with another question: "Remember the night you said I was like my father?"

"Yes," she said, and her eyes were wet.

"You were right," I said. "Only I'm not half the man he was."

"Yes, you are, Rush! You are!"

I still didn't know what the room was going to mean to me, but Marge did. I wondered if she had known I would need it now? I would never ask her, and she would never tell me if I did. It was just there when I needed it. I touched my lips against Marge's eyes and went inside, and she closed the door.

I was alone with myself for the first time in my life. I stood still for a moment, remembering the deep, half-visionary expression in Marge's eyes. Her expression had told me everything about the need to be alone and about the times the need comes.

For me, it just happened to be a time when things were too terrible. But as I stood there in the half-dark, I saw how the need might come in any overwhelming moment, when life is too big or too small, too rich or too sterile.

I saw what a magnificent range of experiences might bring to a man the impact of life: a death may bring it, or a birth; the song of a bird, or a stranger's glance; the coming of spring in a familiar land, or of winter in a wilderness; the sound of laughter or of tears; a woman's lips, or the eyes of a child, or the smell of blossoms in a humid night; the cross on a white church or the echo of prayer in a cathedral; or the too intense asking of all the unanswerables: Who am I? What am I, and why? Wither am I going? Why did I begin, and where will I end? And why, oh why, has this thing happened to me?

The only light in the room came from a street lamp outside, and that was very dim; but I could make out a few familiar things: my old drafting board, a few pictures identified merely by the size and shape of their frames, a table, a couple of chairs, and a sofa.

I went over and lay down on the sofa and put my face into a pillow. I looked at what I couldn't bear to see. I saw the inside of the tunnel again, a hundred feet underground. I heard the racket of the air drills, boring into the rock. I sniffed the silica dust, and through it saw the sheen on men's backs and the corded muscles of their arms.

Then I heard the rock-slide and saw a ton of granite drop from the ceiling, pinning the man to the rock floor of the tunnel. Why, oh, why did gravity and granite choose that man? Why not I? Why not some other? There is no answer!

The man did not die right away. He lay on his back, and his chest was broken. *His* chest, the chest of the one who had trained us all, who had told us with what respect we must regard the earth in which we burrowed. This was the man who was trapped under the brutal weight of stone!

I could see his dimming eyes and in them the knowledge he was going to die. I saw the life running red from his smashed body, staining the gray rock darkly. He said so much, who could not speak, whose every breath was agony! He was young and did not want to die. He was always young, young in his body, young in his spirit, younger in some ways even than his son! His death was like no other death. The man was like no other man. He was the man who began me, and whatever in me is good came straight from him. He was my father.

THE TEACHER COMMENTS

BACKGROUND AND ATMOSPHERE

A tough critic, who is also a successful writer of fiction, was lecturing to a group at a writers' conference. He had been remarking that too many stories by beginners spend too much space describing places, sunsets, storms, the song of birds, the feel of grass underfoot, the sound of wind through pine trees, and white clouds sailing across an inevitably azure sky.

"Fiction is first, last, and always about *people,*" he concluded. "It is not about meteorology, ornithology, dendrology, or even architecture. What interests us is the woe of the heroine; not the state of the weather."

He stopped and glared. You could feel that he was daring someone to challenge him. He didn't have long to wait; a determined lady took him up.

"But what about atmosphere?" she asked.

The timing of his answer was perfect; just then the bell struck the end of the lecture period. He waited several seconds, still staring as though he hadn't heard the question. Nobody moved. Then he turned his head slowly and looked hard at his questioner.

"Madame," he said, *"never have atmosphere."*

The imperative may seem extreme, but the principle is sound. Of course all fictional characters must be located, and definitely located, in time and space, but they mustn't get lost in them. You must remember that the business of story-telling is story-telling. Take it as your motto; write it out in block capitals and paste it on the wall in front of your work desk. Maybe it will help you to stick to your story when you are tempted to wander away from it.

The principle may be stated and developed in a number of ways. Here are a few of them:

Description for description's sake (or for "atmosphere's" sake) is no part of fiction. If you doubt it, analyze the passages you tend to skip in other people's stories.

Look suspiciously on those passages which seemed "to write themselves," that got down on paper in bursts of automatic, creative frenzy, without pain or sweat. They are probably exploiting a pet accomplishment, usually the "description" that got its author straight A's in high-school composition.

Fiction, like drama, music, and the dance, is a dynamic, a fluid art. Its hallmark is motion, motion forward, motion toward the accomplishment of an end, toward the resolution of conflicting forces released into fluidity either during the early part of the story ("Last Trip Together") or before the story is begun ("A Place to Cry"). Any passage not in some way contributing to that motion forward is a static passage and therefore wrong.

Motion is not to be confused with physical action. How important is physical action in the two stories you have so far read in this book? It is not important at all, although both stories have it. The stories move, and they move pretty rapidly, but their motion is dependent on the drawing together of conflicting forces: imagination against reality, restraint against emotion. Progress in fiction is motion toward the end of the story, not the mere transportation of persons from place to place. Many beginners would have confused the importance of Web's trip down-river, of Rush Atwood's drive from the scene of the accident to Boston. What is important about those trips is not the action involved, but the conflicting forces at work inside the characters. Both stories would have been badly damaged, if not killed, by superfluous description of the landscape along the way. Such mistakes in emphasis, such descriptions, would have robbed those parts of the stories of their necessary motion, even though the descriptions emphasized the physical action of a canoe trip and an automobile trip.

That is why passages of beautiful description, done for their own sake, why any passages which "wrote themselves" are highly suspect. Look at them carefully. Does anything happen in them? Is the story farther along because of them? If a passage begins on page two, and carries over to page four, has the story changed because of that passage, has it progressed, or are we still where we were on page two? If there has been no contribution to the story's progress, no push toward its end, then you have a static passage, and you must cut it right out, however beautiful it may seem, whatever was your personal ecstasy during its creation. Beauty and ecstasy do exist for the writer, but only in terms of whole stories, of completed effects, not in terms of isolated and irrelevant bits of exquisite evocation. "You must learn to murder your darlings" is a quotation I cannot run to earth, but it was obviously said by a professional writer of fiction.

In "A Place to Cry" there are background and atmosphere—plenty of them. Plenty, and not too much. Note carefully the *kind* of background in the story. It is primarily the background of a person, not of a place nor even of a profession. Now look back to the preface and retrace Mr. Ware's steps that lead to the creation of Rush Atwood. What is important about Rush Atwood is that he is a person, not that he is a construction engineer. He has to be a construction engineer, yes, because that happens to be the profession that best fits Mr. Ware's plan of the story and his own background and experience. Other people, Mr. Ware points out, would have brought the idea embodied in Rush Atwood to realization in other jobs.

The writer must, of course, be warned against fitting characters with jobs or professions that are totally unfamiliar to him. Meticulous knowledge of detail is necessary to carry conviction to the reader, but the exploitation of that detail for its own sake, the mere showing off of knowledge, while it may convince the reader that you know what you're talking about, will also bore him.

Both Mr. Ware and I have already said that an idea is not a story; neither is an emotion, a feeling, a mood; neither is a set of circumstances or happenings. To greater or less extent, all stories must have ideas, emotions, moods, and happenings, but none of them in itself makes a story. The proportion of them in your stories is going to be determined by the kind of person you are. If you are a person of detached curiosity, of a deductive turn of mind with an interest in psychological subtleties, your stories will probably be what some critics call "intellectual." If you are a person of quick sympathy, deep feeling, and generous impulses, your stories are going to be surcharged with emotion. If you have a love of action for action's sake, you will probably write adventure stories. (This is not to say that all seven qualities may not coexist in one person. If they so exist in you, you are probably going to be a successful writer of mystery stories—

or Shakespeare, reincarnate.) By all means exploit your own peculiar twists of character and your own experiences, but exploit them to the advantage, not the cost, of your stories.

PEOPLE

Fiction is about people, people in relationship to each other. These people are symbols, the physical counterparts of the writer's abstract ideas. And, like stories themselves, they must be "made up," must be created—distorted, warped, changed from anybody you ever knew in "real life." They may begin in fact (Web Rivers), or they may be wholly imaginary (Rush Atwood).

Just as a story idea is not a story, neither is a person idea a person. The person has to be presented to the reader as a flesh and blood illusion. Like stories themselves, fictional characters carry a dual load of idea and reality, of tangibility and intangibility, of symbolism and thing. Review the evolution of Rush Atwood from idea to character. Then reread the story and mark the translation of the idea into the man. The idea is still there, but something more has been added. Rush Atwood remains "a man who . . ." but he is now "the" man of the story, the particular, definite, unique person.

This transition from the general to the specific is an obvious necessity in any art that depicts human beings. "A" man simply does not exist as a factual reality. There are only men—man_1, man_2, man_3, and so forth. The word "people" is only a generalized idea, an abstraction. Fiction must be chary in its use of this abstraction; only when the author wishes to give a dim impression of crowds or of groups which are, to a limited extent, homogeneous (the homogeneity of any group is always relative and limited because it is made up of individuals) dare he use it. A mob, actuated by a common impulse, becomes for the moment as definite as an individual, but only for the moment. Seldom are people members of a mob perpetually. It is true that groups of people are, in life, more or less dominated by single ideas, impulses, twists of character due to environment or other circumstance, loves, hatreds, and so on. The history of modern fiction has shown, however, that mass effects cannot be gained by the use of masses, but only by the use of numbers of individuals, individuals who may possess many interests and inheritances in common, perhaps, but who also possess those differences which in life always make one person distinct from every other.

To say that human beings are complex is to say the obvious, but it is also to resolve this problem of the individual and the many. To some extent every successful fictional character is everyman, or at least manymen, and at the same time he is "the" man of the story. This is the duality of fictional characters; it is also the duality of "real life" people, and of you and of me. In fact this duality is the central premise of all art, of all imaginative projection beyond immediate sense experience—of all social agreements, all liberal politics, the whole fabric of civilization. The writer is forever pondering "the similarity in difference, the difference in similarity"; *e pluribus unum* and also *ex uno plures.*

All this is to say that fictional people must be two things: types and individuals. In order to create a type, however, you must first create an individual. For one example, take Robert Frost's fine short story in verse, "The Death of the Hired Man." Silas is first the definite New Englander, the farmer who has never owned his own farm, a failure in his native country, though a hard and intelligent worker. He exists there, at that level, as a fact, as an individual; unique, definite. On another level, he has another existence, a wider, abstract existence. He is one of the world's incompetents, a man who works hard and fails, who means well and falls short of expressing his meaning; a kind of man the world has always known, a creature of pathos, an embodied idea, a prototype. For the writer, what is important about Silas is that he is first this *particular* man, this man_1. He has to exist at that literal, tangible level before he can exist at all, before he can even begin to assume universality. Although the order of creation in the writer's mind is usually from idea to man, in the reader's mind the process is reversed; the reader sees first the man, then, at the story's end, the shadow of the man, the symbol, the abstract idea for which he stands.

PERSONS

At some point, then, in the growth of your story, you stop thinking about people and begin thinking about persons, about Web and Rush, and Web's Old Man, and Rush's wife and children. You begin to plan how you are going to create them, to present them to the reader as flesh and blood illusions.

And *how* do you do that? How *do* you bring your persons to life on the empty page—even when you know what they must be?

This is the biggest and the most important question you can ask. If you can answer it, and can apply the answer to your stories, you are a successful writer. I am going to give you an answer, and I am going to assume that it is *the* answer, although I know very well that it is not the complete answer; it is, I believe, *one* answer, and I know that it is an answer very helpful to beginning writers. It cannot be a complete answer, because the process of creating imaginary characters is as various and complex as the characters of individual writers, and much of the process necessarily goes on below the level of the conscious. Nobody exactly knows; there are depths to human activity which, despite the investigations of modern psychology, still must be described as mysterious.

But back to the problem. How do you create characters?

You don't. You make them create themselves, and they create themselves in four ways. As in life, people in fiction reveal themselves in four ways, singly or in any combination. They are what they are because of what:

1. They think
2. They say
3. They do
4. Other people in the story think, say, and do about them

This is all you need to know about character because it is practically and practicably everything.

But what about the author? Can't he explain his characters to the reader? Can't he describe them, at least? Aren't physical characteristics very important? Aren't appearances important?

The answer is no.

Those are the rules. Learn them, apply them a hundred times, then when you thoroughly understand them, break them at your pleasure —and also at your peril.

Now for a few qualifications. Of course physical characteristics are important, and so are appearances. But confine your presentation of them within the rules given above. For example, you are writing a story about a very hot-tempered heroine, and it is necessary therefore to convey the fact of her temper to the reader. Do you say, "Mirabelle had red hair and an explosive temper?" No, because that isn't a fact; it is only a statement, a statement about a fact, perhaps, but not the fact. You present the fact something like this:

> Mirabelle burst into the room. She went straight to the table and snatched up the framed picture of Mark, whose firm mouth and cool eyes mocked her turmoil. For a moment she stared at it, then hurled it with all her might into the fireplace. It shattered against an andiron; the picture itself fell out of the frame and lay face up, staring at her, calm, imperturbable as Mark himself.
>
> Mirabelle violently shook her violently red head. She stamped her foot. "Damn you," she said. "Oh—*damn you!*"

There is the temper itself—self-displayed, not author-displayed; presented, not described; the fact, not a statement about the fact. Note also that we've gained something more than the fact of Mirabelle's temper; through her, through her temper, we have also got a glimpse of Mark (rule 4).

It comes down to this: Seeing is believing. Years ago, Bernard DeVoto reminds us, George M. Cohan expressed a necessity of the stage which is also an imperative of fiction: "Don't tell 'em; show 'em." There, concisely expressed, is the difference between stage directions and acting, between fiction and narrative, between idea and realization of idea, between the statement and the fact. It is all the difference between nothing and something.

Rules are made to be broken, yes. But not until you can follow them, not until they have proved themselves inadequate to the depth and breadth of your necessities. To some extent you will see those four rules broken. Mr. Ware breaks them in some of the stories in this book. Doubtless many stories in this month's magazines break them; but many, many more follow them. It is wisdom to follow them, at least for your first dozen stories. They won't thwart you, they won't stifle your artistic impulses. If you genuinely have those impulses, the rules will give them what they need above everything else: resistance to work against.

There is much, much more to say about character in fiction, but it cannot all be said at once. For the time being, get a firm grasp on the principle that fiction is about people, and that people must reveal themselves.

III

THE WRITER COMMENTS

WRITING IS WORK

While rereading "Angler, Beware!" the writer felt certain that his story sounded buoyant, light-hearted, and altogether effortless. He believed for an unguarded moment that his tale was the kind which might be unfolded in a few pleasant hours under a tree. "Angler, Beware!" was written long enough ago so that the writer felt himself happily dissociated from its creation. Someone else might have done the work, if work was at all necessary. From the nature of the piece and its manner of telling, it seemed to have been tossed off, to use a galling phrase.

But presently the writer began to reflect upon the fact of his writing. He remembered his fatigue, his snarling disapproval, and self-criticism, his despondency, his labors of excision, and in general the great sadness of his effort to make people laugh—or even smile.

A great deal has been said about the dark thraldom of writing. One hears writers remark upon the sweating, fruitless hours, while the waste-basket becomes Gorgon-headed with the day's errors. Too much has been proclaimed about the hard work of creation, but too much is not enough unless some of it is believed.

What of the writer's tottering mind when, for the twelfth consecutive day, the children he once thought he loved come by stealth into his office in order to breathe upon his neck, peer over his shoulder, snort, and inquire: "Are you still on page twenty-one?"

And insufficient mention has been made of the writer's bitterness when people whom he has considered his friends say: "I certainly envy you—working only five hours a day. Pretty soft."

There is no way to enlighten these blackened souls, nor any method of penetrating their senses with the truth. They smile in distant amusement when you tell them you would prefer their jobs, or any job, to yours. They simply don't believe it.

Then there are the academic friends—professors, one or two college presidents, and some deans. They have a tendency to weigh you down with the obligation of genius, and they see no reason for spending time on any literary work which isn't conceived for the cultural advancement of mankind.

"What?" they say. "Still fussing over that ending?"

They manage to get a derogatory twist into the word fussing, and just as you are bristling defensively, they soften your anger with words like these: "I don't see how you do it! I wish *I* could do it!"

Your warmth and elation are invariably short-lived, for in the next instant the academicians add: "But don't do it!"

A writer talking about his work is a form of crying in the wilderness. The writer is George Babbitt prattling on the subject of real estate in Zenith. Worse, he is a fisherman telling another fisherman of something mythical and slippery which got away. The trapped listener will be wise to make his escape at once, for in some moods the writer may take hours to tell an audience one of the following trifles:

Fussing over an ending is carrying a pack of crushed rock up a mile-high mountain. You are barefoot, and the temperature is 110 degrees F. Tossing off a story for *The Post* is an infuriating phrase loaded to the boards with ignorance, envy, and injustice. It is easier, probably, to write for posterity than for *The Post*—and when you do both simultaneously, it is no accident, and there is nothing in the process which could evoke the word tossing, unless the epithet refers to sleeplessness.

"Angler, Beware!" was tossed off for *The Saturday Evening Post* in five weeks. This does not account for eleven years as managing editor of a sporting magazine during which the writer learned the vocabulary of authoritative, and even definitive anglers. But whenever one writes a story, he throws in the dividends of his total experience as a matter of course, and then eliminates all of it which isn't pertinent.

"Angler, Beware!" draws heavily on fishing background. Fidelity to background is another of the countless "number one" laws of fiction writing, and if it wasn't invented by *Post* editors, it is most sternly enforced by them. To any editorial jury worth its salt, a background fault is a capital crime. I am of the belief that a jury of *Post* editors would graciously allow the culprit to commit suicide, preferably before publication.

Although "Angler, Beware!" is a fishing story, it could be written about any hobby which a family might enjoy or dislike fervidly enough to enhance story interest. Fishing is noted for the fervor it engenders. The collecting of antiques, however, might do as well, or perhaps the growing of tulips. One useful point about the fishing background is in its anathema, generally speaking, to wives. This anathema at the start of "Angler, Beware!" sets forth the basis for conflict. It is there established that Sue Crane, the wife, tolerates fishing because her husband is obsessed with it as a hobby.

Sue loves her husband, but detests fishing. Her antipathy is personalized in the plodding, unimaginative, solemnly discoursing George Pattengill, her husband's fishing crony. George, of course, is a bachelor and probably deserves it.

The deliberate trick of having the son, Jud Crane, born on the opening day of the fishing season, illustrates precisely a legitimate use of coincidence. Jud's birth date muddies the situation by making Sue's predicament worse. The date indicates to her that she is going to have still another fisherman in her scheme of things. George and her husband's fatuous belief in prenatal influence add conviction.

But coincidence always must be handled with caution. Lucian Cary has given the perfect example of its correct use in story-telling. A man is penniless and hungry. A friend owes him five dollars. If the friend shows up with the five dollars, that is *not* coincidence for story purposes. But, if the penniless man owes an enemy five dollars, and the enemy shows up and demands payment, you have used coincidence effectively.

Coincidence is an instrument for producing added obstacles in the path of an already beleaguered character. The character must fight his way over the obstacles by means of his own strength—never with the help of coincidence. Briefly, coincidence is used against, not for.

Mr. Bailey and the writer elected to discuss "Angler, Beware!" because it illustrates clearly some of the common and useful story mechanisms, of which coincidence is one. Does the reader remember the ingeniously simple framework of O. Henry's "The Gift of the Magi"? It was a Christmas story, and a poverty-stricken young couple were wondering what they would give each other, and how they would find the money. Each had a prized possession, the husband a gold watch, and the wife a lovely head of hair. The husband sold his watch to buy his wife a comb for her hair, only to discover on Christmas that she had cut off her hair and sold it in order to buy a fob for his watch.

"Angler, Beware!" is the same story without the pathos. But it is carried one degree further by means of one added character—Jud Crane, the young son. The wife in "Angler, Beware!" deplored fishing, but bears its tedium for the sake of her husband and son. The husband himself gradually loses interest in fishing, but keeps up the display for the benefit, he believes, of his son. At length, the father discovers that his son, also, has lost interest in the sport, but has faked enthusiasm for his, the father's, sake. The ending of the story will show the step which carried beyond "The Gift of the Magi," in a similar cycle.

"Angler, Beware!" is as full of bald devices, but useful ones, as a jigsaw puzzle is of pieces. This type of story is called meretricious, meretricious being the critic-word for tricky, or the author-word for conscious care. Sometimes, not very apologetically, meretriciousness seems to mean to this writer an economical use of his materials, or inventions.

For example, Sue Crane, as she sits on river banks while her husband and son fish, reads innumerable books. It seems legitimate, if meretricious, to make sly use of the titles of Sue's books in order to emphasize the point of her boredom and sacrifice. This is a method of steering the reader along a certain course—the course at all times, of the story itself. It is a study in emphasis, for the greater Sue's boredom, the more unbearable it becomes, the merrier the tale. Thus she reads *Look Homeward, Angel,* for the title hints that she desires to be elsewhere than on a damp boulder swatting black flies. Speaking of fishing and boredom, *Of Time and the River* is an obvious choice for poor Sue. Another year she reads *One More Spring,* and for the year of greatest strain, she has saved *Anthony Adverse,* a title which is almost a gilt-edged promise to the reader that something bleak is about to occur.

George Pattengill, Sue's husband's dull and humorless fishing crony, is a pure character-device to begin with. But George becomes important not only for perspective on the background, fishing, but as an aid to the motion of the story itself. Everyone in the story changes —except George. He is steadfast to himself, to the background, and/or to fishing. Sue's increasing shortness with George and her husband's increasing doubts create motion—or perhaps something which might be called tension, or suspense, or a progress toward the point where human emotion can endure no more.

The three family characters—father, mother, and son—all reach the end of their restraint by courtesy of George Pattengill's stolidity and his fidelity to trout. Thus the reader presumably is curious about three things which are promised him. How will Bill Crane explode? (And when?) How will Jud Crane, the son, explode? (And when?) And how, above all, will Sue, the wife and mother, explode? (And when?)

These three releases of human emotions are suspense mechanisms, and the reader knows almost from the start that at least one (Sue's) is going to occur. Bill Crane's persuasion from angling is a more gradual thing, since his obsession has been more clinchingly planted. Incidentally, the reader might be interested to know that in the original version of "Angler, Beware!" Bill's foreswearing of fishing was too abrupt. *The Post* editors said: "Make it gradual, or at least forecast it!" Hence Bill's change of passion is thrice-predicted in the finished story.

Jud Crane's deviation from the family fishing tradition comes as an amiable surprise, yet it does have certain foreshadowing. His mother, Sue, breaks in an unexpected, but entirely logical way—which brings up the extremely important point that surprise *must* be logical. That is to say, surprise must be carefully conditioned.

The writer believes that in "Angler, Beware!" there are some interesting time-devices and timing, or its indication, which have appeared in Mr. Bailey's college classes and in other classes, as a problem to students of fiction. How do you indicate time? How do you answer the question, "when"?

The reader of this piece might, possibly, feel more comfortable if he knew that all writers, present and past, ask the same question and answer it not always by courtesy of their talent or by happy accident. Time is intricate in fiction. It is complicated, devious, and without relation to the calendar. But you can begin with your watch as follows: "It was ten o'clock." From there, in added sentences you can further establish time. "The dead leaves rustled underfoot, and the sunlight . . ." So you know it was morning and fall.

That indicates only fixed time. Passage of time is often more difficult, and this writer, although he acknowledges the difficulty where he, himself, is concerned, feels that it can actually be indicated even more easily. There is a tendency to bridge a fictional gap of ten years, say, by writing a paragraph relatively ten years long. But the reader of the story is much more pleased and enlightened if one simply writes something like this: "By the time he was entered in prep school, Jud Crane was a skilled fisherman . . ." or a similar phrase. But that, and similar phrases, have invariably hindered the writer—this writer and others, beginners and veterans. Let the reader think deeply on this: The number of words is never relative to the passage of time within a story. The main action, using up a thousand precious words of a short story—say a fifth or sixth of the entire tale—may occupy a split second in actual time within the story's action. The passage of a decade may take a sentence, no more. Never let time interrupt the story.

In "Angler, Beware!" which takes about twenty minutes to read, something like sixteen years pass by. I believe the process is called compression, which suggests another piece of strategy in the same story. For example, Bill Crane's writing a stodgy book on fishing technique was originally intended merely to heighten the humorous effect. After a little study, it was included to serve many purposes. It bunches a number of points, to wit: It gathers the four characters in a very tight group in which explosion becomes more imminent. The book's dedication leaves out George Pattengill, which again stresses the change of the other three characters away from George. The book's real dedication gave George a chance to imagine one, which further characterized George himself. The popularity of the book made it almost obligatory for Bill Crane to continue fishing, which strained his patience to tight-wire suspense. And Sue's reading galleys and page proofs sent her farther toward a crack-up.

The above illustrates how one piece of simple invention may be used for many purposes; the idea of Bill's writing the fishing book was a natural sequence, or association with the far previous invention of having Sue *read* books on the river bank out of boredom.

"Angler, Beware!" in short, while a story written purposefully for entertainment, has examples in construction which may prove helpful. If you devise a piece of story machinery, make it work for the story, for background, for character, for suspense, for motion, for time, for everything for which it may be suited.

Perhaps, by divine providence, you will occasionally bunch all these in an episode, a paragraph, a sentence, without recourse to the waste-basket. More often, by fussing over an ending, a beginning, or a middle, you will carry that load of crushed rock up a mountain or two, and when people ask if you are tossing off another story, you may fall upon them, rocks and all, with impunity, justice, and the encouragement and well-wishes of all who have known the slavery of writing for posterity and/or *The Saturday Evening Post.*

Angler, Beware!

Sue Crane's obstetrician did not believe in prenatal influence. He would have smiled at the old midwives up around Fredericton who insist that a boy born during the first salmon run will be a great fisherman. He practiced in Boston and believed in prenatal care. With the able coöperation of Sue herself, he brought young Judson Crane into the world, slapped the breath of life into him, and went out to the reception room to see if he could do anything for the stricken father.

William Edward Crane, inventor of the Crane Wing fly and—later—author of *Stream Technique and the Fly Rod,* and George Pattengill, his lifelong fishing comrade, were clinging together for comfort when the doctor arrived. They were dressed in waders, flannel shirts, and hats. It would have been difficult to tell at a glance which man was the father. Both seemed on the verge of collapse.

"How is she?" said Bill Crane, paling as the doctor entered.

"She's great, Bill! Great baby too. Congratulations!"

"What kind is it?" asked George Pattengill, clammy with dread.

"Boy. Just under eight pounds. Got a back like a wrestler."

It was George Pattengill who fainted—relief and ecstasy in equal parts. Had the new-born been a girl, George probably would not have regained consciousness. He had once tried to teach a girl how to cast a fly, which is why he remained a bachelor. George now came to, muttering something sentimental about the new-born's first trout. The doctor, administering brandy, frowned.

"Sue said things began happening on some river bank," he said.

"I shall never forget it," murmured George Pattengill from the daybed. "Sue was sitting under the big pine just above the cement bridge on the Manhan. I had just raised a fair-sized brown—"

"What's the idea?" The doctor turned to Bill. "Taking your wife fishing at such a time! Haven't you got any sense at all?"

"No. Yes. I mean— Oh, gosh! I don't know," said Bill. "It's opening day on trout, don't you see? Sue wouldn't let me stay home with her. Said it would spoil our fishing—George's and mine. 'Course I couldn't go and leave her alone. So, she—"

George Pattengill sat up. He looked better, but was still a sick man. "It's beautiful," he breathed. "It's glorious, Bill! Your son, born on opening day, and all of us out there fishing, when it started. That is, I mean you and I were fishing. Not Sue."

"No," said Bill bleakly. "Not Sue. She was reading."

A wan light showed in George Pattengill's eyes. The poetry in him was not yet exhausted. "If only she had been reading La Blanche, or Hewitt on the dry fly, the aura would have been perfect. I mean to say, the prenatal influence of such a powerful combination—"

"Rot!" said the doctor. "What was she reading?"

"I—George!" cried Bill. "I remember now. It was *Moby Dick!*"

Whether or not there was anything in the Crane-Pattengill theory of prenatal influence, young Judson Crane, at age three, could actually cast a fly out of his lap and some distance beyond. His father, of course, had given him a fly rod before he could walk. George Pattengill—Uncle George now—had provided him with a complete set of celluloid trout for bathtub use. In the ordinary sense, little Jud Crane never wore rubber pants. He was taught to call them waders.

"See, mummy! See! See!" he cried one summer day, following an especially good down-wind cast on the back lawn.

"That's lovely, dear," said Sue, not quite looking up from her book. "Daddy will be so proud. And Uncle George will burble."

Later in the day Jud's mentors returned and went out immediately to see how the boy was coming along. He performed splendidly.

" 'Nother year or two," said Bill, "and we'll have him on the stream with us."

George Pattengill watched his protégé in a kind of steamy trance. "Look! He—he's even getting his wrist into it!"

"How wonderful," said Sue, setting aside her book. "You three boys are going to have wonderful times together, aren't you?"

"You didn't include yourself, dear," said Bill Crane. "You must think of us as four, not three."

"But I do, Bill. You know I do."

At seven, Jud Crane had mastered the roll cast and some of the simpler curve casts in still air. He was catching trout regularly. His picture had appeared several times in rotogravure. Usually you saw him standing between his father and George Pattengill, a lanky, graceful, serious-looking boy. Then, in the background, slightly out of focus, yet somehow dominant, you noticed Sue Crane. She was lovely looking, her eyes invariably on her son. She held a book in one hand and a bottle of fly dope in the other.

During the winter of his ninth year, Jud Crane learned to tie his own flies. One March night Jud completed a specimen and turned to his father for approbation. But this time Bill's chair was empty.

"Where's Dad, Mum? I thought he was right here."

"He went into the study five minutes ago."

"Is anything the matter?"

"I think he's tired. He's been quite quiet this evening."

"Well," said Jud, "how do you like this one?"

"How lovely, dear! It's a—a—don't tell me—Royal Coachman!" said Sue, and went to get the vacuum cleaner to rid the blue rug of feathers, lint, and tinsel.

Jud stared blankly after her and then darted for the study. He found his father lying on the sofa gazing at the ceiling.

"Hi, Dad. Are you awful tired?"

"Huh?" said Bill, sitting up. "Tired? Me? Why?"

"Well, you scratch when you're tired, and your hair's rumpled."

Bill Crane wasn't exactly tired. He was troubled. Bill had lunched that noon with George Pattengill and a visiting fly man from the Anglers Club of New York. They had discussed a trout's cone of visibility in clear water. During the conversation it had suddenly occurred to Bill that Hargrave's glass-tank photographs and diagrams had settled the subject—exhausted it, you might say—ten years ago. There was really nothing left to be said. Yet George Pattengill and that other fellow had said it for two solid hours. Why?

George's voice, hoarse with the lust of angling theory, had irked Bill all afternoon. In trying to rid his ears of the echo, Bill felt a twinge of disloyalty both to George and to a trout's cone of visibility. It worried him.

But Jud's appearance in the study had a refreshing effect. Bill waxed enthusiastic over his son's expertly tied fly. He did not notice that the boy listened in a preoccupied way.

"That's a beautiful Crane Wing," said Bill. "You've even got your hackles slanted just right. Uncle George ought to see this. You're going places, son."

With startling irrelevance Jud said, "Dad, doesn't Mother like fishing?"

"What? What's that? 'Course she does! Love's to come with us and watch us, and everything. What do you mean?"

"Dad, she just called this Crane Wing a Royal Coachman!"

"Don't let that worry you at all. We're a right little, tight little unit—you and mother and Uncle George and I. Always will be."

"She just seems to read, though, Dad. She doesn't fish!"

During the next few seasons Sue Crane read a great deal on the banks of many rivers. She became not only a student of contemporary literature but an authority on fly dope. She tried all the new brands, and in time came to regard fly dope as perfume, which she secretly labeled *eau d'ennui*.

In May of one of these seasons Bill Crane had his second symptom, or qualm, concerning his attitude toward fishing. It was vague and unexplainable, like the first. He had waded out of the Westfield River one afternoon and ploshed up to where Sue was sitting.

"What are you reading, dear?" he said.

"*Anthony Adverse*. Go away, darling. You're dripping on me."

A squeal of delight reached them from across the river. "Darned if Jud hasn't tied into another one," said Bill, and went down the bank again into the stream. A trout rose to a natural within thirty feet of him. He didn't notice the trout. There was a gorgeous white cloud lifting above the ridge. Bill noticed the cloud. He couldn't remember noticing a cloud before while fishing. Nor could he recall wading out of a stream during a rise to inquire what Sue was reading. With a faint shudder, he at once resumed casting.

In the winter of that very year, George Pattengill finally prevailed on Bill to write *Stream Technique and the Fly Rod*. Sue Crane was thus driven into reading her first book on fishing. Loyalty and a taste for the correct use of the English language compelled her to read the typescript, galleys, and page proofs.

Stream Technique and the Fly Rod came out in March and sold eight thousand copies in three weeks. The book was dedicated simply and devotedly: TO MY WIFE AND SON. George Pattengill, now quite bald and more solemn than ever, had imagined a dedication roughly as follows:

TO GEORGE PATTENGILL

My dearest friend and most inspiring companion on the trout rivers of Eastern North America. Without his encouragement and expert criticism this book could not have been written. It will be apparent that his genius is largely responsible for the brilliant chapters on stream entomology, leader calibrations, and the sense perceptions of trout. And I would like to express here an even more personal word of gratitude to George, for it is none other than he who has so loyally aided in the angling education of my son.

When George read the real dedication he felt neglected and lonely, but on the backswing he went a little wild. He arranged a dinner party at Locke-Ober's Café and bought champagne for Sue Crane, Bill, and himself, and an orangeade for Jud. He stood up and raised his glass.

"I want to say just a word," he said.

"Shoot, Georgie," said Sue. "Quick. I'm hungry!"

Nervously plucking at his collar, George began, "The eve of Jud's birthday, coinciding with the publication of *Stream Technique and the Fly Rod,*" George plucked, drew breath and resumed, "finds the four of us together again. And I count it a special privilege to make Jud a birthday present, one that will serve him down through the years."

George reached under the table and produced an aluminum-cased rod. He conferred the gift on Jud and stepped back, perspiring.

"Georgie! You shouldn't have done that!" said Sue.

"I have wanted to for a long time," said George.

"Good Lord, George! It's a Spencer—a genuine!"

"Three and one-half ounces of sheer grace," said George.

"Oh, gosh! Uncle George!" cried Jud, uncasing the rod and caressing the joints. "It's wonderful! Oh, thanks, Uncle George!"

"Just now," said George, his head at a reverent angle, "I am thinking of a day eleven years ago. Your father and mother and I, Jud, were fishing the Manhan above the cement bridge. We—"

"I wasn't fishing, Georgie."

"No, Sue. You weren't. For it was on that day that a sacred—I mean to say, you were concerned with the divine process of—"

"Georgie. On that day Jud was born. Is that what you mean?"

"Yes," said George wringing his napkin. "And now that Jud has a Spencer, I thought it would be upholding a sort of tradition if we all went out to the Manhan tomorrow and wet a line together."

"Oh, boy!" said Jud. "Swell!"

Sue gave a rippling laugh. "All right, Georgie. I'll bring a blanket and a book."

Bill Crane had a miserable time getting to sleep that night. At first he attributed his restlessness to lobster, then to the fact that tomorrow was opening day, then to a curious feeling he had had about George. There was no denying it: a subtle inflection in Sue's voice had made him see George, himself, *Stream Technique,* and—yes, yes!—fishing, through detached eyes. What the deuce was wrong? Nothing, really. Not a darn thing. Good old George! Swell of him to give Jud that beautiful rod. Just like him. Heart of gold.

Bill finally dropped off, but at a shuddery, predawn hour he awoke and sat bolt upright, thus dragging the covers from Sue.

"Bill, darling. Do lie still. I'm freezing."

In the frigid, graying light, Bill stared around the bedroom.

"Did George ring the doorbell?" he asked.

"No. And if he did, he can just wait outside till five o'clock."

Bill imagined old George waiting on the front steps in the cold. The picture made him wince.

"Did Jud call?" he said.

"No! Pity's sake, Bill! What's the matter with you?"

"I—darned if I know. Nightmare, maybe."

"It's opening day on trout, if you ask me," said Sue wryly.

Bill swung out of bed and went downstairs. Jud's fishing gear —waders, creel, wading boots, and Spencer lay neatly on the sofa. By habit and custom Bill's tackle should have been laid out beside Jud's. It wasn't. *Funny,* Bill thought, *darn funny on opening day.*

On the way to the tackle closet, Bill stopped at the living-room table and riffled the pages of a copy of *Stream Technique and the Fly Rod.* Usually this pastime comforted him. This time it didn't. Bill knew now that he was on the verge of a revelation which might be too appalling to face. But an instant later, when the revelation came, he not only faced it but welcomed it. He said the words inwardly. The house didn't tremble. He spoke the words aloud in a low, steady voice, "I don't give a damn if I never go fishing again!"

The thing had come about quite painlessly. He realized that it had been eating away at him for a long time. There wasn't a regret. The writing of *Stream Technique* had simply been the final blow, but long before that he had been quietly corroding. Now, thank God, it was all over. No more ice-water leaking through his waders. No more getting up in the middle of the night. No more interminable conversations about leader lengths, nymphs, bugs, flies, and a trout's cone of visibility. What a heavenly relief!

"Think," mused Bill, "what poor Sue has been through all these years! Just for Jud and me and poor old George! What a girl!"

Bill picked up another copy of *Stream Technique*—the house was full of them—and hurled it into a distant chair. It lay there, pages fluttering, like a bird with a broken wing.

"Here I am," Bill told himself, "at the height of my fishing career, and I hate fishing. Boy-oh-boy-oh-boy!"

But Bill Crane was not at the height of his fishing career or anywhere near it. Presently he understood why. He reached his understanding through an imaginary conversation with George Pattengill.

"George," he said in fancy, "I'm through. You can have my Spencers, and my Caverdi reels, and all my other—"

"What?"

"Just as I say, George. Fishing bores me."

In Bill's piteous, though somehow delectable dream, he saw the pallor spread slowly over George's face. "But the Crane Wing fly, Bill," George seemed to say, "and *Stream Technique,* and—"

"Hell with 'em all. They bore me, too, George. Have a brandy?"

George's next question, though still imaginary, gave Bill Crane such an actual jolt that he nearly needed brandy himself.

"What about Jud?" asked George. "Going to let your son down, Bill? Going to break the boy's heart? Are you?"

Bill's pulse thumped. This was reality. So was the buzzing in his ears. And so was the tinkle of Jud's alarm clock. It was the opening day! Bill gave himself a poignant smile in the front-hall mirror as he passed on the way to Jud's bedroom.

"Hi, Dad! Hi! Hi! Gee, I can't wait to get going."

"Neither can I!" said Bill. "Happy birthday! Yippee! Let's go!"

Bill Crane's casting that morning on the Manhan was effortless, disinterested, and nothing short of magnificent.

"Gad, Bill," said George Pattengill, "you're hot. You're really sweet, man. Never saw you in such wrist. Practically fluid."

"Huh?" said Bill, gazing off at Jud, who was working a riffle just above. "What's that, George? Oh, yuh, sure. Thanks."

Bill was especially attentive to Sue that morning. He hadn't told her of his revelation for two reasons. The first was that he couldn't be sure his release was permanent. The second was that he feared Sue might take steps to lure Jud away from his beloved sport. If Sue really got herself braced, Bill could see the three of them vacationing on a hotel porch in the mountains. No, he had better not tell her. At least not yet.

Sue sat under the big pine, wrapped in her blanket, her nose looking cold, and the pages of *One More Spring* whipping in the breeze. Every other time Bill turned to her, a trout socked his trailing fly. Bill couldn't keep them away. He had his limit by nine o'clock.

"Gee, Dad!" cried the adoring Jud. "How in heck do you do it?"

"That," said Uncle George, "is called stream generalship."

The novelty of fishing purely for sacrifice didn't last Bill Crane very long. His compensation was in Jud's happiness and in the strengthening of the bond between them. But he had come to loathe fishing as much if not more than he had once loved it.

The next season, in prizes for big, bigger, and biggest trout, Bill won four hundred dollars' worth of fishing tackle. He was by now conducting a number of fishing columns in magazines and newspapers. He had a public as well as a son.

George Pattengill blithely arranged dates for Bill to address fish-and-game clubs in winter. George and Jud always sat beside Bill on the platform, while Sue attended the nearest movie. After his lectures, Bill would often have to give a casting exhibition in some bleak gymnasium smelling of old basketball shoes.

There was no peace in winter or even in sleep. In nightmares Bill would hear Jud's clear, urgent, young voice saying, "Dad, let's go fishing!" and Bill would answer, "You bet! Great idea! Come on!"

His one satisfaction was in knowing that he was doing the right thing for Jud. Pretty soon now the boy would be grown up. He would go fishing with friends his own age, and Bill could rest, certain that he had left his son a solid treasure of companionship. Bill decided that when that time came, he would write a stark volume entitled, *Hell with Fishing*. Then he would put a torch to his tackle and take up gardening.

The year of Jud's enrolment in boarding-school Bill determined to give the boy something really big to honor the occasion.

"Son," said Bill severely, "what would you like best in all the world?"

It was an early June evening. Jud looked up at his father and mother, his face brightening. "Don't you know?"

"Haven't the faintest idea," said Bill.

"Can't imagine," said Sue.

"You're trying to kid me. You know darn well what I want. I want a good long fishing trip with you and Uncle George."

"How strange!" said Sue.

"Sure is," said Bill, "because it just so happens I've engaged four of the best guides on the Nipisiguit River. There's trout in that river—squaretails—that'll go six pounds. We start the twenty-sixth of this month. We'll be gone three weeks."

"The Nipisiguit!" cried the boy. "Three weeks! Oh, Dad!"

The joy in his son's voice was balm almost adequate to the wounds Bill had suffered throughout three deadly seasons. But Jud was regarding his mother thoughtfully. He finally said, "Are you going to be with us all the whole time, Mother?"

"Of course, dear. Why not?"

"I was just wondering," said Jud, fidgeting, "if you'd like it."

Always, when Jud had voiced this doubt, Sue had gaily laughed it away. Now Bill noticed that she was steeling herself. There was a barely perceptible tightening of her lips. Bill could understand. Three weeks on a wilderness river in fly season was a heavy stretch.

"Of course I'd like it!" said Sue.

"I mean really like it," the boy persisted, nervous in his effort to make himself clear. "I mean the way Dad and I and Uncle George like it. You know, Mother—the fishing part. You don't ever seem to fish. You most always seem just to read."

Bill had a bad moment. Just when he was sure Sue would revolt, she braced herself and said, "I love being with you and Dad, dear."

"And Uncle George, Mother?"

"And Uncle George," said Sue, her lips now practically a straight line.

Bill remembered this conversation many times in the weeks prior to departure. It had done something to Sue—undermined her. She grew increasingly silent, and at times even grim. Bill felt the tension in her and dreaded that she would reach the point of open rebellion. He could feel her shrinking from three weeks in the close company of George Pattengill. Bill understood only too well. Not that George wasn't a good fellow. It was just that—well, as a matter of fact, George was still talking about a trout's cone of visibility.

Three days before departure, George announced that he would be unable to get away for the full three weeks. Bill felt that this news would be a relief to Sue. He was relieved himself, and a little ashamed. But Sue's reaction to the glad tidings was not as he had hoped.

"Dearest," he said, after Jud had turned in, "old George is acting strangely. He may be in love. He—"

"May be?" said Sue. "He is! I'll tell you who with, too. He's in love with George Pattengill and fish! Fish! Fish!"

"Wait a minute, Sue. You'll wake Jud. Relax, dear. It isn't going to be so bad, after all. George isn't—"

"Damn George!"

"Dear, I'm trying to tell you that George isn't coming up till the second week. He told me this afternoon."

Sue curled up in her wing chair and bowed her head in her arms. Bill was perplexed. His good news seemed to have brought her little, if any, relief. He decided to adopt a gay manner.

"I asked George if his trouble was financial, and he said, 'No.' Then his face got round, and he stared up at that salmon that's mounted over his desk. I couldn't help thinking how he kind of looks like the salmon—the eyes, I guess. Then he swallowed, and mopped his head with his handkerchief, and said, 'Time is of the essence.' That's all."

As if she hadn't heard a word of what he had said, Sue asked in a dull toneless voice, "Where is this Nipisiguit River?"

Bill was thunderstruck. "Why Sue! You know where it is. You've heard George and me discussing it times without number."

"I wasn't listening. Where is it?" Bill thought it best to humor her. "Northern New Brunswick," he said patiently. "It empties into Bay Chaleur at Bathurst. From Bathurst we go sixteen miles up-river on the abandoned mine railroad. You'll love that, Sue.

There's just a flatcar. At the abandoned mine the canoes meet us, and—"

"That's enough. Are there any flies?"

"Flies? Oh, you mean black flies? Why—uh—maybe—a few."

"Bill," said Sue, facing him and speaking with a kind of ghastly gentleness, "I'm not going."

"What?"

She repeated very slowly, "I . . . am . . . not . . . going."

Bill saw that she was preparing herself for his storm of indignation. Smiling at her with infinite understanding, he simply said, "All right, old dear. I know how you feel, and I'm sure Jud knows. That boy's really keen. I'll break it to him gently."

"You know how I feel?" said Sue, almost shrilly. "You? You don't even begin to know! Bill Crane! I've got fly bites on my legs dating back to nineteen twenty!"

"Yes, dear," said Bill. "You've been a good soldier. Jud and I'll go it alone. We'll get along."

Sue came down to see them off on the boat for St. John. As the boat slipped away from the pier, they looked over the rail at her. She was gazing up at them, her eyes streaming.

"Aw, gee, Dad," said Jud. "She's crying. I'm going to miss her awful."

Far down the pier they spied a familiar figure lumbering toward them and waving a Panama. They waved back frantically.

"Uncle George!" yelled Jud. "See you in a week!"

George's pudgy arm had suddenly stopped waving. His Panama hung, so to speak, at half-mast. He had noticed Sue Crane. He stopped beside her. Bill saw him reach out his hand as if to pat her shoulder. Poor old George, thought Bill. Then, turning to Jud, he said, "Well, boy, we're off!"

A few days later, Bill Crane and his son were taking trout on the fabulously beautiful Nipisiguit River. They were camped in those neat peeled-spruce cabins on the high bluff at the Narrows, four miles above the abandoned mine, where the river sings down through the ledges.

For the first time in his life, Bill Crane had taken a book on a fishing trip. The book was Walter Edmonds' *Chad Hanna,* and aside from the parts where Chad went trout fishing, Bill enjoyed the book mightily. When he and Jud were within sight of each other, Bill fished. But when he could sneak around a bend, he would climb out on the bank, apply fly dope, and settle down with *Chad Hanna.*

The evening of the day before George Pattengill was to arrive, Jud reported a very large trout in the pool near the head of the Narrows.

The next morning, he said, "Dad, I'm going up there and work on that mossback. Bet you his tail was five inches wide."

"Wow! Go get him, son. Want me to come along?"

"Well, I— I kind of want to solve him single-handed, Dad. Then I'll have something to tell Uncle George tonight."

"That's the stuff, Jud. Know just how it is. Guess I'll stay around camp for a while and then maybe work the lower pools."

"Okay, Dad. So long. Tight lines!"

After Jud had gone, Bill decided to take *Chad Hanna,* slip down-river a couple of bends, and do some quiet reading.

"Seen that book of mine, Zeb?" he asked his guide.

"No, I ain't. But seems like 'twas layin' on your bunk."

"It was," said Jud's guide. "But Jud took it with him. I seen him tuck it in his creel."

"You—you what?" said Bill Crane.

"The boy took it in his creel, Sir. Like for me to go up there an' get it for you, Mr. Crane?"

"No, Zeb. Thanks. You fellows stay right here and whittle. I'll walk up there and get it myself."

Ten minutes later, peering through the branches of a little fir that grew on the shore of the upper pool, Bill Crane saw his son lying full length on the sun-warmed ledge, *Chad Hanna* spread open before him. The boy was completely absorbed. His Spencer rod, forgotten, leaned against a bush, the line trailing in the water. A small trout had taken the fly. Its antics, unnoticed by Jud, twitched the rod tip violently.

Bill stepped out onto the ledge and said, "Hello, son."

Jud scrambled to his feet. His face turned crimson and his lips worked nervously. "Gee, Dad! Thought you were down below."

"When did you get sick of fishing, boy?" asked Bill, his voice overflowing with affection.

"Sick of fishing? Why, Dad! What the heck do you mean?"

Bill came close. He put his arm around Jud's shoulders and hugged the boy against him. "Well, it's this way: I've hated fishing for three years that I know about. Probably two or three more that I don't know about. How about you, son? Come on! Confess!"

"And—and all this time you've been fishing because of me, Dad?"

"Something like that. But I loved that part of it. How long have you been fishing because of me?"

Jud smiled. "Heck, ever since I can remember. But it was kind of nice, though, Dad. I like doing things with you and Mother, even when I hate the things."

Father and son stood off and looked at each other.

"You know," Bill said, "I think this is about the happiest moment of my life—except, maybe, when you were born."

"Me, too, Dad. Gee, you're a swell guy. Wait till we tell Mother! She'll have ten million cat fits."

"I can hear her laughing right now," said Bill.

"Poor Uncle George, Dad. What will he say? He'll suffer awful!"

"Good Lord! I'd forgotten about that. We better not say anything to him at first. We'll have to handle him with kid gloves."

George Pattengill was on the cabin porch when Jud and Bill got back. This was strange on the face of it, because George wasn't due till evening. Moreover, George seemed distracted, and at the same time complacent, and even a little fatuous. "Left East Boston airport at daylight. Landed in Bay Chaleur at nine. Got here ten minutes ago."

"Great to see you, George. Expensive trip, wasn't it?"

"Worth it. Come here. Look down there at the lower pool."

They stepped to the edge of the bluff. A solitary fisherman stood waist deep in the pool below. George pointed a shaking finger.

"One of the Rollins boys?" said Bill, puzzled and impatient. It wasn't like old George to ring in a stranger.

"Looks like Tiny Rollins," said Jud. "Looks like—Dad! It's—"

"George!" gasped Bill. "My God, George! Is that one of the Rollins boys? Or—or is it my wife?"

"It's Sue Crane," said George, a halo all but visible above his head.

"Mother!" said Jud. "Dad! Look at her cast that fly!"

Bill and his son exchanged a glance. Sue hadn't seen them yet. She was casting over a pocket fifty feet away, and she was casting beautifully. Bill and Jud watched her in stunned silence. No wonder they had mistaken her for one of the Rollins boys. Her hair was tucked up under her felt hat, and they could see a smooch of dirt on one cheek. A cloud of black flies, unnoticed, busied themselves around her. But more than that—far, far more—there was the tense, slightly wild expression on her face —the gleaming, telltale eagerness. Bill glanced again at his son, and his heart soared to the boy's slow wink. Jud, too, had recognized the signs of the true, passionate, and permanent angler.

"Sue!" Bill yelled. "Oh, Sue! Sue!"

She didn't hear him. A twelve-inch trout had looped into her fly, and she had it on. Her rod curved in exactly the right arc. She played the trout expertly, slipped the net under it, and looked up to see her loved ones. She didn't wave her hand at them. She waved her hat!

"Yoo–hoo! Oh, da–a–a–rlings!" she called, wading ashore.

Jud went racing down the steep trail to meet her. Bill started to follow, but George prevented him. "Wait, Bill. I haven't finished."

Bill was now aware that George had been talking for some time. George's monologue was both an explanation and a paean of self-praise. The main facts reached Bill in a badly blurred condition, but he was gradually separating them, while Sue and Jud were exchanging hugs on the river bank below.

It seemed, according to George, that Sue had come to him in secret the day after Jud had been told of the prospective trip to the Nipisiguit. She had said to him, "George, Jud is miserable because I don't fish. He's unhappy because I just read. So I am going to fish if it kills me. It may kill you, too, George. You're going to teach me how!"

George said that he had never seen such savage determination in the eyes of a woman. He had given her secret lessons every afternoon.

Bill again started down the bluff toward his wife and son. George pinioned him.

"Wait, Bill. I want you to know everything."

"Hurry, George!"

"Bill, if I may say so, she was awful! No other word. Three weeks without a spark. I almost—"

"Why didn't she ask me to teach her?"

"Dread of failure. And it is my belief that it might have led to serious domestic strife, perhaps worse. Because after only ten lessons we stopped speaking to each other. That was the day Sue broke the tip of a Spencer by hitting the ground on the backcast. The backcast, Bill!"

Bill now made a third lunge toward the trail leading down the bluff.

George again restrained him by force.

"Bill, you must hear me first. Let her tell Jud. You can see how happy she's making the boy. Look at the way they're smiling at each other."

"Yuh. Sure, George. Hurry."

"Three days before we were to leave on the trip," George continued, "I saw a glimmer of hope. A faint one, Bill. That was the day she tried to strike me. But I had tied her elbow to her side, so that she couldn't use that frightful full-arm sweep. I had just told her—gently, of course—that I had never dreamed anyone could be as awkward as she. Right after that she struck at me with the rod. In that instant she got her first sense of timing. Instead of hitting me, what she did with her elbow tied, was to get a respectable cast—her first. She didn't realize it, but I did. It was poetry, Bill—poetry."

"George! That was the day you told me you couldn't get up till the second week."

"Yes. It was a turning point. She needed a bit more time."

"Time was of the essence," murmured Bill.

"I was constantly by her side, Bill. Of course I wouldn't have done it for anyone else. I gave her everything I knew. It was beautiful to see it taking shape in her and growing. One day she smiled. Radiance simply spread over her. She had got out thirty-five feet and the fly stayed on. The basic fire, the love, must have been there all the time. Must have been lying dormant in her for twenty years. What you have just witnessed is the mere flowering of—"

This time Bill Crane made good his escape. An instant later he held his wife in his arms. "Sue, dearest! You're a marvel. That was pretty casting!"

"Oh, Bill! I'm so glad! Jud said I was good too! When I think of what I've missed!"

"Plenty good years ahead for all of us."

"That's just what I told her, Dad," said Jud. "I told her about my big trout in the upper pool too. But she won't go near him!"

"Cast for another fellow's trout?" cried Sue. "Nothing doing!"

Bill's arms tightened. Apparently, in Sue one of angling's highest principles was already fixed. He stared over her shoulder into his son's tanned, wistfully smiling face. In each other's eyes, father and son saw their future reflected. Year after year they would arise in the cold dawn. They would don flannels, waders, and a spirit of Spartan gaiety. It would be an ordeal by ice-water, alarm clocks, tapered silk, and split bamboo. Their reward would be another's happiness, in the knowledge that, together, they held the key. The trout in the upper pool was but the beginning.

Bill smiled and straightened up.

"Guess it's your trout, Jud. But if you want any help—"

"I'll take this one myself, Dad." The boy came around to face his mother. How strangely real rang his eagerness. "Come on, Mother, Dad. Let's go!"

THE TEACHER COMMENTS

THE OBLIGATION OF GENIUS

In his preface to this story, Mr. Ware touches on a matter most important to any writer. That is the matter of attitude toward your writing and toward your readers.

Whether you wish to write for *Thrilling Adventures,* for *The Saturday Evening Post,* or for *The Yale Review*—or as some have done, for all three—be sure of this: You cannot condescend to the magazine or its readers. You cannot "toss off" your story and expect it to get you anything but a rejection slip. Mr. Ware's "blackened souls" are indeed ignorant; they think that to be saleable is to be spurious.

The very young and the very self-consciously literary are much given to criticism of magazine fiction. It is, they say, mawkishly sentimental, unreal, stupid. Most of this criticism is silly because it violates criticism's first canon, which is to judge an object in terms of its purpose. It is true, of course, that fiction has done its greatest service to humanity when it has been most profound. But profundity is not the only purpose of fiction. To be gay, to be amusing, to provoke laughter are also legitimate, and to deny their legitimacy is to exhibit ignorance of the history of fiction or snobbishness toward the public's reading tastes. You may reject the public's tastes, and that is your right. You may not like Gilbert and Sullivan, and Cole Porter, but you do not hold their influence to be wicked or roast them for failing to be Verdi.

It has always amused me that many of my intellectual friends unashamedly enjoy the movies, second-rate detective fiction, popular music, and even the comic strips, but consistently denounce slick-magazine fiction. If they would take the trouble to analyze that fiction, perhaps they would stop trying to compare apples and oranges.

To that end, therefore, it is appropriate to quote several paragraphs of an extremely acute analysis of slick fiction. This was written by Bernard DeVoto when he was editor of *The Saturday Review of Literature:*

Writing for the slicks is a branch of the amusement business. People read the magazines primarily for entertainment. There are other important reasons, too—they read to have their ideas confirmed and their emotions ratified, to have their phantasy life stimulated, and to increase their knowledge of the minor sanctions and rituals of society—but first of all they want to be amused. It is a harmless desire.

It necessarily follows that, though they may like to be threatened or thrilled, they do not like to be scared; that, though they may enjoy a seasoning of horror, they must not be appalled or disgusted; that, though they may play with ideas, they will not wrestle with them. Satire flourishes in the slicks, but it is a satire of manners. Few themes or subjects are tabooed but every subject must be treated in such a way that basic fears, disgusts, and prejudices are not roused. The "unhappy ending" . . . is a commonplace in the slicks, but genuine tragedy would be as out of place there as a chorus from *Antigone* interpolated between innings at a baseball game. People do not read the slicks to encounter the brutalities, the profundities, or the complexities of experience. That fact, not the timidity or hypocrisy of editors, determines the nature of magazine fiction.

. . . . . .

In short the magazine story does not and cannot explore the profundities of human experience, probe psychological intricacies, or describe life brutally or cynically. It is frequently thoughtful, pessimistic, or satirical, it is sometimes extremely unflattering to human nature and human belief, but it must be so in pursuit of an agreeable end or in vindication of a more optimistic ideal. It is only rarely intellectual, and its ideas are seldom weighty. It works with simple emotions, and, except for heroism and fortitude and honesty and similar primary virtues, it works with them superficially. And it uses any theme primarily as material for the creation and resolution of a situation. "In this office," an editor once remarked, "a story is defined as a narrative in which something happens." That is the complete definition of the slick story, and when it is understood everything else is clear. The slick writer is a story writer.

. . . . . .

Nevertheless, though the greater part of slick fiction is superficial and conventional, the best of it has many virtues. Not all human emotion is complex or profound and not all experience is frightening or disgusting. At its highest level, the slick story is gay, ironical, sophisticated, adventurous, immensely entertaining or exciting. It has a shrewdness of its own and it is the vehicle for some of the sharpest observation of the contemporary scene, especially contemporary manners and fashions, that is to be found in our fiction. Its realism, though light and shallow, is frequently quite as good as any in the contemporary novel. You will not encounter realism about homosexuality, let us say, or strikebreaking or adultery, but you will find superb realism about women at matinees or literary clubs or the A. & P., men in the locker room or the bar or the commuters' car, married people worrying about expenses or the children's diseases, adolescents adjusting themselves to the high-school world. In many of the trades and businesses, in many of the common activities and minor relationships of life, and especially in fashions of behavior and belief and amusements, the best slick fiction is frequently better than any except the very best novels. The historian is going to recover the surface of American life—at least of middle-class life—much more fully and with less distortion from the slicks than from the novel of our day. The slicks render the surface more honestly, more accurately, and with greater respect. The slick writer, unlike the novelist, is penalized if he loads the dice.

. . . . . .

Unlike the novelist, also, he is forced to master his medium. Serious fiction would be greatly improved if every novelist could be required to serve an apprenticeship as rigorous as the slick writer's. There are occasional meteors who make the *Post* with their first story and have no trouble thereafter, but most slick writers travel a long and laborious way. . . . Writing for the slicks is a skilled craft which must be studied seriously, and there is no way of shortening the learning process.

It is a craft which requires exactness, compression, flexibility of intelligence, and versatility of style. The writer must do his job under the tyranny of space limitations, and he must be crystal clear. He must learn to do without inessentials and he must think things through—he can afford neither the verbosity nor the vagueness that sometimes creates reputations in the novel. He must practise an economy of means that would seem parsimony to the most conscientious novelist. He must master the form—the effects of the slick story result from a technique as intricate and interdependent as that of the sonnet. And he is held to his job as, in the circumstances of our publishing system, no novelist is held to his. If a given scene can be done in three hundred words, a novelist may fumble it through three thousand—or may let the first, sloppy approximation slide into the book. Very few publishers, none if he is an important novelist, will discipline him. There is another publisher around the corner—and the difference doesn't show in a novel of a hundred thousand words, the reader may skip the passage if he wants to, and if fifty thousand people won't buy the book, why, five thousand will. But in the slick story that job must be done in three hundred words. If it isn't, there will be no sale at all. And there can be no contradictions, no opaque places where the writer isn't quite sure but maybe the reader will be, and no debauches of beautiful but irrelevant rhetoric. If book publishers held novelists to standards of workmanship as high as those uniformly enforced by editors of the slicks, fewer novels would be published and fewer novels would be flops.

The writer who thinks he will just toss off a story for the *Post* gets it back because his craftsmanship is bad. He is usually too contemptuous to study the form he is trying to work in, and may go on for years sending in misconceived and flabby stuff and confirming his belief that the editors are enemies of art. . . .

There is no conflict between writing for the slicks and writing serious fiction. True, any time spent writing a slick story is time which cannot be spent writing a psychological novel, but so is time spent earning a living in any other way. The slick writer is not debasing himself or prostituting his art. He cannot expend his profundity, forthrightness, and subtlety on magazine stories, but working in an office, writing for a newspaper, or correcting freshman themes sets the same limitation on him. Within the areas of experience which the slick story touches, he can utilize all the shrewdness, humor, observation, intelligence, and skill that he possesses. He will enjoy himself more and exhaust himself less than he would in an office job, and he will have more time for the work that most interests him.

Furthermore, he will gain a good deal. He will learn economy, clearness, compression, and polish; he will learn a lot about sheer style. Serious fiction in America owes the slicks a sizeable debt for having made better writers of a considerable number of novelists. And finally, the man who is making a comfortable living from the magazines will not feel a pressure that degrades some of our most ambitious fiction. His serious novels do not have to be aimed at the box office; he is free to write them as he pleases.

So much, then, for your attitude toward work. Beginners, like other writers, must begin, and it seems to the writers of this book that magazine fiction offers excellent models for the study of fictional techniques, whether you intend to write fiction aimed at the multitude or at the few.

WHEN?

Mr. Ware tells us that "Angler, Beware!" is full of "bald devices," or, more euphemistically, technical solutions to fictional problems. So is almost any successful story at a given level of excellence. As Mr. Ware shows in these prefaces, his stories have often worked themselves out in terms of answers to questions that the writer puts to himself. I have earlier said that "why?" is the most important question a writer can ask and answer about a story. "When?" is a close second in importance and often holds the key to "why?" Why did Sue Crane decide to take up fishing? Because, at that time, at that *precise* time, in her life, her resistance to it, which had sustained her (and the story) broke down. It could have broken at no other time. Very often causes and motivations which puzzle a writer, which seem to block the progress of his story, become clear if he asks himself: "When did it happen?"

PRESSURE

Whatever happens in a story has to happen because of pressure. Mr. Ware speaks of coincidence, and we may define coincidence as that point in time when two or more converging pressures meet. What is important is that the reader must see or feel these pressures converging, and he must see them converging in one of three ways: throughout the story ("Last Trip Together"), somewhat throughout the story and completely by the story's end ("A Place to Cry"), or suddenly and completely, at the story's end ("Angler, Beware!" and "The Gift of the Magi"). What may be coincidence to a character in a story is never coincidence to the reader.

Actually, for the reader, *there is no such thing as a story with a surprise ending*. Surprise is a misnomer; the term is recognition. The only story in the world with a surprise ending is "The Lady and the Tiger," and the only thing that can be said about that story is that it is unique and has already been written.

Innumerable stories by beginners fail because their writers are confused on this point. Part of their confusion is due to their lack of grasp of the principles discussed in Chapter I. It is true that people in real life fall dead at unexpected times and places, but you cannot visit your villain with a conveniently lethal attack of coronary thrombosis at the moment of his ascendancy over the hero—you cannot unless other pressures already set in motion toward convergence are apparent to the reader either at the time of death or earlier. If the villain earlier in the story exhibits symptoms sufficient to account for his demise under the emotional stress of victory, then the laws of fiction permit you to kill him. Ingenuity may hold off the definite threat about the villain's heart (just as in "A Place to Cry," information as to the identity of the man killed in the tunnel is held off) until the end of the story, or information may be given in such terms that it will seem to be something other than what it is. When the story is ended, however, the reader must recognize that what has happened has happened because of the logic of cause and effect, not because of the machination of chance or even because of the visitation of divine justice.

There is, however, one place where coincidence will be accepted by the reader and that is before the story really opens, when coincidence is presented as a *fait accompli.*

> He found it hard to believe that all these things had happened to him. First, to have his pocket picked—that didn't really happen to people, but it had most assuredly happened to him. Then, of all the people to run into under the circumstances, it would have to be Sam Sykes, whom he hadn't seen for five years, but who had not forgotten a certain poker game and an unredeemed I.O.U. And now, to be seated in the city's most expensive restaurant, sipping coffee and liqueur, and gazing into Julie's violet eyes, while the waiter approached with the check for which there could be no payment—

Only outside the time-frame of a story can coincidence of this sort—call it luck, good or bad—play the inscrutable rôle that it so often plays in life. Whatever happens, either to or within a person, must happen clearly as the result of pressure, the pressure of personality, of place, of circumstance, if it is to happen within the story proper.

Pressure itself is of two kinds: There is the pressure of *continuing time,* the pressure that, over a period of years, months, or hours, as the case may be, slowly wears away resistance or fortifies resolve. In "Angler, Beware!" the same pressure, operating over the years, accounts both for the wearing away of Sue's resistance and the fortifying of Bill's resolve. The second pressure is the pressure of the moment, the pressure of *now,* the specific, particular pressure that forces the story's final action, or part of it. In "Angler, Beware!" there are two examples of pressure of now. One, when Sue, in Mr. Ware's prefatory word, "explodes," that is, when she reaches the belief that she is being unfair to her family (it is interesting to note that information about this pressure although foreshadowed, is held off until the closing paragraphs; it is more interesting to note that *it must be given somewhere in the story*). Two, when Bill discovers Jud's antipathy to fishing. To refer again to "The Gift of the Magi," there are two pressures of continuing time: one, the couple's love for each other; two, their poverty. The pressure of now, or the instant, is the imminence of Christmas.

These two kinds of pressure always work together: The one leads to the other; the other precipitates the action foreshadowed by the one. Also, taken together, these pressures must be strong enough to force what happens to happen, and yet not too strong, not of a kind which promises the reader more than he gets. Anything less than the long ennui of George Pattengill, of Sue's hours of reading on river banks, of the jargon which she must endure, would have cast suspicion on the validity of her motive when she "explodes." Anything greatly more than such pressure—say the danger of a family break-up or Sue's being led toward serious nervous collapse—would have been pressure too great for what it causes and would therefore result in absurdity. Conversely, pressures of the instant must not exceed in force the sum of the pressures of continuing time. Had Sue, for example, threatened suicide because she was bored with fishing, the reader would have lost sympathy for her. Indeed, the pressure of definite time may often be something quite small in itself and only distantly related to the more diffuse pressure of continuing time. In "Angler, Beware!" the pressures of the instant happen to be closely related to the pressure of continuing time, but in "A Place to Cry," for example, the presence of Rush's young son in the bathroom is but distantly connected with the accident. There must be, of course, *some* connection; in this case the connection is the father-son pattern plus the reminiscent revery in which Rush had earlier been indulging.

Let the writer ponder the pressures in his story. Are they sufficient to account for what happens? Are they greater than the story requires? Are they less? Do the pressures of definite time bear sensible relation to the pressures of the instant?

HOW MUCH TIME?

The actual time shown in a story may be as much as twenty years (De Maupassant's "Diamond Necklace") or a few minutes (Katherine Mansfield's "A Dill Pickle"). The amount of time necessary to the story is always relative to that particular story, what the story shows and how it shows it. One generality, however, is useful: Other things being equal, start your story as close to the end in point of time as you can.

In stories that show change in a character's attitude or personality, long time lapses are necessary to account for that change. These time lapses may occur either within the time-frame of the story or in material antecedent to the time-frame. "A Place to Cry" is framed in time between afternoon and early evening—say six hours at most. Time mentioned and accounted for, however, goes far back of that particular afternoon and evening. "Last Trip Together" depicts current action within three hours, but past events are brought into the story. The majority of modern stories are likewise compressed into a time-frame that is actually much smaller in type-space than in time-span.

"Angler, Beware!" however, is a story that must show the passing of time within its framework because the showing is essential to an understanding of what the characters do. We have to see Sue sitting on those river banks through the years in order to build up sufficient pressure to make her explosion valid. We have to see Bill losing his rapture in the sport with each passing season, and we have to see Jud growing from birth to the age of sixteen in order that Bill's discovery of his defection shall have importance. No sudden (to the reader) change in character is convincing. There was a time, perhaps, many years ago, when characters in a story could suddenly account for their unaccountable changes by one device or another; a favorite one, for example, went something like this:

> Then, suddenly, in his moment of triumph, Derek Beardsdale tasted ashes in his mouth. He looked at the beautiful form of Mildred, standing dejectedly beside her defeated mother, and for a moment all the evil passion he had for her welled up in him. Then, slowly, as though he were in a dream, he began to tear up the mortgage. When the last shred had fallen to the floor, he looked up, and there were tears in his eyes.
>
> The face of Mildred was beautiful to behold, as the full significance of Derek's act began to dawn upon her. With brimming orbs that bespoke more gratitude than ever words could convey, she stared dumbly at him. At last she spoke.
>
> "I—I don't understand," she quavered. "I thought you wanted—"
>
> "I did," he replied harshly. "And I don't understand either." From habit his hand began to twirl the end of his sinister black moustache. "Unless," he went on, his voice almost a whisper, "unless it is that your beauty and goodness, Mildred, have made a different man out of me!"
>
> So saying, he turned on his heel and went forth into the world, a truly changed and better man.

Nowadays, however, readers of any kind of fiction demand more logical solutions to fictional problems. Fundamental changes in character cannot fortuitously occur; they must be accounted for either by the pressures of time and circumstance taken together, by cause and effect, or by repeated yet unobtrusive information which tells the reader by the story's end why things were other than they seemed.

How much time a story shows, and the way it shows it, depend, then, on the kind of story it is, the way the writer chooses to tell it, and the kind of circumstances he employs. A story showing the impact of an overwhelming experience on a man ("A Place to Cry") must be altogether different in treatment from a story showing how a man and his wife ironically exchange attitudes toward a hobby.

INSIDE THE TIME-FRAME

It is helpful to put a time-frame around your story and to make it definite. Within the frame will occur the events which comprise the core of the story. This frame, as was said above, varies in size with the kind of story you are writing. In "Angler," it extends from Jud's birth to that particular day on the Nipisiguit River, sixteen years later, when all the pressures in the story converge and settle the family's angling future. In "A Place to Cry," it extends only from "the afternoon sunshine" until shortly after supper that same day. Stories which deal with the impact of a single experience are usually thus compressed within a relatively small time-frame. Let the writer ponder carefully the dimensions of his time-frame before beginning the later drafts of his story. The smaller the frame, other things being equal, the greater the story's intensity. It is sometimes advantageous, if you are floundering about in your story material, to impose an arbitrary time-frame on the material, and try to work out the story within that frame. Say to yourself: "The story must begin at noon and end at six that evening," or, "The story begins Monday morning and ends late Wednesday night." Such an exercise may help to solve a number of problems which, because they were vague, eluded or confused you. The arbitrary frame you choose may not, of course, be the right one for the story, but it will probably show you how much time your story is going to require and the kind of treatment you will give it.

OUTSIDE THE TIME-FRAME

A time-frame, however, by no means limits the total amount of time covered by the story; it limits only the amount of time shown in direct presentation. For example, the time-frame of "A Place to Cry" is a matter of hours, but the total time covered is three generations. There are, that is to say, two kinds of time in a story, or rather, two kinds of time treatment: direct, and antecedent. Stories require varying amounts of time outside the frame: "Angler" requires only a few hours, those immediately preceding Jud's birth, while "A Place to Cry" requires dozens of years. The author must select from those years particular highlights which have bearing on the events within the time-frame, and he must give them, nine times out of ten, dramatic presentation. The tenth time, he can present them in terms of summary or straight narration; but summary and narration, particularly in the pluperfect tense, have very little place in fiction.

This presentation of material outside the time-frame is what Hollywood has aptly called the "flashback." The flashback is at once the most useful and dangerous of all fictional devices. Its usefulness is that it enables the writer to construct his story in its most dramatic form; to keep the intensity of a compressed time-frame and yet range, when necessary, over long periods of time. Its danger is that, in unskilled hands, it runs away with itself. A beginner grasps the principle of starting his story in an interesting situation, and then, through the flashback, explaining how the situation came to pass. In so doing, however, he is likely to tell entirely too much, to become so involved in the background of his story that he forgets to carry it forward. It is true that backward motion in a story often seems to satisfy fiction's demand for dynamics, but watch out! Motion backward in time must accomplish motion forward in the story; it does this by increasing pressure (or tension or conflict, call it what you will) simultaneously with the giving of information. You may think that it is necessary to explain how your characters got where they are (the old newspaper questions of Who? What? When? Where? Why?) and you are right, but it is only half the problem. The other half is keeping your story fluid, pressing onward toward its end. Motion backward in time which fails to achieve some heightening of pressures is another form of statics, and hence fictional death.

This is a point worth considerable laboring. Take the problem of information by itself. How much information about character and place and circumstance is necessary for the reader to understand the story? A categorical answer says, a whole lot less than the beginner believes. I recall a student's story that opened with a fight between a young married couple. The fight itself was well handled, and the reasons for it, the points of irritation that had worn thin the nerves of the man and wife, were self-evident in the dialogue. The story was told in the first person, through the agency of the wife's brother. We see a word, spoken impatiently, taken up, worried, tossed back and forth between husband and wife, expanded to whole strings of accusations and counter-accusations, and ending, finally, in a scene of intense bitterness. Then, instead of carrying the story forward, the narrator begins a reminiscence that ran for eight pages, starting with the three of them as childhood playmates, and carrying through the wedding and the first four years of marital living. Nothing in that reminiscence told the reader what was not explicit or implied in the fight itself. All those eight pages, therefore, were simply redundant.

Turn now to "A Place to Cry" and analyze Mr. Ware's flashbacks. Notice particularly, that much of the background information about Rush Atwood is given within the time-frame. A beginner might have been tempted to range backward, somewhere in the first long paragraph on page 31 and explain all about Rush's profession, how he came to embrace it, what it meant to him, and a great many other matters that are not at all necessary to the reader's understanding of what is taking place. The first flashback begins on page 33 with the sentence: "My father was shaving in the bathroom of a house I can't remember." There are two points to notice about that flashback: It is brief; it pays enormous dividends later in the story. It may not appear, at first glance, to give a very strong push to the story's forward motion, yet closer analysis shows that it does increase the intensity of Rush's emotion, and that it whets the reader's appetite to know what it was that happened in the tunnel.

And so with the others. They all give information about Rush's character and simultaneously, in one way or another, contribute to the progress of the story.

SCENES

Fiction has been accurately described as a series of interrelated, integrated scenes. After you have written the first or second draft of a story, it is a good idea to look carefully at the scenes that compose it. How many are there? Are they arranged in their most effective order? What ones come inside the time-frame and what ones outside? You may often find that the most effective order of scenes is not chronological. If, for example, you have eight scenes, you may find the most effective order to be 3–4–5–1–2–6–7–8 or any other combination, even to starting with scene 7 or 8! Normally, however, extreme deviations from chronological sequence pose many difficulties that the beginner is wise to avoid. At this point, it is recommended that the reader turn ahead to Chapter VIII and read "Some Have to Get Hurt," noticing how the scenes in that story are arranged with reference to their chronological order.

Not all fiction is composed entirely of scenes. There is often some summary and even some narration. Summary and narration, however, should generally be kept to a minimum and are useful chiefly as transition. Mr. Ware, for example, speaks of bridging a fictional gap of ten years with the sentence, "By the time he was entered in prep school, Jud Crane was a skilled fisherman." But if the writer finds long paragraphs in his story, *telling* the reader what has happened, rather than *showing* him, watch out! Notice how brief are such passages in "Angler, Beware!" how much of the story is directly presented in scenes.

IV

THE WRITER COMMENTS

SUPPOSING

There is usually a great deal of excess supposing in organizing a work of fiction; but aside from the rare burst of insight—the unheralded and exalting sense of form—I do not know a good way to start a story from zero, except to suppose something. The process of supposition at least has movement and occasionally gets somewhere.

Dog-biting-man is our most ancient starting line. It is no story because it is too common. Man-biting-dog, on the other hand, is a story. There the old newspaper editor used to end his lesson in reporting. But the fiction writer carries on. Supposing, says the fiction writer, that the dog bites the man, and the man, in retaliation, bites the dog. As a result of supposition, there is more of a story. But no one really cares very much, so it is waste supposing. Why don't people care? Perhaps it's because the biting act is devoid of what Plato called universality. Writers call it reader identification. That is, to make the story a convincing illusion of reality, the writer must create characters and situations in which the reader feels a sympathy, or a parallel in himself or his experience.

Suppose there is a middle-aged man whose dreams have never been even partly fulfilled. In that man, you have supposed a large number of people. A lot of readers, young, middle-aged, and old, could identify themselves with your man's smoldering ember of romance. Everyone, even an American husband in the bosom of his family, is due one solo flight, or one act in defiance of the domestic law of gravity and convention. When a steady, plodding, dependable soul makes a sharp left turn, you have the way paved for an interesting situation. Why? Because his friends and family see something strange happening—something unthinkable for poor old Henry Barstow—

and they react in various ways, and their reaction is the beginning of a story.

It is apparent that the more ordinary and conventional the man, the more dramatic will be his change. Conversely, a man with eccentric habits would make no story at all if he did something unusual. For him, the unusual is expected. But for Henry Barstow, any variation from his habit-worn route is news.

It was this simple observation which prompted the writing of "Mr. Barstow's Infidelity," and the title indicates what form his rebellion took. The title was chosen deliberately as a suspense-device. One wonders how a man named Mr. Barstow, as harmless as he undoubtedly is in name and instinct, can commit adultery. It is a leading question, designed, or hoped to be leading enough to allow the writer time and space to limn Mr. Barstow's habits and family in detail and to set forth his almost tranquil conflicts.

Already Mr. Barstow presents difficulties as a character. By original concept, he is so usual as to be uninteresting. How, then, can an uninteresting man be made to perform something as interesting, not to say shocking, as marital infidelity? Mr. Barstow simply isn't that sort of character. He is kindly, sweet, faithful, and rather dull.

Here the process of supposing makes the story move. Suppose Mr. Barstow were caught in some compromising circumstance? That is one way to make him appear unfaithful and still save his morals. He must be innocent, even though he looks guilty to everyone—except the reader.

One other way, after much fruitless supposing, presents itself. Like everyone else on earth, there are times when Mr. Barstow dreams of himself in rebellion, in a great rôle, in the ecstasy of wild freedom. He can dream dreams, and still maintain his security, and keep his faith with family and accepted forms. He can dream, moreover, and by so doing work his way deeper into the reader's heart, for the reader knows that everyone dreams, and he identifies himself with Barstow, who also dreams.

But how can an act so innocent as dreaming impinge with reality upon the characters surrounding Barstow? They—those antagonistic characters—obviously must discover Mr. Barstow's dream, and mistake it for actuality. At this point in his story's development, the writer is delighted with his own ingenuity, for through his laborious supposing, he sees light and laughter ahead. Supposing, he now says, that poor Mr. Barstow, blunted and dulled by his pedestrian life, has a dream of love, all clean and visionary and harmless and sweet—but his family, learning about it, thinks it real!

The story now has everything but a conclusion, everything but a few inventions. By what device will Mr. Barstow's "infidelity" be discovered? How will his wife, son, and daughter react when their pudgy pillar of dependability appears to totter? And above all, how will Henry explain himself? This constant questioning inheres in all fiction-writing. What will happen? What will he, or they, do? What will they say? Where will they be when they say it? Why? It is this writer's advice and Mr. Bailey's, to explore characters and stories by similar repeated questioning, for each question may have a variety of answers, and each answer may open up all kinds of possibilities.

In the case of Mr. Barstow, this questioning solved the story, as I believe it solves all stories. If Mr. Barstow told his family he was merely dreaming of a love-affair, what would they say to him? Answer: They would either say he was lying, or they would say he was crazy. Being smart enough to know this, what does Mr. Barstow do? What *can* he do? He is in a dilemma, more recently called a situation, predicament, or spot.

Here the story is at its cross-roads. It can go left or right. Left: He admits he was dreaming of love. His family ridicules him unmercifully, till at length he translates his dream into adulterous action because they drove him to it. That might be one story of Mr. Barstow's infidelity, and it might be a pretty good one. Yet somehow it doesn't fit Barstow's character, as already described.

Supposing, then, that Mr. Barstow turns right at the story's cross-roads. Facing his family with dignity and some humility, he admits falsely that he is in love with a girl who is non-existent. In this new situation, Mr. Barstow is reacting true to character. There is opportunity for a fine and sweetly ironical scene—the family shocked and accusing, Barstow gently but firmly defending himself for something he hasn't done, but only dreamed of doing. Here is the scene where all the characters in the story begin to change and gain stature. It's the first shocking thing that's ever happened to any of them. They are, for the first time, faced with a stark reality—which only Barstow and the reader know to be a dream.

As for the inventions in the story, the reader will at once perceive the reasons for them. He will realize why Mr. Barstow's profession was so carefully selected, why his wife liked goldfish, why the weekly mutton was cold, and why things were as they were.

For example, if Mr. Barstow hadn't run a travel agency, he wouldn't logically have been able to write excellent circulars. And if he hadn't been able to write circulars, he wouldn't have been able to write himself the incriminating love-letters. This is a case where invention and plausibility are one—or at least parallel.

The tone, or the style of writing in "Mr. Barstow," was chosen to conform to his character—slow, patient, yet with a suspicion of reserve and dignity. This reserve and dignity, if in fact they were achieved, make a contrasting harmony with the slang dialogue of Mr. Barstow's son, Junior, and with the harsh criticisms flung by Mr. Barstow's wife, Muriel.

As the frame of the story now stands, with Barstow convicted, the reader will realize the possibility of alternative endings. Having confessed that his dream is real—in other words, having been forced to lie himself into a difficult place—what will Barstow do? What happens next? It is an interesting exercise in supposing. Will Barstow at last break down and give his family the full and true confession? Or will he keep his secret forever?

If he confesses, he will have lost what he has gained: the curious and unprecedented focus of his family's attention, which at times is almost admiration. He will, in short, have lost a trick. Supposing he keeps his secret forever? What will his family think of him? Will they regard him as a reformed adulterer, and will he thereby suffer for his innocent dreaming?

The story might have been concluded either way; but Barstow, like all writers, was obliged to choose but one, and make it stick.

THE STORY

Mr. Barstow's Infidelity

ONCE, in his dim-remembered youth, Henry Jennings Barstow must have thrilled to a sunset, a starlit night, or the marching of majestic clouds. Somewhere he must have looked upon a beautiful face and in the attic of his soul, stored a measure of the poetry of love. Albeit Mr. Barstow still believed in these things and even advertised them to others in his skilfully worded circulars of the H. J. Barstow Travel Agency, he supposed that far horizons and the tang of adventure were not for him.

In Mr. Barstow's own life, romance had been stifled by innumerable realities, of which his wife, Muriel, was one. Mr. Barstow didn't blame Muriel for being a reality. He didn't blame anyone for anything. Once in awhile he dreamed that Muriel might give him a larger share of the devotion she bestowed on her two docile goldfish; and sometimes he imagined, just for fun, that Thursday night suppers might consist of bread fruit and African lobster tails, instead of mutton, peas, potato, and wrinkly apricots. There were still other times when he thought mistily of going somewhere besides his office, and of returning anywhere but home. But Mr. Barstow had never done anything about it. He believed he never would.

At forty-two, Henry Jennings Barstow was a patient prisoner in routine, a trusty in a brown suit, brown shoes, and brown overcoat. He had no regrets, save for the fact that the second World War had brought travel to a standstill and caused the rationing of gasoline. Mr. Barstow uncomplainingly accepted an A-card, which found its way inevitably into the pocket of his son. Junior was seventeen.

"Pa, c'n I have the car today?"

"Well, Junior, you had it yesterday, and what with the gas shortage, and our tires smooth, I don't think it's patriotic to—"

"Aw, gee, Pa! I wanna go to the movies with Eddie Macon. And besides, what good's my driving license if you won't let me drive?"

In habitual support of her son, Muriel Barstow asserted that Henry didn't really need the car. "Why don't you walk to your office?" she asked. "Mr. Forbush walks, and he's a banker."

So, because Junior had a driving license, and because Mr. Forbush was a banker, Henry Barstow relinquished all claims on his car and walked to his office. He continued to walk. He rather enjoyed it. With pleasant irony, he told himself that the walk freshened him for his work—of which, currently, there was none.

But even with his car monopolized and his business dead, Mr. Barstow was grateful for many things. There was the sanctuary of his office with its golden oak desks and four superfluous typewriters, including one which wrote French, and a little one with elite type; there were the large cardboard cut-outs of ships sailing in a dusty sea atop the filing cabinets; there was the comfort of sufficient money saved. And of late, ever since the chimney fire in his home, there was a ray of understanding from his daughter, Gladys, who was a year younger than Junior.

The night of the fire, Junior had rushed out dramatically to ring in the alarm and had seemed vaguely disappointed when the fire department extinguished the blaze in a mere five minutes. Muriel, in dressing gown and curling clips, had stormed at the water damage to her living-room rug.

"Henry, I don't see why you didn't have the chimney cleaned last fall! Just look at my rug! It's ruined!"

Mr. Barstow, who had prided himself on thinking first in the emergency of Muriel's goldfish, stood in the open front doorway holding the bowl. Within, the fish swam idly, oblivious to peril. Water had slopped from the bowl and trickled down the front of Mr. Barstow's bathrobe. His initial sensation of gallantry in action had changed to one of clamminess.

"I didn't think about the rug," he apologized. "I just thought about the goldfish. First thing that came to mind."

"It's a wonder," said Muriel, rescuing the bowl from his arms, "that we weren't all burned in our beds. Incinerated!"

"Well, now, Muriel, really, I—"

"Anyway," interrupted Junior, "you should have had the chimney cleaned, just like Ma said. Eddie Macon's old man had theirs cleaned."

It was then that Mr. Barstow's daughter took his part. He was strangely moved by the sound of a voice lifted in his defense. The sensation was unique and heartening. He thought Gladys extremely pretty in her blue kimono and slippers. It was as if he had noticed her for the first time—or, rather, as if someone nice were noticing him.

"Pa's not to blame," said Gladys. "Why don't you leave him alone? It was just one of those things."

"But my rug! Oh, my poor rug!"

Turning to his wife, Mr. Barstow said: "I'll carry it out to the car, dear, and take it to the cleaner's tomorrow."

"You use the car *tomorrow,* Pa? How'm I and Eddie Macon going to get to the hockey game?"

"Maybe," said Henry, "you could leave a little early, and just drop the rug on the way to the game."

"Me drop the rug? *Me?*" Junior sighed tragically. "After all, Pa, the fire was your fault."

Gladys' blue eyes sparkled warningly in her brother's direction. "Selfish! Go ahead and take the old car! I'll simply telephone the cleaner and have him come and get the rug. So there!"

"Why, that's an idea, Glad," Henry said. "Never occurred to me. Settles the whole thing. Well—guess it's time we all got back to bed."

Muriel replaced the goldfish bowl on its accustomed pedestal, and after murmuring words of endearing solace to its occupants, started toward the stairs. She paused to touch her eyes with her handkerchief. "There'll be precious little sleep for me tonight."

"Count sheep," said Gladys, gently.

His daughter's rôle in the chimney-fire episode was a bright spot in Mr. Barstow's family life. In fact, it was so bright that he half-doubted its reality. To test Gladys' affection, but perhaps more to savor it again, he invented the dog proposal. Purposely dawdling over his coffee one morning, even though Muriel repeatedly declared her wish to clear the table, Mr. Barstow contrived to leave the house just as Gladys started for school.

"Glad," he said, walking along beside her, "what would you think if I got a dog?"

"Why, Pa? Lonesome?"

"No, I wouldn't say that. But—" Mr. Barstow hesitated cautiously, "—I've noticed how much pleasure your mother gets from her goldfish, and I thought maybe if I had a dog, I'd enjoy him too."

"Better just keep him in your office, Pa. The rug, you know."

"That's right, the rug. Maybe I could get one to match the rug, though—eh, Glad?"

She looked up at him and laughed. "Do they have green dogs, Pa?"

For an instant, seeing into his daughter's eyes, Mr. Barstow was almost elated. But the instant passed swiftly. Two of Gladys' school friends hailed her, and as she rushed across the street to join them, he felt himself futilely trying to keep her near to him a little longer.

"Glad," he called, hastening after her, "here's something for you. A dollar—for movies and ice cream. Wait a minute!"

"Never mind, now, Pa!" she shouted over her shoulder. "I'm having my hair done this afternoon, anyway. Good-bye!"

Mr. Barstow stepped back onto the sidewalk and watched the three girls greet each other. He knew Gladys' friends well, but in their eagerness at meeting, they failed to notice him. They did not, however, fail to notice Mr. Forbush, the banker, who at that moment emerged from his house, pulled on his suede gloves, and started off to his office, swinging a cane.

Mr. Forbush was a splendid figure, dashing, white-mustached, and long-striding. As Mr. Barstow observed his daughter and her friends following the banker with admiring eyes and whispering in his exalted direction, he felt summarily forgotten. Perhaps he, too, should carry a cane instead of an umbrella. Perhaps he should have been a banker.

On that morning and for many mornings thereafter, Mr. Barstow wondered if his office weren't a trifle too much of a sanctuary. Where once had been a comradely secretary, there was now a vacant chair. Mr. Barstow missed the flap and flutter of mail dropping through the slit in his office door. The telephone no longer rang, except when Muriel wanted him to stop at the bakery for éclairs, or when salesmen called.

In his yearning for friendship, Mr. Barstow invited salesmen and became an easy mark for them. He thought it unfair to take up their time, without making a purchase. This had led to his acquisition of the superfluous typewriters, now five in number. He would undoubtedly have bought more, if typewriters hadn't been frozen along with foreign travel.

During the winter, Mr. Barstow pondered quite earnestly about dogs. He visited a number of kennels and scratched the ears of many setters, spaniels, and retrievers. He bought a thin volume entitled *Your Dog, Its Care and Training*. But he put off making an actual choice, partly because there were no green dogs, but mainly because of a jolly vendor of printing who called at his office one afternoon in February.

Mr. Barstow regretted that he had no excuse at this time for printing circulars, but he engaged the young salesman in an hour's conversation, in return for which he ordered a wanton assortment of stationery. Some was plain, some monogrammed, some bore the H. J. Barstow letter-head—complete with a half-tone of a full-rigged barkentine, hull down on a blue horizon.

To Mr. Barstow, a union between his new stationery and his five typewriters seemed predestined. It provided an outlet for his imagination, and filled his days with fanciful correspondents and fictitious business relations. Seating himself at one of the typewriters, he would insert a sheet of stationery, spin the roller, and address himself as follows:

My dear Mr. Barstow:
I am eager this year to extend the range of my travel, perhaps as far as Czechoslovakia. An acquaintance has assured me that you are able to give me excellent advice. Therefore, will you kindly . . . ?

It mattered not to Mr. Barstow's revery that Czechoslovakia was now as unreachable as the stars. In the course of a business day he wrote himself several such letters, mailed them, and jubilantly received them next morning through the slit in his door. He prided himself on his ability to write inspiring and authoritative answers, even though his own travel experience had been limited to Atlantic City and Bangor.

Dear Mr. Harper:
I strongly recommend that you spend some time in Prague, which is one of the world's oldest and most beautiful cities. You will see traces of Moorish architecture, and you will find an atmosphere of refined antiquity.
The Hotel Alcron is modern, however, and very comfortable indeed. The rate of exchange between the American dollar and the Czechish kron, is currently . . .

Or,

My dear Miss Moresby:
Manaos is approximately two thousand miles up the Amazon River. The trip is long, but not difficult in the proper season. The tropics have always held deep fascination for wanderers, bringing to mind a line written by the late Rudyard Kipling:

"Have you heard the steaming stillness
Of the orchid-scented jungle . . . ?"

Toward the end of a rainy day in March, Mr. Barstow was in the midst of one of his finest letters. He was planning a honeymoon for a mythical young couple who enjoyed outdoor life. Oblivious to the gusts which flung the rain against his dreary windows, he wrote with all the passion and poetry in his lonely heart:

> . . . for certainly I not only appreciate but encourage and abet your desire to be alone on this, of all occasions. That is why I suggest Mystery Lake, north by plane from Hudson, Ontario. In this vast wilderness, the stars hang low at night, and the silence is your friend. By day there are beaches of white sand, and the wind is washed by eight hundred miles of forest. I wish that I might, for my own sake, have some small part in making your trip more beautiful, and I . . .

Reluctantly Mr. Barstow left his typewriter to answer the intrusive telephone. His abrupt return from the land of midnight sun to a view of the rain-swept street below unnerved him. Muriel's voice, coming over the wire, was petulant and disheartening.

"Is that you, Henry? Why didn't you answer? They've been ringing and ringing. I heard them. Where have you been?"

"Why, right here, dear. I was absorbed in some work. I guess I just didn't hear the phone."

"Well, I wish you'd be more wide awake. Now, listen, Henry: On your way home, stop at the Goodie Shoppe and get a dozen macaroons and a box of cream cheese."

"Yes, dear. Anything else?"

"There is. It's about Junior and the car. He had to drive all the way home from the movies on a flat tire. The spare's no good. Can't you get him another second-hand tire?"

"I'll try, Muriel."

"Well, do it tomorrow. I don't want you to be late to supper. Gladys is going to the high-school dance tonight, and she can't help me with a thing. Don't forget the macaroons and cream cheese. And—wait, Henry, don't hang up till I'm through! Stop at the pet shop and get some more goldfish food. That's all."

As Mr. Barstow pulled on his rubbers, took up his umbrella, and prepared to leave his office, he was disturbed by an unkind thought about the goldfish. It seemed to him that in the past six months, they had grown even more obese, ignorant, and footling. Or was he simply comparing them with the flashing trout and muskellunge native to the north country of which he had so recently been dreaming?

In the puddled street below his office, Mr. Barstow opened his umbrella, crossed to a mail-box, and mailed the day's letters. He made his purchases in the Goodie Shoppe, which smelled of stale chocolate syrup instead of wind-clean pines. The pet shop smelled alarmingly of pets.

A further sense of the unchanging dullness of his life penetrated Mr. Barstow as he tucked his bundles under his arm and trudged homeward. He was examining the sensation rather guiltily, for he felt it disloyal to Muriel, Junior, and Gladys—when, suddenly, the lights of the city went dark. He was startled for a moment before he remembered that at six-thirty there was to be a practice blackout. All lights were to be put out, and all cars, except scheduled buses, were to turn off their headlights.

In the rain and darkness, Mr. Barstow's umbrella grew companionable. So did the bundles. Dark figures of pedestrians loomed terrifyingly toward him, then passed in the night. A small spirit of adventure awoke in him. He clutched his umbrella as though it were a weapon and walked sturdily into the wind.

As he paused uncertainly at an intersection, feeling for the curb with a cautious toe, he was startled by someone standing near him—a shadow among shadows. A swooping gust of wind tugged at his umbrella and tore it from his hands. He groped helplessly, but the shadow before him, moving with sprightly precision, retrieved his umbrella and handed it to him.

"Here you are! Dark, isn't it?"

The voice was a girl's. It was clear, gay, laughing.

"That was awfully nice of you," stammered Mr. Barstow. "And very quick too. I—I like quick people. I'm ever so much obliged."

In the sudden-sharp lights of an approaching bus, her face and figure took shape before him. She was wearing a camel's hair coat, and her chin nestled attractively in the upturned collar. As the bus drew nearer and slowed toward the stop, Mr. Barstow noted that the girl's hair was raven black. In a wind-blown strand that had escaped under the side of her jaunty hat, raindrops glistened like pearls.

But not until the bus drew to the curb did he see the wraith-like loveliness of her face. The wide, star-shot eyes glowed full upon his. She smiled and said: "It was fun. I'm glad I could catch it before it blew away. Isn't the rain wonderful? Good-night."

"Good-night," he said, and watched forlornly while she swung away and up the step of the waiting bus.

That she should appear and vanish so swiftly seemed to Mr. Barstow like a kind of tragic miracle. He heard the bus door clank shut behind her. To him it was the portcullis of a castle. The engines roared, and between him and the girl-of-the-darkness, a moat widened and became a gulf. Just once again he saw her high-boned, lovely face framed in the silver-streaked window. He waved, and her white hand flashed against the pane. Then the bus showed its dwindling red lights, and on the rear platform an illumined globe across which blazed the names of remote destinations: Chicago, Kansas City, Denver, Los Angeles!

Mr. Barstow didn't remember the exact moment when the blackout ended, but he found himself looking at his umbrella, which he held still open, point down on the sidewalk. He suddenly relished the sting of wind and rain, and his heart awoke and sang a tune of gallantry. Armor gleamed in the sun! Spears clashed in the dust and shock of tourney. In fancy, kneeling before the girl-of-the-darkness, Sir Barstow touched his lips to the hem of her skirt, and in his mailed fist held her satin hand.

In defiance of the storm, Mr. Barstow recklessly closed his umbrella, tilted the brim of his hat, and started homeward at a brisk pace. His shoulders were back, his chin high. His sordid bundles contained incense, myrrh, and precious stones. His umbrella, now tightly wound, was a cane—or, no! It was a rapier! Squaring off to a threatening telephone pole, Mr. Barstow made a thrust, and cried: "On guard! Have at thee, sir!"

He marched on victoriously and at length arrived at his home. In the front hall, he furtively opened his umbrella, stepped into the view of his family and closed it. He smiled at them, said "hello," and awaited their blessing.

"Henry, you're soaking wet, and late, too! Did you get the goldfish food? Can't you just carve before you change your clothes?"

"Hey, lissen, Pa! It's insulting to not have a decent set of tires on the car. Here I and Eddie Macon had to drive on a flat all the way back from the movies, and people laughing."

"Does your umbrella leak, Henry?"

"No, dear."

"Why didn't you use it?"

"I did use it."

Unassailable in his vision of the girl-of-the-darkness, Mr. Barstow didn't even wince when Gladys turned on him, saying: "Pa, with a flat and no spare, how'm I going to get to the dance without getting my new slippers simply soaked?"

"Call a taxi," suggested Mr. Barstow, as he carved the cooling mutton.

The next day Mr. Barstow did not open his business letters. He didn't even hear them flutter through his door. His thoughts of the girl-of-the-darkness enchanted him, filling the empty wells of his heart. He had named her Evelyn, since it was the most beautiful name he could think of, and since, shortened to Eve, it took on a profound and stirring significance. He was grateful now for the small typewriter with the delicate keys and elite type. It seemed wondrously suited to the purpose of his dream.

Eve, my dearest: Last night when I met you, all things I have wished for lived within me. Your nearness, your love, your beauty, have given me something all human beings need and yet so seldom have. The ache to tell you of the fullness of my heart is like a wound. Eve, my darling, what change have you wrought me—and what have you brought me? What is the nature of this light, where once was darkness? All I know is that the dark is gone, and I am happy, lifted now above the run of men, because you love me, dear, as I love you.

Please write me soon, and tell me of your journey, of all the smallest things of your life, that I may see you in your day and night, and find myself with you. I love you.

Henry

This, the first of his letters to Eve, Mr. Barstow mailed to a hotel built of grass, which, he had been told by a former client, rested among palms near a coral strand in Tahiti. He gave Eve the surname of Crevecoeur, remembered from a book. The envelope was plain, with no return address. But Mr. Barstow, after an appropriate interval, eagerly tore open the reply, as though it were fresh from the pen of Eve herself, and as though he had not written and mailed it to himself the day before.

Dearest Henry: Your beautiful letter reached me at last; and you, who are so far away, are close to me once more. I think I know and feel, the things you need to say—and one of these is the very need itself, the human need to speak and to be answered.

Do you remember those times, when, together, we both had the same thought at the same time? That was speaking, dear. It was understanding. We saw through the same eyes, felt through the same hands, and this awareness is our unity of spirit.

And the light you see—the light that once was darkness. What is that light but the hope and will to live? What was the dreary dark but the dust of small, interminable duties through the creep of time? We must not let ourselves succumb, my darling! We must not die the sleepy death of the commonplace, for there is something extra to be wrung from this, our life! It is of the stuff of dreams, and we shall steal it to combat reality. It is the sparkle of dew on white flowers, the sound of a stream speaking among the stones of its bed, and the web we shall weave from the contemplation of starlight. These, through our love, we have created, until our hearts are full. These are the children we may never have. Oh, darling —please hold to this, to me, forever! Don't let them tear you away from me, for how can a love as beautiful as ours be wrong? Can it be wrong, when it hurts no one?

Write soon, dearest one. You, too, must tell me of the days, of your family, of the smallest detail of your life. I love you.

Eve

For months Mr. Barstow lived in ecstasy with Eve Crevecoeur. Their romance ripened through April, May, and June. Eve's replies to his letters, to be sure, bore the local postmark—but Mr. Barstow blithely destroyed the envelopes, preferring the effect of the addresses within. These addresses were of places he had always longed to see: Cairo, Dakar, Trinidad, San Cristobal. In all her fanciful, far wanderings, Eve's eyes turned ever toward him, making him happy and insulating him against such things as goldfish, cold mutton, the transportation problems of his son and Eddie Macon, Muriel's shrill orders to stop on the way home and buy peanut brittle, lard, or soap, and Gladys' casual "hello-Pa-good-bye."

Mr. Barstow guarded his love with all the reticence of grief or loneliness. He showed no outward sign, until at last the spirit of Eve prompted him to buy a new suit.

Not since he could remember, had Henry Barstow worn anything but brown. He bought one suit a year, and the new one, within two days, invariably looked exactly like the old. But the suit he purchased this cloudless day in June was a happy exception. He went, rather sheepishly, to a clothing store where he was not known—a fashionable and expensive shop.

"Light-gray, darling," whispered the voice of Eve. "With a fine, blue stripe in the weave."

And as Mr. Barstow tried on the suit and gazed upon his reflection with an outwardly placid eye, it seemed to him that Eve rested her hands on the bold lapels, kissed him tenderly on the cheek, and said: "There! You see? How young you look, how straight, and strong."

After some minor alterations extending the waistline of the trousers, Mr. Barstow called for his new suit and decided to wear it home. He changed in the clothing shop, and, refreshed by his appearance, stepped merrily into the street, carrying the old brown suit in a box.

His family greeted him like a mildly incredible specimen. Gladys, however, awarded him a glance of interest and a smile. When he arrived, she was about to leave for a friend's house for supper. She met him at the front door. "Hello, Pa! Say!

Snappy! Going to the races, or something? Good-bye." And she was gone.

Junior, sprawled on the sofa, raised himself to one elbow and stared with languid disapproval. "Huh! Where'd you locate that, Pa? They saw you coming, all right. Collegiate! 'But Sam! They made the pants too long!' "

"You don't like my suit, Junior?"

"Aw, maybe it's okay. But Eddie Macon's old man, he wouldn't—"

Mr. Barstow didn't learn what Eddie Macon's parent wouldn't do, for Muriel came from the kitchen to frown critically and to observe: "But you've always worn brown, Henry! What's come over you?"

"I thought I'd just change to gray."

"But your brown suit had months of good wear. Isn't it early for you to buy your new suit?"

"Why, yes, dear. It is—a little."

"What have you done with the old one?"

"Oh, it's right here. Right in this box. I can use it for an extra, after it's cleaned and pressed. I'm—I'm sorry you don't like the suit."

"Well—what's done is done. Supper's ready. How much did the suit cost?"

"Seventy-five dollars," said Mr. Barstow, limply.

The next evening, partly to quiet his family's objections, and partly by way of guilt-payment, Mr. Barstow came home bearing gifts. For Muriel, he had selected two gardenias—not the small ones, but the dollar size. For Gladys he had chosen a silk scarf, and for Junior, at great effort, a second-hand tire with practically two thousand miles of wear left in it.

As he came in, cheerfully banging the screen door, he felt pleased with himself and even a little debonair. Junior's tire hung over his shoulder. He carried the other offerings under his arm.

"Hello, folks," he said. "See what I brought you? Something for everyone!"

He was greeted with a bleak and penetrating silence. Muriel lay on the sofa, her head turned away from him, a damp-looking handkerchief pressed to her face. Junior, after an uncontrollable jerk toward the tire, settled back in his chair with an outraged look, while Gladys gazed pensively into space. A sense of catastrophe traveled along Mr. Barstow's spine. He dropped his gifts, took off his hat, and came on into the living-room. He said "hello" again. There was no answer.

"Why! What—what's the matter?" he blurted.

"You've just wrecked the whole family," mumbled Junior. "That's all. That's absolutely all."

"What?"

Mr. Barstow, staring from one to another of his family, was bewildered. A low sob from Muriel added to his confusion. Gladys' strange, sidelong glance filled him with dread.

"I wish you'd please tell me what's wrong," he begged. "And—Muriel, dear. I brought you some gardenias—the biggest kind."

Muriel sat up on the sofa. After a single, heartrending look, she covered her eyes and reclined again. "I don't want the gardenias," she said quaveringly. "You can save them for—for *her!*"

"Who?"

"That woman!"

"What woman?"

"She means Eve, Pa," said Gladys, her wide, wistful eyes on her father's. "She found the letter from Eve in your old suit. She was going through the pockets before sending it to the cleaner's."

"Oh," said Mr. Barstow, slumping into the nearest chair, "oh!"

Junior, who had furtively arisen, strayed toward the second-hand tire and stood peering at it contemptuously. "It's a disgrace," he said.

"What?" Mr. Barstow spoke in a dazed tone.

"I said it's a disgrace."

"It—they said—the tire man said it had two thousand miles left in it."

"I don't mean the tire. You know what I mean!"

Gladys drew in her breath sharply. Muriel reveled in a sob. Mr. Barstow licked his dry lips, and said: "There isn't anything to it—I mean, not really. Eve is just—well, she's just a—"

"Just a pal," supplied Junior.

"Oh, be quiet, Junior," Gladys snapped. "Let Pa talk!"

"What can he say?" wailed Muriel.

Mr. Barstow, his brows puckered, guessed that the letter had been read by his entire family. "Which—uh—what letter was it?" he asked, confusedly.

Muriel groped under a sofa pillow and found the letter. She passed it to him with a wan and drooping hand. "All about passion flowers," she cried, giving way to hysteria, "and moonlight, and—oh—oh—!"

Henry glanced at the letter, read the first line, and shuddered. In this one, he remembered, he had really let himself go. It opened forcefully with: "Henry, my dearest one," and went on up the scale to tell of Eve's plucking a passion flower for him and touching it nightly to her lips, and of how she recalled swimming with him in the moonlight, and how the waters of the lagoon were like cool velvet, and—

Muriel's tortured questions broke in. "How long has this been going on, Henry? Where did you meet her? How often do you see her? What—oh!—what shall I do?"

"Do?" Henry swallowed painfully. "Don't do anything. We'll just go on, as before. I—just let me explain. I—that is, you see—"

Mr. Barstow abruptly realized that he couldn't explain. If he told them the truth, that Eve Crevecoeur was a fantasy woven from the wraith of a girl who had rescued his umbrella, they wouldn't believe him. If they did believe him, they would judge him ridiculous or demented. With curious relief, Mr. Barstow saw no course other than to substantiate Eve's reality. His family's appalled interest in him, moreover, contained an element of admiration which caused him to tingle pleasantly. Very well! Let them believe!

"I am very sorry," said Mr. Barstow with a new and mounting dignity. "I'm sorry you found the letter. I have nothing more to say, at the moment."

Mr. Barstow's family were momentarily stunned, including Junior. Muriel was the first to recover. Her voice was so piteous that Mr. Barstow restrained himself with difficulty from taking her in his arms and patting her.

"How do you think I feel?" she asked. "Haven't I—? Henry! Haven't I been— I mean, haven't I tried hard to be a good wife? And the children, Henry! Didn't you think of them when you were in this other woman's arms? How will the children be able to face their friends, knowing of their father's—uh—infidelity?"

"You've broken Ma's heart," remarked Junior, who was examining his tire for possible defects. "And when Eddie Macon hears about this, he'll prob'ly never speak to me again."

"You dare tell Eddie Macon one word about Pa's affair, and I'll—!" Gladys' outburst ended in a lethal hiss.

"Perhaps," said Mr. Barstow, "we had better not discuss the matter any further at this time. Is supper ready?"

"Guess no one's very hungry, tonight," sighed Junior.

"I am," said Mr. Barstow.

At supper he was subjected to the hurt-silence-and-untouched-food treatment. Even Junior managed to starve himself, eating but a single helping of hamburg and two pieces of bakery pie.

Mr. Barstow bore up extremely well. His appetite, heightened by his family's shocked attention, was excellent. He felt marked, for once in his life singled out, their eyes covertly upon him, wondering, accusing, grieving, yet vaguely respectful.

During the next few days, Muriel was sad and spartan by turns. She varied these attitudes with an occasional touch of martyrdom, spending much time alone in her bedroom with the door closed.

She brought up the subject of Eve at frequent intervals, sometimes in the presence of the children and sometimes not.

"Henry, have you told her—that woman—that you have been discovered?"

"Why—uh—yes. I wrote her at once."

"What did she say?"

"She—uh—she hasn't had time to answer. She happens to be out of the country."

Muriel, for a moment, suffered in silence. Presently her eyes filled with tears. "I've always wanted to travel, too, Henry. Does Eve travel a great deal?"

"Yes, dear," said Mr. Barstow gently. "Practically all the time."

The yearning so plainly sincere in Muriel's voice touched Mr. Barstow. So did the expression of wondering uncertainty in the eyes of Gladys. But what touched him most deeply of all was the subtle change in the perquisites of home.

One morning, to his thoughtful amazement, he found an ash tray placed conveniently on the breakfast table.

"Smoke, if you want, to, Henry," Muriel murmured. "I really don't mind."

He delectably smoked and read the unravaged newspaper which Gladys brought to him without even looking first at the funnies. On two consecutive evenings, Muriel ordered Junior to vacate Mr. Barstow's arm chair in the living-room. Mr. Barstow pondered long over his shaving the morning he found a fresh package of blades waiting in plain sight on the bathroom shelf. And he felt a definite ache in his throat the night he went to his lonely bed to discover that someone had folded back the covers invitingly, as in a good hotel.

In the dark watches of that very night, Mr. Barstow was awakened by a plaintive knock on his door.

"Henry, can I come in? I can't sleep. I want to talk. Please, Henry."

"Why, yes, dear. Of course."

The door opened. Muriel's shadowy figure approached. She

stood beside the bed, hesitant and uncertain. "Can I—do you mind if I get into bed with you, Henry? Or shall I just sit on the edge?"

"Get in," said Henry, moving over.

Muriel had treated herself with a drop of perfume, and as she settled herself beside him, Mr. Barstow sniffed pleasantly.

"What disturbs you, Muriel? What is it?" he asked.

In a thin, frightened voice, she said: "What does she look like? Eve, I mean."

"Oh, she's—well, she's hard to describe."

"Is she young, Henry? Is she much younger than I? Young and beautiful?"

"Yes," said Mr. Barstow, truthfully but reluctantly, "she is young and beautiful."

"Do you want to leave us, and—go to her?"

Mr. Barstow had intended to speak solemnly of "this thing which has come into my life." The vision of Eve was clear and beautiful in his fancy, beckoning always, elusive, inspiring, ineffably dear. Yet he could not withstand the hurt despair in Muriel's voice, and as he lay beside her, his hand crept out and caressed her shoulder. Surely Muriel, too, had felt the long, dull pain of monotony. She, too, must have breathed the dust of interminable duties—sweeping, cooking, washing, worrying, waiting for him to come home, all the while yearning vainly, even as he had yearned, for the tang of romance, the dew on white flowers in a jungle, the sensation of starlight, and the wonder of far wandering.

"Muriel, dear," he whispered, "I—maybe I have done wrong."

"No, Henry. I don't blame you. But—but—" She struggled to keep back the tears "—it's just that I can't compete with Eve, Henry. It's so hopeless! I'm not young any more. I'm not beautiful any more. But I was, once, Henry—wasn't I?"

"You still are," said Mr. Barstow.

"I want to make you happy. I want to try so hard. It's all I have to live for, Henry."

Mr. Barstow's heart ached unbearably. It ached not only for Muriel and himself, but for the tragically vanishing ghost of Eve Crevecoeur, as he said: "I'll give her up, Muriel. Yes, I will. I'll write her tomorrow. I'll write and break it off—forever!"

"But—do you *want* to? Are you sure? Do you truly want to?"

"I—yes!"

"Then you *do* love me!"

"Yes."

"And Gladys and Junior, too!"

"Yes."

The eager happiness and relief in Muriel's voice flooded through him. It was compensation—almost.

"Oh, Henry, dear! You mean it! You do! Oh, you really, truly do!"

The rest of the night, while Muriel slept peacefully by his side, Mr. Barstow lay wide awake, composing in his mind his last letter to Eve. He was tortured by a feeling of divided fidelity. On the one hand, his loyalty drew him powerfully toward Eve for the strange, fantastic beauty she had given him. On the other hand, he was drawn as powerfully toward Muriel and the children for the life of day-by-day. He perceived that the letter would be the most difficult and delicate of his career. He decided to write it at home, wishing to get the task over with quickly, and fearing that in his office, away from his family, his resolve might weaken.

When, in the morning, he sat down before a small cleared space on the table beside the goldfish bowl, Mr. Barstow's eyes were haggard, and his pen stubborn. It was Saturday, and the children had no school. They didn't interrupt him, although they remained in the house. His only interruptions were Muriel's whispered orders to the children not to disturb him.

"Junior! Sh-sh-sh! Your father's writing to *her!* He's giving her up!"

"Huh? Give her the air? Boy-oh-boy-oh-boy!"

"Gladys, please stop rustling that paper. You'll distract Pa."

Meanwhile, seated at his table, Mr. Barstow, after protracted staring at the goldfish, had written: "My dearest, dearest Eve," and come to a stop.

Out of penitence or loyalty, or both, he destroyed this beginning and made a new one limited to a single "dearest." This brought him to a second stop. Just when it seemed to him that the flame of composition had expired, an oriole sang in a tall elm outside the window. An urchin whistled in the street. A white cloud billowed in the sky. The goldfish suddenly cavorted like rainbow trout, and, without once stopping, Mr. Barstow wrote:

> My dearest Eve: It cannot be. Perhaps there is no change but death. The roots of family, of children, wife and home, have struck too deep within me. We must part. For us, there is no destiny, my darling—none save the memory of the pale nights when the stars burned down upon the lonely secret of our love. This we may have and hold in all its sweet, transcending glory. I am pledged to write no more, yet the fountain runs full. And, forever, darling, you are the flame in my darkness, the song in my silence, and in my heart the knowledge of the birth of time.
>
> But I love my family, and belong to them, and with them. If the flesh of my flesh may some day know the beauty you have given me, then have I lived to high purpose. I want my son to be a finer man than I, and my daughter to know the poetry and music of life. And above all, my dearest one, I want my wife to have my last, unswerving loyalty.
>
> Farewell, my lovely.
>
> Henry

With something akin to awe, Mr. Barstow watched the slowly drying ink. He capped his pen and wiped his beaded forehead. Then, glancing up, he observed his family silently peering at him from the living-room doorway; and—whether from the desire to exhibit proof of his future fidelity or from pride in the creation of his pen—he held the letter toward them, saying: "Here it is. Read!"

Breathlessly they grouped around the letter, and breathlessly they read. Mr. Barstow was impressed and pleasantly thrilled by their reactions. Junior, confused by the phrase about the fountain still running full, sought enlightenment.

"What d'ya mean, 'fountain,' Pa? Fountain pen?"

"No, Junior. I do not mean fountain pen."

"He means," said Gladys, in a small, quivering voice, "the fountain of—of—his soul. Don't you, Pa?"

"I do."

Muriel, half smiling through her tears, looked wistfully toward her husband, and said: "Henry, dear, I liked the part about the family best. The part about how you love us."

Mr. Barstow nodded agreeably. "Yes, Muriel. That part was good."

The appraisal over, Mr. Barstow addressed an envelope to Miss Evelyn Crevecoeur, Empress Hotel, Victoria, British Columbia, Canada. He folded the letter, tucked it inside, and after sealing the envelope, glanced thoughtfully toward the front door.

"Henry," said Muriel coöperatively, "I have plenty of stamps."

"Stamps? Oh, yuh, sure. Thanks, dear."

"And an air-mail sticker, too."

"Splendid."

Henry kissed Muriel good-bye and left the house, carrying the letter all riotously stamped and labeled for its journey to oblivion. He paused uncertainly at a mail-box at the corner. Just once he turned and looked back toward his house. Then he touched the letter to his lips, dropped it into the mail-box, and whispered: "Good-bye, Eve, my darling."

He had walked on some distance toward his office, when Gladys overtook him. She put her arm through his, hugging his elbow against her side. Suddenly averting her eyes, she held his arm still tighter, and said: "Pa, I wish—some day—someone would write to me, like that. I mean that part about the memory of the pale nights, and the song in the silence, and how in your heart you felt the—you know, Pa—the bigness of time."

"Someone will, Glad—some day."

But it was not his daughter's understanding heart that really lifted Mr. Barstow to the skies triumphant. Nor was it wholly

Muriel's warm, almost passionate kiss of welcome when he came home that evening, nor yet the fact that on Saturday night, when baked beans were not only tolerable but almost obligatory, there was steak for supper—thick, juicy porterhouse. It was Mr. Barstow's son, Junior, who, with gangling gestures, nervously working lips, and strangely enlightened eyes, approached him in the privacy of the front hall, to say:

"Pa, I won't need the car tomorrow."

THE TEACHER COMMENTS

GETTING STARTED

"I always think I am going to have plenty of ideas for stories," a student complains, "until I sit down to write one for your course. Then they all evaporate, or if I do remember anything of them, they become impossible the minute I face that blank paper!"

There are two things to tell the student, one of comfort, one of advice. It may be cold comfort to tell him that many professionals suffer the same frustration, but there is warmth in the knowledge that the professionals were once beginners themselves, and that they manage, at least some of the time, to produce completed stories. The advice is to follow Mr. Ware's method of supposing by actually writing.

Like the remedy for the ills of Democracy—more Democracy—the remedy for most of the ills of writing is more writing. Beginners do not write enough, do not sufficiently use the manual tool of their occupation, be it pen, pencil, typewriter, or a combination of them. The small-note-book-always-in-your-pocket idea is not a bad one, though it may engender self-consciousness in the very young. It is useful as a means of translating fleeting ideas into something at least slightly tangible. If you sit down at your desk, and you have a few notes before you, you are ready to make some kind of start; you can transcribe the notes to that sterile blank paper, and the act sets in motion a complex of nervous, physical, and intellectual energies without which no story can ever be written. But if you merely sit frowning, chin in hand and pencil between teeth, you accomplish nothing. All well-fed mammals share an instinctive resistance to work, and the only way to break it down is to expend physical energy. "How do you learn to write?" a naïve soul once demanded of a professional writer. "Write!" was the monosyllabic imperative. It must be taken literally.

HOW TO SUPPOSE

Stories must grow; they must grow first in the mind, but there is no measure of their growth save written words. Therefore, do your supposing on paper. For illustration, let us try to suppose Mr. Ware's story with him.

"Suppose you have a middle-aged man," says Mr. Ware. All right, put it down: "middle-aged man." Look at the words on the paper and suppose further: ". . . whose dreams have never even partly been fulfilled," continues Mr. Ware, and so do you, perhaps in slightly different words: "Never been anywhere or done anything, but always wanted to do something romantic."

Here, perhaps, you are ready for a first tentative generalization. "This man is like a great many men, for almost everybody's dreams exceed realization," or something to that effect. The point to be made is that even the preliminary thinking about a story should be set down in words. Then you have them, and you can direct the growth of the story in a straighter line than if you merely allow a few tags and half-formed generalities to swirl about in the mind. Of course, the mind works at an infinitely greater speed than the fingers, but it is necessary, or certainly helpful, to train the fingers to record the mind's activity. Remember the disparity between intentions and deeds, and the composition of the pavement on the road to hell! Writing is a deed; thinking only an intention.

In an earlier chapter, we said that stories and the people in them are made up, that they are not transcriptions of actual persons and episodes. Actual persons and episodes, however, are sources of fiction. Let your mind play over a number of men you know who are middle-aged, solid, selfless, sweet, and rather dull. You cannot know about their romantic dreams; you have to make them up out of your own and out of your reading and total background, distorting them and giving them emphases appropriate to your inchoate character. What you want is a kind of distillate of middle-aged romanticism.

Perhaps at this point your supposing has led you to understand something of what must happen in the story—your character must burst out of his earthly cocoon, flutter gaudy wings, and sail off on a "sharp left turn." You write, therefore: "takes sharp left turn."

The story now has grown from a dim conception to the statement of a big part of the total idea. Write it all down: "Middle-aged man, never been anywhere or done anything, takes sharp left turn." Though still very vague, the story now has a skeletal outline of character and action. It has direction: You know something of what you must do. You have made a start. Only a bare start, to be sure, but you have employed your time to far greater advantage than if you had done nothing but make tooth marks on a pencil.

KEEPING GOING

It is one thing to begin a story, to suppose it through to its end, and quite another to get it written. On page 21 we spoke of "literary damp-off" and suggested some general means of preventing it. More specifically, we now suggest that you keep writing. "But," the student asks, "how can I keep on writing when I'm stuck?"

The first thing to do is ask "Why am I stuck?" Sometimes analysis will show up the trouble. For example, suppose you had been writing "Mr. Barstow's Infidelity." You felt that you had a good story in hand, yet by the time you had arrived at page 104, at the end of Eve's letter, you reviewed the whole situation and found it utterly unconvincing. That a sane man should begin writing love-letters to himself good enough to convince his family, is in truth a pretty preposterous idea. Remember, however, that in the realm of light romantic fiction, anything is possible. Treatment is everything. You carry your analysis a step further and begin examining your treatment. You find, let us imagine, that instead of adopting Mr. Ware's "tone" in the writing, you have unconsciously been writing about Mr. Barstow as though the reader were to take him with utmost seriousness and not with a kind of amused detachment. You have made him, let us say, a person whose rebellion is too near the surface, and whose causes for rebellion are too uncomfortably realistic for the purposes of light romantic fiction. This changes Mr. Barstow from Mr. Ware's conception of an ordinary conventional man, and that change will have corresponding change on the emphases of the story. Up to page 104, all the events have been leading toward a story with comic, if slightly poignant, overtones. If it is your desire to write a story with serious and biting irony in it, that too is possible from this material, but only one story can be written at a time, and its tone must be consistently maintained.

At this point, then, write in the margin the word "tone," and go on with the story. It is better in most cases to wrench the story through to an end before you begin to rewrite, to adopt changes as you go along rather than to attempt to get the whole thing perfect at once. Some writers do work the latter way, but the danger of bogging down completely and never finishing the story is increased the further away you allow the end of the story to remain. When you have trained yourself to finish every story you start and have had some success, then you may profitably work more meticulously over the individual passages as they are first written.

Sometimes you will find yourself stuck because the general idea of the story is too hazy. It is often good practice to write the last scene first; this will give you completed action to work toward and may sometimes solve many of the minor problems of plausibility. It may help you to realize some of the "inventions" Mr. Ware speaks of on page 92 of the preface to "Mr. Barstow." For example, if a man by writing a letter has falsely convicted himself in the eyes of his family, how could he do it? Immediately, you know one thing about him: He must be able to write pretty well. But this ability conflicts with the overall simplicity of Mr. Barstow's character. Hence, you choose some normal business for him that requires a kind of romantic cliché in its advertising or correspondence. It would, for example, be possible to write this story about a man in the spice-importing business, or the cosmetics business, or any of several other businesses. Your choice depends on two or three factors, such as your familiarity with a specific business or your opportunity to become familiar with it, and its adaptability to the needs of your story. The travel business was an excellent choice for Mr. Ware's story because of its useful topicality. It had been brought to a standstill because of the war, a fact which accounts for Mr. Barstow's necessary leisure, which in turn accounts for the purchase of the excess typewriters. Note, however, that one minor problem arises in connection with the typewriters. By the time the story was written, typewriters had gone off the market. Now, it is most important to remember that all inventions, big or little, must ring true, must be verifiable in the world of experience. Consequently, we seem to have a knotty little difficulty here. But the difficulty was solved, very simply, by timing. Mr. Barstow bought the typewriters just before they went off the market, and it is worth noting that Mr. Ware has protected himself against any carping reader by unobtrusively yet specifically mentioning the time sequence. The point is that a great many of the minor problems in popular fiction are as easily solved. Don't let them block the forward progress of the story's first draft; leave them temporarily unsolved, if necessary. Eventually, of course, you must get them absolutely right, but don't waste precious energy fuming over them on the first draft.

Sometimes, as you are writing along, scenes, bits of dialogue or characterization, that belong in a later part of the story, will form suddenly in your head. Jot them down at the moment of their conception. The chances are that you will be able to use them, or part of them, but if you fail to put them into writing you are likely to forget them. Perhaps it is a good idea to keep a note-book for each story. Stenographers' dictation pads are good for this purpose, since they are cheap and plenty big enough.

Suppose, then, that you have kept going and have written the story through to its end. You yank the last sheet from the typewriter, assemble the messy pages in order, and read them through.

Alas! Even you, the author, can sense that what had once gleamed so brightly is but a poor thing grown dull and unconvincing. Or, if you are a person incapable of detachment, you read through the story, paying no attention to its faults, dwelling on its pathetic virtues, and loving it wholeheartedly because it is yours.

If your reaction follows the first pattern there is hope for you. But if it follows the second, you are herewith advised to read no more in this or any like book, and to take up a different form of self-expression. You won't follow the advice, of course, and if you are one in a hundred thousand, you will succeed anyway, but nothing anybody can tell you will help you. Learning to write is, to coin a brand new aphorism, slow and very hard work. But it is also slow and very hard work to achieve competence in anything that returns satisfaction in any form.

You are, then, forlorn yet stubborn. You are going to make this story better than it is.

The first thing is to try to spot the sources of trouble, and to make marginal and interlinear comments and changes. Next, run the whole story through the typewriter again (if you compose on the typewriter). Now check it against the technical discussions in this book, or in other books, and against your class notes, if you are a student in a course, and make other changes, rewriting whole pages if necessary—and it will almost always be necessary. Next, through the typewriter for the third time. If your work has been done at all effectively, the story is now ready for your instructor's reading or for a period of rest while you turn to another. In all events, you have finished with it for at least a week. If you have given it to your instructor, he will undoubtedly suggest other changes which, together with your own fresh reëxamination, will require yet a fourth trip through the typewriter and maybe more. It is nothing for a professional to send a story through his typewriter from six to a dozen times or more, either in whole or in part. The present writer recommends entire rewriting rather than patchwork because it helps the beginner to gain a sense of story structure, of the relation of part to part, and gives him opportunity for polishing and repolishing his writing.

So much, then, for what may be called "working methods." The methods are far less important than the work, however. No story, certainly no beginner's story, is going to "write itself," though you may occasionally hear professionals using that phrase. Mr. Ware's experience with "Last Trip Together" is, as we have mentioned, most unusual. Recently, a former student wrote to me of her first published story: "The ideas suddenly jelled in my head and the story wrote itself in about three weeks." Those three weeks mean twenty-one days of constant hard work, somewhere between sixty and eighty hours of actual writing. The student, who had written more than a dozen previous stories, was gratefully surprised that she had been able to accomplish this particular story in so short a time!

V

THE WRITER COMMENTS

ANYBODY'S FIELD

The things that happen to everyone, day by day, are a free and splendid field for any writer. These things are so many that it is frequently difficult to see the woods because of the trees in some more distant and attractive field. For some reason, a grass hut in the South Seas is more tempting as a story background than one's own home on Elm Street. Nothing ever happens on Elm Street, and the houses appear to sleep in the summer sun. There are the familiar sounds of the lawn mower, the garage doors being opened, the caterwauling of children, the radio, someone practicing scales on the piano, the evening paper being deftly flung on the porch steps by the paper boy.

The background of the house on Elm Street is so familiar it is almost irksome. To write about it seems a dull chore, requiring no adventurous researches. And yet it seems likely that all people like to read about familiar things. The home-town newspaper is most eagerly sought. Why? People want to know what their neighbors are doing, who gave a lawn party, who was there. A familiar name always seems to leap from the page. You know that person, hence somehow it strengthens your own identity.

Without consciously reasoning it out, the writer once attempted to produce a story about a commonplace family doing commonplace things. As it turned out, he finally wrote twenty-six stories of the commonplace doings of this same commonplace family. At Mr. Bailey's suggestion, three of these stories follow. There are several reasons why three were chosen. First, in all the stories, the same basic characters appear: Jeff Raleigh, the earnest, somewhat harried American husband, who is in the automobile business; his bright, decisive, musically inclined wife, Alice; and the three Raleigh children—James, a boy in the earliest stages of adolescence; Joan, a mysterious and demanding girl-child with an elfin love of horses, and baby Charles.

A second reason for lumping these three commonplace tales, is the very commonplaceness of their origins and development. In none of them will the reader find any drama or high emotion, any violence or death, any love or any longing beyond the simplest desire for family unity.

Another reason that the Raleigh stories might be of interest, or perhaps assistance, is their illustration of simple and natural dialogue. The speech of all the characters is familiar to everyone who has observed or participated in average American life.

Finally, the story behind each tale revolves around something so familiar as to be almost threadbare at first glance. Thus, "The Rampage of Baby Raleigh" is merely the story of the baby being temporarily mislaid, or lost. "The House That Jeff Built" is merely the story of the Raleighs building a house. And "In The Reign of Jeff Raleigh" is the story of the Raleigh household while Alice is in the hospital with appendicitis, and Jeff is at home, in charge.

In reviewing this series of stories about a single group of characters, the writer was astonished by the importance of the commonplace—food, clothes, houses, business, summer vacations, garden hoses. In his opinion, the Jeff Raleigh series was successful, not because of any special talent in their construction, but because people like to read about themselves, things they have done and seen, and places they have been. The South Pole is interesting to read about because it's different. Home is interesting to read about because it is familiar.

In this connection of the commonplace, the writer gives in to the temptation to describe some of the other stories in the family series: "Jeff Raleigh's Piano Solo" is the story of Jeff's buying a piano for his wife's birthday present. "Home Is the Hero" reports the travail and trivia of a vacationing husband returning home from a fishing trip, carrying an unsuspected grippe germ. There is still another story of the Raleigh family away, except for Jeff, who remains home alone, after having fancied that it might be soul-satisfying to recapture the joys of bachelorhood. To this story, the editor of *Good Housekeeping* applied the attractively familiar title: "No Milk Till Further Notice."

Home, to repeat, is anyone's field because everyone knows it at first hand. Perhaps that is one reason why home is difficult to write about. Perhaps, that is, one's observation has been dulled by too much repetition of home experience. But if home is to be a theme, then the observation must persist and grow keener. It seems to me that in a home, the eye, and ear can receive much. The table-talk of any lively family will have at least as many topics as there are people, and often no two interests coincide. The resulting confusion is story material—sometimes. At least, it was from such ragged and protesting dialogue that the writer got his first idea for the series upon which Mr. Bailey makes further comment at the end of the chapter.

THE STORY

The Rampage of Baby Raleigh

To Thomas Jefferson Raleigh, as he began a ninth, distracted circuit of his living-room rug, it seemed preposterous that Alice should blame Mr. Corfu for the disappearance of their baby, Charles, age three. Why, Jeff wondered, did his beloved add blame-fixing to the torture of doubt? And by what devious brand of feminine reasoning did she accuse Mr. Corfu? Mr. Corfu, a total stranger, had blundered into the Raleighs' life—and right out of it—four whole days ago. Yet Alice harped upon his memory so that it hovered about like an everlasting woe.

Jeff paused in his pacing to glance at the mantel clock. It was half past one. Little Charles had been missing more than an hour. Jeff wondered whether he should make a third search of the neighborhood, but decided it would be better to await the return of his two older children, James and Joan, who were cruising the town on bicycles.

As Jeff resumed his pacing, Alice, her face drawn with anxiety, entered the living-room from the front hall, where she had been telephoning the neighbors again.

"Any luck?" said Jeff.

"No." Alive swept a strand of hair from her forehead. It was a gesture of distress. "Oh, I wish we'd never gone on that ghastly trip!"

"So do I."

"If only you hadn't indulged your genius for attracting weird, human creatures, Jeff! If only you could discriminate!"

"Mr. Corfu again!" said Jeff, strickenly.

"Yes!"

In accusing Mr. Corfu, Alice Raleigh indirectly accused her devoted Jeff, for it was as she had hinted: through Jeff's blind and trusting friendliness, Mr. Corfu had attached himself to the Raleighs; and, like a pudgy, lonely, and well-meaning parasite, he had clung to them on the tour of the White Mountains from which they had returned only two hours ago.

"But we shook Mr. Corfu at Twin Mountain!" said Jeff. "That was days and days ago. How could his influence possibly—?"

"Jeff! Charles was angelic till you dragged that ghoul into our midst. After that, during the whole trip, Charles *seethed!* At the Brightwell House, he simply—"

Jeff shuddered violently. "Alice, I beg you on bended knee: Never mention the Brightwell House in my presence again. Besides, the Brightwell House was your idea, not mine."

"Kindly remember," said Alice, "that we went to the Brightwell House in order to *escape* your Mr. Corfu!"

"*My* Mr. Corfu! *My* Mr. Corfu!" Jeff looked at the ceiling, as if in last appeal. "As I've told you forty times, Alice, if we'd stayed that first night in Windsor, Vermont, as we agreed, we never would have gone near the tourist camp in Lisbon. You suggested driving on, Alice! And of course the children sided with you—as you knew they would. And where, I ask you just once more, did we meet Mr. Corfu? At that tourist camp!"

The very tension which threatened to come between the Raleighs in their hour of trial now suddenly drew them together.

"Jeff! Oh, dearest! What shall we do?"

Two, long, hungry strides, and Jeff caught her in his arms. "Guess we must be tired and wrought up—talking like this, and Charles lost."

"Do you suppose my baby's all right, Jeff? Do you?"

"Yuh. Sure. 'Course he is," Jeff growled.

"But the automobiles! And the river. Jeff—the river!"

"Calm down right away and stop imagining."

While his own imagination ran wild, Jeff's thirteen-year-old son, James, came clattering in through the front door. One of James' pant legs was rolled up, after the fashion of the younger cycling set. Slamming the door behind him, the boy careened into the living-room, banged against a chair, looked at it disapprovingly, and flopped into it. "Whew!" he puffed. "Can't find him anywhere. Been all over the place. Asked cops 'n' everything. Prob'ly kidnaped. Now c'n I have something to eat, Mother? And a clean shirt? This one's crummy."

"Yes, dear," said Alice, remembering that life, meals, and laundry must go on. "There's a clean shirt in your top drawer. Lunch is on the table."

Joan Raleigh, who was eight, reported a few minutes later. Joan was a beautiful and strangely elfin child. She was dressed in a striped slip-on sweater, jodhpurs, and something made of clothesline and haywire which resembled a bridle. She entered with dignity, her neck arched like that of the sensitive horse which as usual she was both impersonating and riding. Delicately lifting first one hoof, then the other, she assumed the expression of a courier loaded with tidings. The suspense which she generated with a single, huge-eyed glance, was more than Jeff could bear.

"Heavens' sakes!" said Jeff, as always slightly mystified in his girl-child's presence. "Tell us what you found out!"

Joan turned on a look which indicated that he knew nothing of the throes required to transform oneself from a horse to a girl. "I am simpully uxaspurrated!" she remarked.

"Why? Where's Charles? Anything happen to him?"

"Jimmy left his bicycle uxackly in the *uxack middul* of the sidewalk!"

"Oh, lordy!" Jeff moaned.

"Jeff, dear. Be patient," said Alice.

Having enlisted her mother's support, Joan slowly unburdened. "I know one place where Charruls has been."

"Where, dear?"

"Mrs. Morrison's!"

Alice quailed. Mrs. Morrison, who helped once a week with the heavy housework, was a splendid person and one of Charles' most loyal companions—but she lived some distance away in the tenement and railroad belt. Alice pictured her baby toddling across intersections. Brakes squealed as cars swerved to avoid him. Drivers leaned from their windows to excoriate him, but were softened by his round, dark eyes, and his sun-bleached curls. "What," said Alice, controlling a shudder, "did Charles want at Mrs. Morrison's?"

"He wanted to go to the bathroom."

"Was he all right?" said Jeff. "Tell us the rest, can't you?"

"Yes, Daddy. But I prufer to tell it to Mother."

Joan's attitude changed subtly, filling Jeff with a new uneasiness. He didn't know whether Joan's enormous eyes were courting or condemning him. Having sidled close to her mother, Joan spoke directly to her, as through a sorrow which she felt could be savored only by womankind.

"Mother," she said. *"Charruls un-quired for Mr. Corfu!"*

Jeff's shoulders wilted. Fearing to call the police, and fearing not to, he leaned wearily against the mantelpiece, while the misery of doubt, the shade of Mr. Corfu, and the recollection of the nightmarish White Mountain trip awoke to harrow his soul.

They had started out so bravely, so confident of escaping heat, boredom, and reality in the far, dim region to the north. At the T. J. Raleigh Automobile Agency, of which he was owner, Jeff had had the new demonstrator groomed for the trip. In his eyes the car had taken on a special splendor. It was transportation to happiness for his loved ones!

"Mother," Joan had asked before they reached the outskirts of Northerst, "where shall we spend the night?"

It had seemed to Jeff that Alice's answer was inspired. "We're leaving everything to Dad," she had replied. "We'll do exactly as he thinks best."

Jeff announced that they would spend the first night in Windsor, Vermont. Certain that Jeff had never visited Windsor, Alice smiled to herself as he limned the beauties of the town. Jeff had learned about Windsor from his crony, Pat Morgan, but he had not mentioned this. Alice did not approve of Pat. He smoked cigars, split infinitives, and read nothing but Westerns. So Jeff himself took full credit for Windsor.

"And I want to say right now," said Jeff through the sweet steam of pride, "that there isn't a better-looking family touring in a better car in this price-class between here and Dixville Notch!"

Jeff had scarcely got the words out when, with a smooth purring sound, a flash of red, and the squirl of tires, there passed a car of highly competitive make. It was driven by a superior being in a white suit. One thought of exclusive clubs and Harvard, class of 1910. The driver was tanned and distinguished. So was the woman who rode beside him. Quite clearly the two children in the back seat would some day be enrolled in Groton or St. Paul's.

Jeff's brow wrinkled. His fingers tightened on the wheel, and a strange, boyish bitterness made him step hard on his accelerator. "Some gall," he growled, "passing us like that!"

"Go get 'em, Dad!" urged James, who sat beside his father.

Jeff got them just out of Greenfield. He passed them, staring haughtily at the road ahead. James cried: "Yah-yah!" Joan said: "Good, Daddy!" A thin smile of well-being had formed on Jeff's lips when a motor-cycle cop, above the nerve-blasting shriek of his siren, yelled: "Pull over!"

Tremblingly, Jeff drew to the curb and produced his license and registration. He was aware that Alice was staring at him from the back seat, where she sat tense, tiny, electric. He was also aware that, on all possible occasions, he had boasted to Alice of his clean record, his superb driving skill, as an automobile man. He answered the officer's questions with restraint. His courtesy availed nothing.

"You'll have to appear in court Monday," said the officer.

Jeff blanched. It was now Saturday afternoon. "Look, officer—I can't be in court Monday. Taking the family for little tour in the mountains."

"Monday morning at ten o'clock," said the officer.

It was Joan Raleigh who came to the rescue. Fearlessly she leaned from a rear window and eyed the vast minion in blue.

"Are you a policemun?"

"Yeh."

"Are you supposed to pree-tec' peopul?"

Erroneously sensing in Joan's interest an admiration for himself and his profession, the officer smiled. "That's right, girlie. I protect people. That's my duty."

"Then why," said Joan, her eyes shooting brownish sparks, "are you dulliberately dupriving a littul girl of her vacation?"

The officer's neck turned a deeper shade of crimson as he mopped his half-acre brow. "Girlie," he said, after brief meditation, "you got me. Where'd you get them eyes?" He tore the incriminating page from his note-book and handed it to Joan. Then, turning back to Jeff, he said: "Drive on, Daddy—an' take it easy!"

The experience of being stopped for speeding only eighteen miles from home had shaken Jeff's confidence. He felt singled out by fate. The open road, once so glamorous, now seemed charged with pitfalls. He proceeded from Greenfield so slowly and cautiously that Alice, her patience strained, demanded that he let her drive. And at Windsor, Vermont, where they had planned to stop for the night, Alice abruptly reassumed charge of everything.

Deftly slipping through the Windsor traffic, Alice said: "Oh, let's drive on and on! It's early!"

"Now, Alice, we agreed on Windsor. Pat Morgan told me about a nice little farm place called the Bide-A-Mite—"

"Ugh! Bide-A-Mite! Pat Morgan *would!*"

"Erky!" said Joan, as if tasting poison.

Even James favored going on. "I say we get up into some good mountains tonight. No sense staying here. Waste of time."

"Like to have you all do just as you wish," said Jeff, meekly.

Alone of Jeff's children, little Charles had taken no part in the discussion. His angelic behavior had as yet aroused no suspicion. But Charles was quietly making his medicine. Standing in back, his hands manfully clutching the rug rail, he sniffed the ingredients of which adventure is made: the rush of speed, the sweet winds, the wood smoke, and the blue distance. Cannily he eyed the hills. His dream of independent rampage was formless, so far, but a pleasant pain in his heart. In order to explode, Charles required only a suitable detonator. Even now, at the Musgrave Cabins near Lisbon, New Hampshire, the detonator awaited his coming.

According to a purple neon sign, the Musgrave Cabins excelled in clam chowder, balsam pillows, breakfast, privacy, eggs, sweet corn, the view, and opportunities for happiness and swimming. The Raleighs arrived after dark and were shown to a cabin suitable for five.

"Listen children!" exclaimed Alice. "Hear the river! Just like camping out. Isn't it heavenly?"

They agreed in unison; but to Jeff's ear the river sang of the sadness and uncertainty which is life. He could not see why Alice, having denounced a place because it was named Bide-A-Mite, should now go rhapsodic over a moldy smelling cabin entitled Glad-U-Kum. But Alice, as they settled in the creaking bed together, was alert to Jeff's mood. Perhaps she had reassumed leadership of the family a little too heartlessly. She kissed him tenderly and whispered: "You'll feel better in the morning, dear."

Jeff did. In the early sunshine, he peered from a window in Glad-U-Kum to the cabin directly opposite. The name of the cabin was Wel-Kum-U, and parked beside it was a sleek and gorgeous automobile, a gray, gleaming, and intensely gratifying automobile—in short, a car of the very same make as that handled by the T. J. Raleigh Automobile Agency. It was the age-old case of man, lonely in Samoa, Mazatlan, or Lisbon, New Hampshire, suddenly coming upon the print of a poem he has written, a gadget his firm manufactures, or the picture in a forgotten newspaper of a familiar face.

"Alice! Oh, gosh!" cried Jeff. "Fellow 'cross the way with a 1941 torpedo job! Boy-oh-boy!"

Alice, though still half asleep, responded adequately. "Dearest! How perfectly marvellous."

A steep path led from Wel-Kum-U to the swimming pool in the river. As Jeff watched, a huge, grampus-like man emerged from Wel-Kum-U's door and lumbered down the path. From the man's massive lips protruded a before-breakfast cigar. He was wearing a bathrobe of turkish toweling, a straw hat weathered by many summers, and a pair of broken slippers, from one of which mushroomed an immense toe.

"Say, Alice," Jeff blurted, "know what? Think I'll go for little swim before breakfast. Make me feel swell."

"Take me, Daddy!" squealed little Charles.

When Jeff, with Charles mounted on his shoulder, had gone down whistling to the river, Alice awakened the two older children. Dressed for swimming, they descended the path toward the pool. No one would have suspected that Alice Raleigh had borne three children. In her bright yellow swim-suit, she looked twenty-five—until, in the middle of the emerald pool, she saw her baby. She then became a small hurricane of maternity.

Charles was enthroned on what seemed to be a hairy, whitish island. Smoke rings wafted skyward from one end of the island. Little Charles sedately watched them disintegrate. Then, before Alice's eyes, the island heaved upward and became a man smoking a cigar. Charles easily maintained a position on one of the upper terraces of the man's stomach. The man wore green swimming trunks.

"Alice!" greeted Jeff. "See Charles out there?"

"Yes!"

"Completely over his fear of water."

"So I notice."

Charles and his new-found friend had started toward shore. Coming to a deep place, the man lay on his back, mounted Charles securely in the valley between his chest and stomach, and kicked ashore, his feet working like paddle wheels, his puffing cigar doing smoke-stack duty.

"Alice," said Jeff proudly, as the liner docked on the ledge, "I want you to meet Mr. Corfu. Mr. Corfu, this is Mrs. Raleigh."

Mr. Corfu, Charles still riding, climbed out and stood up dripping. "So this is Mrs. Raleigh. Well, sir, I'm certainly happy to make your acquaintance. Mr. Raleigh, you certainly got a wonderful little woman, and children, too. Children allus seem to like me right off. Don't know what there is about me. Guess it's maybe 'cause I like children so much myself."

Alice's chin grew firmer as Mr. Corfu ran on. She gave Jeff a lightning glance. In a mere ten minutes, Jeff and this—this person—seemed to have become brothers. Jeff simply welcomed everyone, with no thought of what the influences on the children might be. This great bear of a man had blandly referred to her as "a little woman." And now James and Joan were staring at him, their eyes fascinated.

"Fact is," continued Mr. Corfu, horrifyingly, "we're the only people staying here at Musgrave's. Mighty lonely here till you folks come along. But now we can have plenty good times together. I'll personally take it upon myself to—"

Mr. Corfu paused to blow water from his nose. Alice seized the opportunity to get in a dainty word. "I'm glad to meet you, Mr. Corfu. I—"

"Forgot to tell you," Jeff excitedly interrupted. "It's Mr. Corfu owns that '41 torpedo job, dearest!"

"Of course, I understand," said Alice and returned to Mr. Corfu. "I'm so grateful to you for entertaining Charles. But perhaps I better take him now."

Charles recoiled from his mother's outstretched arm. He glued himself to Mr. Corfu's bosom, squealing. "No, Mummy! No! Don't touch me!"

"Guess the li'l fellah kind of took to me, Mrs. Raleigh."

Charles, leaning perilously over one of Mr. Corfu's many shelves, now pointed downward. "See, Mummy! See! See!"

Alice shudderingly perceived that Charles was indicating Mr. Corfu's appendicitis scar, part of which was visible above the green swimming trunks. In spite of her natural modesty, she couldn't resist a glance. The stitches were startlingly apparent. Quite likely the surgeons, in sewing together so massive a fissure, had employed very stout material, such as telephone wire or sash cord.

To the lonely and friendly Mr. Corfu, his scar was proof of the one magnificent adventure of his life. He was touched and honored by even the fleeting interest of a creature as lovely as Alice.

"Had me on the table two hours and forty-one minutes," he explained. "Used seven cans of ether."

James and Joan, pop-eyed, inched nearer to examine Mr. Corfu's stomach. And it was not until then that Jeff felt the first, faint chill of Alice's disapproval. Hastily he sought to reassure her that the occupant of Wel-Kum-U was a noble friend.

"And—uh—oh, Alice, dear! Forgot to tell you: Mr. Corfu has invited us all to breakfast, the whole family."

Alice stiffened imperceptibly. "I'm afraid we couldn't allow Mr. Corfu to—"

"Mrs. Raleigh, I insist," said Mr. Corfu. "'Course it's all at my expense, and—"

There was, Alice saw, no possible escape. But after breakfast, while the children surged into Mr. Corfu's cabin to be treated to a lethal-looking kind of candy which he always carried, Alice opened her mind to Jeff in Glad-U-Kum, across the way.

"Jeff Raleigh! I don't understand your propensity for picking up stray dogs. He's got the children completely undisciplined already. Candy after breakfast! Purple candy! And he murders —simply *murders*—the English language."

Jeff was not altogether nonplussed. He had felt it coming. His reply was already carefully planned. "You have always had," he began, "an intolerance for people who haven't been to college and got Phi Beta Kappa keys. Mr. Corfu is a kind, and a lonely man. Maybe his language isn't so—"

She turned, her eyes flashing. "I think of my children! I want them to be cultured! I want them to discriminate! You—you simply can't resist anyone. You're weak. Just because that creature happens to own a '41 torpedo job, you think he's a splendid person for our children to associate with."

"Well, it's all over now, anyway," said Jeff weakly. "He can't do them any harm in an hour's association."

There was a knock on the door of Glad-U-Kum. Alice opened the door to admit Mr. Corfu and her three children. Mr. Corfu didn't want to intrude, he said, but he was now ready to take the Raleigh family on a tour of Lost River and the Flume. Possibly they might even drive to the summit of Mt. Washington on the toll road. Be no trick at all, of course, for the 1941 torpedo job. Mr. Corfu said he had happened to mention the idea to the children, and they had all seemed enthusiastic. He had promised to stop at a place he knew along the way and give Joan a ride on an actual horse. He knew of a trout pond where he, James, and Charles could catch trout, too.

"You, an' me, an' the li'l fellah could ride together in the front seat easy, Mrs. Raleigh. 'Course I'm so big an' you an' him so tiny like. That way, we'd kind of equalize, see how I mean?"

"Oh!" said Alice.

"But Mr. Corfu!" said Joan, her sorrowing eyes on his. "*I* wanted to ride bu-side you!"

It is possible that Alice Raleigh, who had adopted a spartan-like calm, might have endured Mr. Corfu for the entire holiday if it hadn't been for his interest in music. But the interest didn't manifest itself till the third day.

On the first day, Alice had only to withstand the trip to Lost River and the Flume. Jeff and Mr. Corfu, with frequent interruptions from the children, conversed learnedly on streamlining, efficient cruising speeds, the profit in gasoline, valve beveling, and caster angles in the front wheels of the '41 torpedo job.

Alice once tentatively switched to more cultural matters.

"What books do you read, Mr. Corfu?" she inquired.

She had intended to let Mr. Corfu's answer be punishment for Jeff, but when the big, ponderous man replied that he read nothing but the Bible, she was herself punished. "Mighty fine piece of literchure," said Mr. Corfu reverently. There was no questioning his taste.

But Alice did take exception to Mr. Corfu's old-time rule for immunity from poison-ivy. The second morning at Musgrave's, she came down to the pool for a plunge and found Charles and Mr. Corfu rolling gleefully in a growth of the deadly vine. She was horrified.

"Charles! Get up this instant. Mr. Corfu! Don't you realize what you're—?"

Mr. Corfu, with a slow and gentle smile, lurched to his knees and stood up, bringing Charles with him.

"Give me my baby!"

"No!" screeched Charles. "Go away, Mummy!"

"Mrs. Raleigh," said Mr. Corfu, "here's a li'l thing maybe most of these modern mothers don't know. But what I allus say, if you just let 'em roll in the stuff, it don't hardly ever seem to affect 'em at all."

"Ridiculous!"

"Well, Mrs. Raleigh," said Mr. Corfu, beaming and unperturbed, "just wait an' see if I ain't right."

By a miracle—and a point for Mr. Corfu—Charles' skin remained smooth, brown, and lustrous. That night he insisted on moving over to Wel-Kum-U and sleeping in Mr. Corfu's spare bed. Alice, though on the verge of tears, permitted it rather than to undergo Charles' tempestuous wailing. But in the dead of night, she awoke Jeff to voice her protest.

"What's matter, Alice? Why you 'wake, anyway?"

"Jeff! I'm—I'm afraid."

"What of, dear?"

"Mr. Corfu. He—he's the sort of man who might carry—carry—"

"Carry what?" said Jeff, now wide awake.

"Carry—uh—vermin!"

"Oh, lordy!" groaned Jeff. "You're out of your mind. Why, he takes four swims a day. And this morning his underwear was pink, and—"

"Oh, Jeff! Pink underwear on a fat man! Oh, I can't stand—"

"But tonight, when we dressed after our swim, it was white."

"Horrors!" cried Alice, sitting bolt upright. "The dye wasn't fast! It—it *ran!*"

"Oh, no, no, no, *no!* He changed it, Alice. Changed it! He put on clean underwear. Why, oh, why are we lying here in the darkness talking about poor old Corfu's underwear?"

Alice, in a tone which blamed Jeff for ever bringing up the underwear, said, "I don't know, I'm sure," and moved to the other side of the bed.

The next morning at breakfast, for which Mr. Corfu again insisted on paying, the subject of music came up. The musically brilliant Alice who had a *magna cum laude* from Radcliffe for history and appreciation, said brightly, "Why, I never dreamed you liked music, Mr. Corfu!"

"Nothing like really good music, Mrs. Raleigh. Very elevating, inspiring you might say—and kind of sad, too."

"Did you attend the music festival at Stockbridge last month?"

"No—didn't happen to take it in."

"Koussevitsky conducted—Bach's B-Minor Mass."

"Huh? How's that again? A Mass, you say? Someone pass away?"

"Koussevitsky. Bach's B-Minor Mass. Tremendous."

"Oh, yuh, well—prob'ly okay, if you like that kind of stuff. But me, I play the banjo. I play 'Someone's in the Kitchen with Dinah,' an' all them nice, old pieces."

While Jeff felt the least bit faint, Alice said: "Oh, indeed."

"You like the banjo, Mrs. Raleigh?"

"Oh," said Alice again, "indeed."

Twenty minutes later, as Mr. Corfu started his banjo serenade at the door of Glad-U-Kum, Alice Raleigh had begun packing. Jeff looked on in hulking silence. Before Mr. Corfu had finished a second, poignant rendering of "Old Black Joe," Alice was ready to leave. In white slacks, her head wound in an orange silk bandana, she looked superb. Her smile, as she came to the door to greet Mr. Corfu, was crystal hard—yet very lovely.

"Mr. Corfu, I can't thank you enough. That was—well, really, it was amazing."

"Not bad, huh?" said Mr. Corfu, quivering in his pleasure.

"It was," said Alice unblushingly, "divine!"

Peering inside the cabin, Mr. Corfu noted the packed bags. A look of disappointment shadowed his face. "You goin' to leave?"

"Right away," said Alice. "We're going to drive on to—uh—" her mind shuffled speedily through the names of many towns "—to Twin Mountain."

"Say! That's fine! I'll meet you all there. You just drive on ahead, and I'll pick you up there. Mighty fine set of cabins up there—kind of in a valley, like. Mountains all around."

Without batting an eye, Alice said: "Splendid. We'll see you there."

But later, as the Raleighs swung into Twin Mountain, and as Jeff spied the cabins eulogized by Mr. Corfu, Alice snapped: "Jeff Raleigh! Keep right on going! We're spending the rest of our holiday at the Brightwell House!"

"Huh? Brightwell House? Eight dollars a day apiece!"

"There's riding for Joan."

"Extra!" croaked Jeff.

"Golf for you and James."

"Extra!"

"Jeff! I'm handling the family budget, remember—not you!"

To Alice, the Brightwell House, though extreme, was justified. It was the perfect antidote for three days of Mr. Corfu. The cultural advantages for the children were many. There was a good orchestra. In the dining-room they could order from menus in French and hear mannerly people conversing of books, Beethoven, and business while the ceiling echoed to the pronunciation of i-n-g's. Alice scintillated. She was so happy in the absence of Mr. Corfu that she said to Jeff as they lay in their silk-canopied bed the first night: "Oh—poor Mr. Corfu! Was I mean to him, Jeff? I wonder where he is? Do you suppose he's lonely down there in some cabin at Twin Mountain, strumming on his banjo, and wondering where we are?"

But if Mr. Corfu was absent in the flesh, his specter appeared frequently. It seemed to Jeff that Alice held Mr. Corfu over him, like a sword. For example, she wielded Mr. Corfu on the occasion when little Charles, enjoying himself mightily, broke up a game of Chinese checkers between two maiden ladies. Prior to Charles' cyclonic arrival, the maiden ladies had been bored to death. Now, joyously, they helped Charles pick up the checkers which had rolled afar on the lush red rugs of the Brightwell House lounge. The ladies sought to decoy Charles to their hearts with glancings, and cooings and dear-little-boyings. Charles would have none of them. His standard for companionship had been set at Musgrave Cabins.

The specter walked again on the evening when Joan Raleigh borrowed some roller-skates and roared around the veranda among the heavily paying guests. As a matter of fact, the guests were disappointed when Alice rushed in to hiss the cease-skating order. The guests hadn't heard a really good noise all summer, but there was no convincing Alice. Roller-skating on hotel porches was a Corfu-ism of purest ray.

A more terrifying episode occurred on the last day of the

Raleighs' stay at the Brightwell House. During the Father & Son Golf tournament for guests only, James Raleigh, with his tee-shot on the seventeenth hole, hit a banker in the ankle. That was bad enough. It was only through Alice's tenderest ministrations that the banker was persuaded not to sue. But the golfing party didn't realize that the worst had happened until, with Alice charmingly assisting the wounded banker, they arrived at the club house. There a shaken greens-keeper informed Jeff that his little son, Charles, had committed a crime punishable, according to the golfers' code, by death.

"Look, sir—I awsk you to look there, sir," said the greens-keeper, who was English. "Little devil spaded up nearly 'arf the eighteenth green, 'e did."

Jeff went white to the teeth. "Charles! Why did you do that?"

Charles smiled dreamily. He held out a small pail, which he had borrowed from the children's sand-box on the hotel lawn. "Oh, boy! I dug wor-r-rms, Daddy. W-or-r-r-ms!"

"Why?" Jeff chokingly asked.

"Go fishing, Daddy. With Mr. Corfu!"

Alice distractedly inquired why the golfers couldn't simply play around the turfless area. She was answered with a horrified silence. The hotel bill, which she paid the next morning just before departing for home, included an item of twenty-three dollars for two square yards of something called creeping bent.

Six hours later, as she opened windows and aired out her own beloved house back in Northerst, Alice was saying: "Oh, Jeff! Home at last. Isn't it wonderful? But we did have a nice vacation, didn't we, dear?"

"You bet we did," said Jeff, coming in with a week's accumulation of newspapers, "but, same time, nothing seems to take the place of our own home with our own things. Guess I ought to mow the lawn."

"I'll have the lunch ready in a minute, dear—if you and James'll carry in the suitcases. Where's Charles?"

"Charles? Right here, isn't he? Saw him a second ago."

"Oh, *Char*-uls! Oh, *Char*-uls! Joan, have you seen Charles?"

But Charles had silently and thoroughly vanished. Three searchings of the immediate neighborhood proved vain. The older children had enlarged the radius on their bicycles; but the only trace of Charles was reported by Joan, who had cut his trail at Mrs. Morrison's. One hour—two—then three. And Alice managed to get out the fateful words: "Jeff, I—I think you'd better call the police."

Alice sat with her eyes closed, her hand pressed to her forehead, as Jeff telephoned the description of her youngest.

"Three years old—nearly four, in fact—brown eyes, big brown eyes—friendly with everyone—wearing a—uh—"

"Sun suit," supplied Alice. "Sun suit."

"Wearing a sun suit," continued Jeff. "Blue, with white—white—"

"Shoulders straps, Jeff."

"Yuh, white shoulder straps. Been gone about three hours. Name Charles Raleigh."

Turning from the telephone, Jeff looked at his beloved. Her eyes were moist, her face white, her hands twisting in her lap. He went to her and patted her shoulder. "Guess there's nothing to do now but wait," he said, hollowly.

Little Charles Raleigh, in sallying forth so soon after arriving home, had intended merely to retrieve a red ball which had rolled through the back-yard fence. But once beyond the fence, he had looked at the sky, the trees, the grass of the adjoining yard. He had felt sweet, inward strainings, and he had uttered a squeal of freedom. The farther he wandered, the sweeter the sensation within him, until his tiny heart swelled with a new, tempestuous ecstasy.

On the first part of his journey, he gathered many toys—some from the yards of children he knew, some from the yards of strangers. These toys included a croquet mallet, a used golf ball, an automobile lacking two wheels, and a steam-shovel in excellent condition. His load growing unwieldy, he appropriated a small green express wagon on upper Elm Street. The toys heaped upon the wagon, he proceeded more efficiently, stopping only to add to his pelf.

By following dimly familiar streets, through which he had passed many times in the family car, he arrived at Mrs. Morrison's. After a brief stay and one lollypop, he departed—solemnly assuring Mrs. Morrison that he was homeward bound. But, a few minutes later, Charles had lost his way. He was not at all concerned. Everywhere he went, people treated him royally. He sat for a time with some workmen, who were eating their lunch. He had bites from several delectable sandwiches, and, with full stomach, drifted into an alley, and thence through the wide doorway of the Northerst Machine Tool & Welding Company. For half an hour he enjoyed the rich experience of making sparks on a Mr. Hennesey's emery wheel. Then, fatigue overcoming him, he took a nap on a heap of greasy burlap, together with one of Mr. Hennesey's tolerant hounds and her seven young.

He awoke in the middle of the afternoon, at about the time Jeff was calling the police. "I'm going now," he told Mr. Hennesey.

"Okay, kid—drop in any time."

"Tank you berry much," said Charles, and, catching up the handle of his express wagon, went his way.

His next stop, aside from one on King Street, where he fell down and skun his knee, was at a fascinating place called the Power House. He was first attracted to the Power House by the sound within of happy, laughing voices. He had trouble getting his express wagon into the Power House, because it had two doors—swinging doors. A lean man, who smelled like medicine, came smiling to his assistance. "Come right in, kid!" said the man, holding both doors open. "Hey, you guys! We got a visitor!"

"Tank you berry much," said Charles, entering.

The Power House was cool, dim, and vast. It was well named, though the power which was generated there was measured not in kilowatts, but in alcoholic units. A fan, circling its wide arms from the ceiling, cooled Charles' ruddy cheeks. Flies buzzed in a torpid way, as though pursuing something easily overtaken. Charles, noting the smiling faces all around him, felt that he was welcome. "What's your name?" he asked of the man who had helped him get his cart through the door.

"Bozo," said the man.

"My name's Charles. I'm three'n'half."

"I'm thirty-seven," said Bozo. Then, turning to a man in a white coat who stood behind a long counter, Bozo said: "Hey, Jerry—give the kid a lemonade."

Some time after Charles had begun on his second lemonade, his mother, at home, had reached the point of desperation. Jeff, holding her in his arms, told her for the hundredth time that there was nothing to do but wait.

"I know! I know! B-but I can't stand it, Jeff! The uncertainty! The—the dread."

"Dearest, we've just got to face it, that's all."

"Call the police, and ask them—ask them—"

"Ask them what, dear?"

"Ask them if they've found—anything."

Jeff fearfully dragged himself to the telephone. He was informed that the cruise car was at the moment patrolling the river district. Jeff didn't say this to Alice. He merely said: "They've found nothing."

Half an hour later, Alice forced herself to begin supper preparations. Only by work, she felt, would she be able to hold herself together. Little Charles' high-chair, standing empty in its place at the table beside hers, seemed to accuse her. She began to blame herself.

"Why did I leave him out of my sight, Jeff? Why did I?"

"Now, Alice! Stop that!"

"I'm not a good mother! I've failed in my job! If I only—"

Jeff caught her by the shoulders. "Alice—you're a wonderful mother. I won't have you torturing yourself by saying those awful things. I—"

The ringing of the front doorbell froze them. A sick, cold dread crawled numbingly through them. "I—I can't go, Jeff. I can't face it."

And she promptly went, Jeff following. Dimly visible through the screen—the door itself was open—Jeff and Alice beheld a huge, familiar bulk. Perched somewhere near the peak of the mountainous man who grinningly entered, was little Charles Raleigh—sound asleep.

"Mr. Corfu—oh, Mr. Corfu! You've brought my baby back! Where, oh where did you—?"

Alice nearly fainted with relief. She sank into a chair, cuddling Charles to her heart, while her words came incoherently. "Where did you—? Why? How did you get here, Mr. Corfu? Oh, you lovely man—for bringing Charles. Oh, you're so kind—you must stay to supper. And spend the night—of course."

Mr. Corfu and cigar, both eloquent, explained the miracle. Having lingered two days at Twin Mountain, brooding over the fact that he hadn't found the Raleighs there—probably some mix-up in the plans—Mr. Corfu had turned the nose of his '41 torpedo job toward home. He had proceeded down U.S. Highway 5, which brought him through Northerst. He had stayed two days in Northerst, planning to visit the Raleighs on their return. He had dropped into a little place called the Power House, just an hour ago, to refresh himself with a glass of beer and there had found Charles.

"Mrs. Raleigh, the li'l fellah just run to my arms. Certainly was glad to see each other again, me an' Charles was. So I looked in the phone book, an' found your address, an' I was goin' to phone—but thought I'd just drop in an' surprise you, like."

"It was I," confessed Alice, "who decided not to stay at Twin Mountain. We went on to the Brightwell House. It was my fault."

"Brightwell House? Kind of toney, ain't it?"

"Yes. Horribly. Jeff! What's the matter with you? Go right

out and buy some beer for Mr. Corfu. You always ought to have some in the house."

Jeff dizzily went around the corner and returned with some beer. Alice's welcome to Mr. Corfu, by the time Jeff returned, had become all but monumental. She insisted that Mr. Corfu witness Charles' bath—a rite hitherto reserved for a few of Northerst's most refined mothers. Mr. Corfu was duly appreciative, and subsequently listened, with bowed head, to Charles' prayers.

But to Jeff, Alice didn't really reach the heights till long after her delicious supper, when Mr. Corfu was being lionized in the living-room.

"Oh, just once again, Mr. Corfu—won't you get your banjo and play 'Old Black Joe,' the way you did at Glad-U-Kum?"

Trembling between the desire to please his lovely hostess, and the desire to do nothing that wasn't for the best, Mr. Corfu shook his head in sacrificial negative. "Well, Mrs. Raleigh—kind of you to ask, an' I sure would like to please you, on account of you appreciate good music. But you know, fact is, I'm afraid I might wake li'l Charles. An' Mrs. Raleigh, maybe you don't fully realize it, but that li'l fellah's plenty tired. Ought to get plenty sleep."

THE STORY

The House That Jeff Built

In the cruel winter moonlight, Jeff Raleigh stood beneath a naked oak tree on a hill which was his own. His wife, Alice, informed him that her ankles were frozen, that the children were alone in the house, and that they must go home at once. But the unheeding Jeff was in the midst of a monumental dream. . . .

The hill and the wind-moaning oak were real. But Thomas Jefferson Raleigh was standing on a flagstone terrace before a house as yet unbuilt, as yet unplanned. The house was low and rambling, of brick painted white, with a slate roof and blue blinds. Each window had an awning. Lawns swept off in all directions. He called into creation a putting green, which eventually became a small but interesting six-hole golf-course. He wafted the golf-course into oblivion. Too ostentatious! He substituted an apple orchard, rich at all times of the year with blossoms. He demolished the brick house, and rebuilt it of field stone, then of shingles, and finally of white-painted brick again.

There was no omen in Jeff's dream of the Bitter Site-Selecting War, or even of the Terrible Beam Argument. The Raleighs had never built, always rented.

"Jeff—*please,* dear," Alice begged, hunching her shoulders, "I'm sh-shivering!"

Jeff looked steadily at the ghostly oak: "A *white* oak," he murmured. "We could sort of frame things around that oak."

"Jeff! The children have been alone for an hour."

But Jeff beheld the ripened fruit in his vision, and the cold could not penetrate him. "Week-ends, if we went away, we could leave the key to the house with Pat Morgan or Val Williams, and—"

"What?" cried Alice, her chill forgotten in counter-irritation.

"Sure. Pat could keep an eye on things while we were gone."

"Not—on—your—*life!*"

As they turned down the hill toward the car, Jeff explained: "Leave a swell place like this alone, and strangers come prowling around. Why, I heard where some fellow had an oil burner taken bodily right out of his cellar when he was—"

"Then," said Alice, in her clean, decisive voice, "I'll leave a key with the State Police. I'd *far* prefer vandals to either Pat Morgan or Val Williams. They'd have every rug simply foul with cigar ashes."

Jeff stumbled over an ice-glazed boulder and swore, not wholly under his breath. "I think I'm capable of deciding who to leave a key to our own house with. I know character when I see it—read it right off at a glance. Never fail."

"You certainly sight-read that ghoul who sold you the mining stock," reminded Alice. "The key," she added, casually, "will be left with the State Police."

By Jeff's abrupt silence, Alice was warned that crisis-foundations had been laid and needed prompt crumbling. She respected the creative value of Jeff's dreams, but knew she must check and redirect him. It was his nature to plunge toward fulfilment without sufficient cost-counting. Quite aside from that, she realized that all life, especially married life, was a series of disconnected crises, great or small. It was time to reduce the present one to atoms. With a bright laugh, improved by the chattering of her teeth, she said: "Just thought of something weird!"

"What now?" grunted Jeff, cherishing his pique.

"We—you and I—are about to quarrel over a non-existent key to an imaginary house."

"Huh. That's so." A few moments later, as they drove toward

home, Jeff added: "But you got to look ahead to those things, Alice. I'm the one who always looks ahead."

Some poignant comparisons between looking ahead and pure day-dreaming formed in Alice's mind, but she smothered them judiciously. "You know, dear," she said, "it's going to be wonderful—building our own home. I—I hope that young architect is all right."

"He's okay," said Jeff. "They never get it on the first try. Give him time." Jeff sighed ecstatically. "I've always said, if I had a place of my own, I'd take an interest in it. You know, the lawns and so forth. Have a little shop in the basement, with tools—good ones. *Make* things."

"Yes," said Alice, thinking again of the children left to themselves in the present home for a treacherous hour.

While Jeff put the car in the garage, Alice rushed indoors to survey the carnage. It was not as bad as she had predicted, but 'twould do. James was thumping the piano with the loud pedal down. Joan had transformed herself into a horse. She had fashioned a bridle and bit from some rope and a bent spike, and was riding herself around the house.

"Sh-sh-sh-*sh*—" hissed Alice.

James finished the first three chords of Rachmaninoff's *Prelude* in C-sharp Minor, spun 'round on the stool, and said: "Why?"

Joan reined herself in and reared, her mane tossing. In the quieting of the nearer tumult, Alice heard the squawling of baby Charles from his crib upstairs. "You woke Charles," she accused. "You children are old enough to realize part of the responsibility for your baby brother."

"We didn't wake him, Mother. He never went to sleep."

This, thought Alice, sounded as though it had come from the lips of Jeff Raleigh himself. "Well," she told James, her temper in fine control, "would you mind easing off a bit, till he gets asleep?"

"Sure, darn it," said James. "I suppose so."

"He," announced Joan, indicating her brother with her right front hoof, "was making pratickly the un-*tire* noise. 'Boom . . . Boom . . . BOOM . . . ,' over'n-'n-over. I told him it was ux-*tremely* horrible. He would not bu-live me." Having delivered this stinging criticism, Joan became wholly quadruped again. She gave herself her head and cantered to the kitchen.

The instant Alice had gone upstairs to determine what remained of Charles besides his voice, James tiptoed for the kitchen to avenge himself on his younger sister. He had got no further than the front hall, when Jeff came in.

"Hi, Dad—where you been?" James noted with interest that his father's face wore what was virtually a Christmas look. In swift succession he thought of new skis, an English bicycle, an envelope of stamps from Tahiti, and a twenty-two rifle with unlimited cartridge supply.

Jeff put his arm around his son's shoulders. "Come on in the living-room, and I'll tell you."

Suffering in suspense, James sat beside his father on the big divan. "Say, look, Jim," Jeff began. "If you could have anything in the world you wanted, what would it be?"

"Just *one* thing, Dad?" James asked, cautiously.

"Sure, but a *big* thing, see?"

James put his elbows on his knees, braced his chin in his hands, and thought hard. Then he said, rapidly: "Pair of Marius Ericksons with steel edges, fiber upturns, Bildstein springs, and regulation Dartmouth-bindings."

"What?" said Jeff, perplexed.

James quoted himself verbatim.

"But what *is* it—or what are *they?"*

"Skis! Don't you *know?* Gosh, Dad, but you're dumb."

"Dumb?" said Jeff. "When I was a boy we used to—"

"Yes, you told me that. You skied on barrel staves. Must of been fierce. When do I get the Ericksons?"

The unexpected topic of skis had led Jeff far from the trail to the house on the hill. He decided to switch back to the main theme, salvaging what drama he might. He put his hand on James' knee: "Know what? We're going to build a *house!"*

"House? What for?"

"What *for?"*

"Well, I only meant, Dad, we've got a house. But I haven't got only that old pair of last year's skis."

There was a moment during which Jeff listened to the whining of wind around the eaves; another of wondering how he might infuse James with the house-building idea, in order that father and son might share in the joy of creation. During a third moment, Joan loped into the living-room, shied at the bridge lamp, circled warily, and drew herself to a stop.

Joan was a beautiful, saucer-eyed child, just beginning to lengthen. She was dressed in blue jeans and a lighter blue pull-on sweater. Her light hair framed her high-boned face. She had a determined and lovely mouth, and her mother's chin, precision, and directness of thought. Her wild vocabulary was due to an acute ear and memory. By her bearing alone, she commanded attention.

"Well?" inquired Jeff, as always in her staring presence the merest trifle uneasy.

"I am not ready to speak to you yet," Joan replied. She had removed the bent-spike bit, and was adjusting a grocery-twine-and-dog-leash halter.

"That spike'll ruin your teeth," said Jeff.

"Not only do you not know hardly anything about a horse's teeth," responded his daughter, "but you have interrupted what I was thinking of saying." Silence.

Calmly, at an unalterable pace, Joan completed an intricate series of halter knots. She ignored James' stare which promised retribution for her remarks concerning his musicianship. When everything was to her liking, she said: "I have been Eve dropping. I heard you say about building a house. I pru-ssume it will be on my hill which you bought, one time ago."

"That's right—*our* hill," said Jeff. "Are you glad?"

"No. You see, Father, you speak just only about a house. I do not care for a house."

"Don't? Well, say! What *do* you care about?"

"Barns. For horses."

"What horses?"

Joan's lips straightened in bitter outrage. "Several," she said, shying, and quieting herself with an inexorable hand.

"Well, couldn't you store them in the garage?" said Jeff.

The teeth of the several horses seemed to click menacingly. "I wish to un-form you: you do not store horses. You *stay*-bul them! And you do not stay-bul them in garages. You stay-bul them in *stay*-buls. Which are parts and par-shuls with *barns!*"

Jeff's magic and mysterious girl-child wheeled in her tracks, shouted over her shoulder, "Or *corrals!*" and pranced. Then she batted her bottom with a fly-swatter riding-crop and rode away to the shimmering canyons of the dining-room.

When Alice came downstairs from blanketing Charles, Jeff was engrossed in a stack of magazines, old and new. As usual of late, he was garnering advertisements of boilers, oil burners, coal burners, paints, piping, pumps, rugs, materials for road construction, cement, shingles, sheet metal, sinks, fixtures (bathroom), fixtures (kitchen), tree surgeons, landscapers, and lawn seed. He was so blissfully lost in his winnowing that he did not hear the telephone. Indeed, he was but half conscious of Alice's excited voice, saying: "Yes—this is Mrs. T. J. Raleigh—please read it to me. Oh! Oh, thank you very much."

Alice replaced the receiver and glanced radiantly toward her husband: "Oh, Jeff! The most wonderful news. *Sue* just wired."

"Unh? Huh." Jeff turned a page in the *Monthly Home Builder*. "Says here where if you use Besto-Wool insulating you can save twelve to twenty per cent on your fuel bill. Call it fifteen. Practically pay for itself in five years."

"Father is coming next week with Sue and her husband. Ray's on sabbatical from his university. Father's taking a trip with them."

Jeff worked his way slowly back into his immediate surroundings. "What's that you say, dear?"

"Father, and Sue, and Ray Inchlock. They're coming Friday."

"Oh. That's fine. Great." Jeff's eyes dropped to a picture of a Colonial house surrounded by elms. "Look, Alice, I was wondering: Where, exactly, do you think we ought to locate the house? Behind the oak tree or in front?"

"Beside it," said Alice, sitting on the arm of Jeff's chair. "So I can see it from the living-room windows."

"No. Seems to me we ought to have the site out further—just a little, of course—toward the brow of the hill, where we can look—"

"I want to see the tree from the windows."

Glancing downward, Alice saw on her husband's face what she knew secretly as the thinking-up-retort-expression. He said: "Do you have to see a tree out a window? Can't you go outdoors and take a look at it, when you feel the urge?"

Alice was dead-tired, and the sting of the cold night had made her drowsy. She wanted to go to bed and feel the warmth of three wool blankets filling her with sleep. "We've got plenty of time to decide, Jeff, dear. Maybe when Father and Sue and her husband come, we could *all* decide."

"Yes," Jeff agreed. "Darn good idea. Then you'll see I was right."

Joan Raleigh, up late, insisted on being the last one to go upstairs. Thus might the shadowy folk ahead be seen as wild horses, and she nipping at their flanks, urging them away from incredible dangers. From a half-remembered tale of the West, came her secret prayer-line. As she unsaddled and tumbled into bed, she whispered it to the ceiling: "The rider on the Palomino stallion was sill-wetted on the canyon's rim."

Several times during the next week, at the expense of the Raleigh Automotive Agency, Jeff took secret drives into the surrounding countryside. He said to Miss Ephraim, his secretary:

"Got to see a customer. Back 'n hour or so." He saw houses—little, big, tall, squat, rambling, compact. He had Miss Ephraim buy a large papier-mâché folder, and label it, House, Etc. Without mentioning it to Alice, he asked the advice of the bold, beefy men he knew: Pat Morgan, Shorty Cornwall, and others. They drew powerfully on their cigars, struck attitudes, and said: "Well, tell you what, Jeff, if I was doing it myself, I'd—"

Pat Morgan had one formidable admonition: "Don't let 'em try to make your new house into an antique. There's nothing worse'n antique houses that ain't real." Jeff figured up his assets several more times. He never got the same result. He delved into the loan propositions of the HOLC, the Coöperative Bank, and two rich acquaintances. He called his young architect on the telephone, trying to sound patient.

On Friday evening, a little haggard, he flopped into his living-room chair with a new batch of home-building magazines. "Gosh, honey," he sighed to Alice, "I'm as much house as Joan is horse."

An unaccountable excitement in Alice robbed Jeff of her usual quick and sympathetic response. "They phoned from Brattleboro they'd be here for supper," she announced.

"Who?" said Jeff, scowling at the prospect of interruption.

"Why, Father, and Sue, and Ray Inchlock, silly. I've been hustling, I can tell you."

"Who?" repeated Jeff, his memory stupefied with considerations of copper flashing and pegged-oak floors.

Alice's arms flew akimbo with the speed of exasperation. Beyond her, Jeff noticed his two older children, who were painfully well dressed. "Jeff Raleigh," snapped Alice, "are you losing your *mind?* You knew perfectly well they were coming. We discussed it right here a week ago and a dozen times since."

"How do you get that way? It's the first time I've heard—" Jeff paused and finished lamely, "Oh, sure, that's right. Just seems to have slipped me."

Alice smiled and brushed the hair from Jeff's forehead. Poor lamb. He'd been living, breathing, and dreaming house. "Well, never mind, dear. Run up and shave. Makes you look so handsome."

"Blarney," said Jeff, with moderate conviction.

Sue was Alice's older sister. Sue's husband, Professor Raymond Inchlock, on sabbatical from his university (where he taught Romance Languages), was the Raleighs' connection with the academic world. They arrived dead on the minute, which was the unveerable custom of Alice's father. At sixty-one, Cornelius Ross was a bald dynamo of information, vitality, and decision.

Supper that evening was an uproarious meal. Mr. Ross expatiated on the British foreign policy, the National Labor Relations Board, the philosophy of Whitehead of Harvard, the physics of Bridgman of Harvard, methods of feeding babies, the economics of Cornelius Ross, and the larval stage of the dobson fly as related to bass fishing in Squam Lake, N.H. Meanwhile, Sue and Alice talked of their children, and the strains and delights of domesticity.

"We're going to build a house," remarked Jeff Raleigh, when there came a kind of interstice in the monologues.

No one interrupted himself in homage to this news.

"Going to build it on our hill," Jeff went on, in a slightly louder tone.

"For instance," Cornelius Ross was saying to Professor Inchlock, apropos of the difficulty of mastering the Czechoslovakian language, "*czonek* means down. And *porto*—you'd swear it meant door—means floor."

Alice's sister Sue had suddenly switched to some beams she had seen for sale in an old New Hampshire barn: "My dear, they're hand-*hewn!*"

"Marvelous," sighed Alice.

It was long after the children were in bed that Jeff finally inserted the house-building theme into a small fissure in the general conversation. The theme stuck. Jeff felt as if his tongue were heavy-laden with precise information on the small American home. Now was his chance to share in the talk and to contribute something of value. He went so far as to offer two or three suggestions in the matter of his and Alice's own house. But everyone strictly attended the broader views of Cornelius Ross, which were delivered in a deep, booming voice. With no logical association of ideas, he was deep in the drilling of artesian wells. Jeff, duly respectful of his father-in-law's knowledge on this as on all other subjects, mentioned that there was a city hydrant within two hundred feet of his home site. This made no difference. A well had to be bored. Alice, Sue, and Ray Inchlock wanted to collaborate. Together, they bored a well.

The next day, at noon, a tumult of Raleighs, Rosses, and Inchlocks swept up Jeff's beloved hill over the slushy cart road, driven by Cornelius Ross. Jeff loved his father-in-law and admired him deeply. Frequently he had told Alice: "Outside of you, he's the greatest single influence for good in my life." It was difficult now for Jeff to remember this. He had struck the ceiling of the car twice on the way up the hill. And no sooner had the car arrived at the white oak than his in-laws began to decide exactly where he should put his own house on his own property, earned by his own sweat. Jeff felt that his house, his hill, his pride, and his identity were being drained from him. He sat on a damp boulder, a man alone, the echoes of their wrangling in his ears.

Professor Inchlock, although but a year older than Jeff, laid a fatherly hand on his shoulder. The professor tipped his poet's head back and closed his eyes impressively: "Here on this hill," he said, portentously, "I can see a house of Norman persuasion, with turrets. Ah, those charming turrets!"

Inwardly, and purely for relief, Jeff said: "If there's so much as one-half a turret on my house, Inchlock, I'll personally cut your heart out." Aloud, in a dull tone, he said: "Turrets? Yuh, sure, Ray—be nice, huh?"

Professor Inchlock seemed to purr with pleasure at his contribution and its acceptance. He was about to offer larger advice when Cornelius Ross following a period of intense thought, reached a decision and swayed in among them.

"I've got it, Jeff! Everything settled! A log cabin! One of the knock-down kind. You see, they have the cabin all prefabricated. A crew brings it up in sections. They work a day, two days—and you've got a house all ready to live in. Think of the saving in labor cost!"

"I—we—Alice and I—" stammered Jeff, "don't really want a log cabin. We sort of thought—"

"Of course you want one!"

Jeff's sigh appeared to elongate him an inch or more. His fists closed convulsively in his topcoat pockets. "No, Mr. Ross—Dad—we don't."

"But I am *positive* you do! A log cabin, all decided. Perfectly adequate for your needs."

Beads of moisture, despite the season of the year, formed on Jeff's forehead like dew on a chilled pitcher. There were several layers of utterance in his throat, the first two of which were dynamite. He was striving to dig out the more refined layers, when Sue and Alice agitatedly joined them. Alice's voice, crisp and bright, acted like oil on the churning waters of Jeff's soul.

"Jeff, darling! We've found the perfect site. Come on and see."

He could have flung his arms around her and kissed her. She had spoken straight to him, and *not* to her father, *not* to Ray Inchlock, *not* to her sister Sue. After all, she knew the house was for Raleighs and Raleighs alone. Darned if she hadn't brought a ball of line and two steel tent stakes. She had hammered in the stakes, frost or no frost, and strung the line for fifty feet—allowing for future expansion toward the oak tree.

"See, darling?" Alice cried, pointing triumphantly. She stood at a point near the middle of the line and stretched her arms out straight. Jeff saw the torn place in the lining of her last year's fur coat and swore an inward oath he would buy her a mink next season.

"There," she called. "Come closer—right here. Now, see? Living-room windows right along in here. I just have to turn my head, and I see the oak tree."

Jeff, deep in his soul, felt the house should be nearer the brow of the hill, but decided to keep still.

"Absolutely perfect," said Sue Inchlock, with a threatening glare at Jeff. "Don't you dare move it an inch."

Jeff's decision to remain silent weakened.

"Gad," breathed Professor Inchlock, honoring the house-site-line with his scholarly scrutiny. "I believe you've struck it."

Jeff was now positive the line should be moved forward, in strict accordance with his original plan. Meanwhile, Cornelius Ross was pacing up and down the string-line like a small, competent lion. He weighed the situation carefully, checking points in a bass mutter: "Sunset over there. Prevailing winds in summer, south and southwest." On the final lap, he progressed by carefully spaced stops and starts. He studied the view, with relation to oak tree, sunsets, and winds, every six or eight feet. There was a time of quivering suspense while his daughters awaited his final word. Abruptly he nodded in the affirmative!

"Smart girl, Alice—you're dead right."

At this moment, little Joan Raleigh, at the head of a posse of twenty riders, all on Palomino stallions which left no tracks in the snow, slipped like a wraith from a clump of leafless birches. She took in the house-site situation at a glance, said: "Ux-tremely perfick," and rode away.

Jeff Raleigh took a numb-legged step toward the south stake. Humbly he pointed to the stake at the northern end of the locating cord. "Alice," he said, apologetically, "pull that one up, do you mind?"

"What? And lose the *place?*" protested Sue Inchlock.

"Tsk-tsk, I wouldn't," said Inchlock, regarding Jeff with cultured disapproval.

"Make a mark in the snow," pleaded Jeff, forlornly, "and we'll put the stakes right back. I—I just want you to see what it's like, twelve feet nearer the brow of the hill. But parallel—absolutely parallel—to the line as you've got it now."

"Well—," said Alice, pulling the stake, "all right, but it won't do any good."

They moved the stakes twelve feet toward the brow. They pushed them down as best they could in the hard ground. The stakes sagged weakly. Jeff straightened, looked at the view, turned to his relatives, and asked: "Now just come out here and look it over."

They came. They looked. They shook their heads in a solemn communion of negation. And they moved the line back twelve feet to its exact original position.

From an unexpected quarter came the loyal support which kept Jeff Raleigh from being one against the world. With a confidential arm-pressure and whisper, Jeff's son, James, said: "Darn it, Dad. You put it right where *I'd* put it!"

During the next twenty-four hours, when it seemed that his sanity was about to go, Jeff remembered his son's splendid opinion. He held out finely until Alice's relatives departed for New York. Scarcely had the pebbles of the driveway settled after Cornelius Ross's hair-raising getaway, when Jeff announced to Alice: "Going down town."

"Down town? Sunday?" said Alice, alarmed. "Why? Where?"

"Office," replied Jeff and left without kissing her.

In his brief absence, Alice pondered his sullen behavior. Was he worried about money? Engrossed to the point of abstraction with plans? Tired out? Or what?

"Hi, dear," she called airily, as he reëntered the house. She held out her arms to him. He ignored them, growling: "Might think I'd been gone a month."

Obviously some kind of strategy was necessary. She brought him a bottle of beer, opened it, poured it, and placed the glass at his elbow. "There," she said. "You deserve it."

"Why?" he said, brusquely.

"Oh, for being so sweet—to Dad, and Sue, and Ray. I think it's wonderful, and extremely unusual, for a husband to get on so happily with his in-laws." Half-way through her compliment, Alice felt the sticky creep of doubt; but she carried on. Without a word, Jeff stood up and handed her the papier-mâché folder which he had brought from his office.

She accepted it and looked at him wonderingly: "What's this?"

"That? That's the house—all the plans, the work, the ideas, the sweat—all of it. I say the hell with it, see? *Hell* with it! *You* take it. From now on, I wash my hands of—"

"Jeff! Please—*Jeff!* Don't look at me like that."

"And the next time that bunch of deciders-of-other-people's-business comes to town, warn me. Just warn me, so I can go away somewhere and stay on some desert island while they're here."

Alice's lips went numb and gray. She clutched the folder labeled, HOUSE, ETC. She thought her fingers might shake to pieces.

"Jeff, oh, I didn't know. They didn't mean anything. You know how Dad is, and—I didn't have any idea—"

"You're *right,* you didn't! You speak of how happy I am with them around me. How the flaming hell can you be happy with anyone that—that—*turrets! Artesian wells! Log cabins! God Almighty!*"

She sank down at his feet and put her arms on his lap. "Jeff, please take this folder back. You love it so. It means so much to us—both of us. I—I beg you, dear."

"It's yours, see. *Yours!* From now on, you decide everything. I obey. That's my job. Obeying and—just earning the money. You and your people are the experts. They know. I don't."

No matter how terrible the temptation, Thomas Jefferson Raleigh did not so much as peek into HOUSE, ETC. for eight days. Trying desperately to recover the lost bond of mutuality so essential to home-building, Alice would invent things which could not be settled without him. Jeff answered her hopeful questions with exaggerated meekness: "Just as you say, dear." But when he saw the young architect's second group of house sketches, he dashed from the office at eleven in the morning and charged into the house shouting: "Hey, Alice—oh-migosh! Look what I've got!"

Together, gibbering in enthusiasm, they poured over the sketches. There it was! A solid central part of white-painted brick—garage and ell of white-painted shingles. There was the oak tree, setting off the whole thing. Here and there a bit of suggested landscaping with some low, field-stone walls.

"Oh, Jeff! It's *exactly* what we—"

"Darn right. Mighty good architect."

"I *knew* you would pick the right one, dear."

Without a single pang, Jeff took HOUSE, ETC., dumped the contents on the floor, kneeled down, and reunited himself with its hallowed litter.

From that time things moved swiftly. There were sweet, savage disagreements on details. There was the delight of compromise. Then, the actual breaking of ground in April and the building of the driveway. "Jeff! We're actually *building!* You can *see* it! The walls going up." With a grave look in his eyes, Jeff said: "Yes, dear—and you know, I'm the first Raleigh in three generations to really own his home and land."

"Oh, I know, it's so wonderful. You've worked so hard."

"Well, I did it for you—you and the kids. I love it, too."

As the house took form, Alice Raleigh became busy to distraction with interiors: wall-paper, light fixtures, bookcases, closets, stoves, kitchen-arrangements even unto the precise location of a new spring-lid garbage pail.

Jeff tacitly headed the construction and grounds department. He became an expert in plumbing, heating, cement mixtures, four-course brick-laying, roofing slate, insulation, and driveway drainage. In May his good friends asked: "Got her started, Jeff?" In June they asked: "How's the house coming along?" And in July, it was: "Say, there! How about that housewarming you promised us? When you going to have it?" These manifestations of interest pleased Jeff immeasurably, filling him with a singing sense of well-being and appreciation from his kind.

Just before the plasterers went to work on the living-room ceiling, there came an unexpected telephone call from the freight depot which turned Jeff into a furtive, alley-seeking creature. "Your name Raleigh?" inquired a hoarse, warlike voice.

"Speaking," said Jeff, mellow in visions of his castled hill.

"Say, d'ja order some beams from New Hampshire?"

Jeff blinked. "No. Certainly not. Must be a mistake."

"Thomas J. Raleigh? Raleigh Automotive Agency? Third 'n' Main?"

"Yes. And I didn't order any beams, and I don't *want* any beams."

"We got about a quarter-carload consigned to you."

"What?"

"Beams! See? Oak beams. Like for firewood, or something."

"I don't *want* any beams!"

"Well, you *got* beams!"

Jeff slammed down the receiver and thought of Pat Morgan, his staunchest and most cynical friend. He thought of Pat's curling lips, as Pat excoriated people who tried to make new houses look old. As the ghastly significance of the beams sank into him, thoughts of a housewarming grew unbearable.

He tried gamely to discharge the whole thing by saying: "Our house is our personal business." It didn't work. He arrived home in a smouldering wrath, and found Alice in the bathroom preparing to bathe Charles.

"I want to know where those beams came from? And *why?"*

Through a mouth bristling with safety pins, Alice said: "Meams? Ohm—yum." She removed the pins. "Beams? Why—oh, yes! Of course. Sue had them sent down from the old place she—"

"Alice, there will be no beams! Flatly and finally! I refuse to accept them or pay the freight."

"Very well. *I'll* accept them."

"You knew about them? All the time? You sneaked them in? You're going to scatter them across our living-room ceiling? Trying to make a new house look old?"

Alice's arm automatically prevented Charles from taking a head-long dive from his dressing-table to the floor. "Jeff, look here! We've been getting along so beautifully for months. Happiest days of our life. Let's not—"

"There—will—be—no—beams," said Jeff, with ferocious emphasis. "What do you think Pat Morgan and Val Williams and the boys would think of that four-flushing, antique stuff?"

Alice's cheeks flamed. She stamped her heel. "Do you suppose I care a *hoot* about those two? I don't care if they never cross our threshold. I want *beams!* I don't like to remind you that you once *gave* me the house folder, and told me to make *all* decisions, and—"

"If you think I'm going to stand for that sister of yours worming her way into our house with beams—"

Tears appeared suddenly in Alice's eyes. Charles regarded his mother ponderously and emitted a trial yowl of sympathy. Jeff's fatal brute-feeling closed heavily upon him. He could not compete with it. He backed wordlessly from the bathroom and fled downstairs. On the hall table he discovered a postcard from Cornelius Ross to Alice. It was postmarked Taos, New Mexico, and showed an adobe house. On the back of the card were the words: "Look this over before building house. Love, Dad." Jeff tore the card in tiny bits. He did not know that Alice had tactfully destroyed house-idea cards from her father from New York, Columbus, Ohio, Denver, and several way points.

By the first of August the beams were in place in the living-room ceiling of the house that Jeff built. He had become almost psychopathic about them and imagined them dropping on his head. He hated them so he dared not look at them, and he feared them so he was always glancing upward. He dreaded the day of the housewarming and tried to avoid his lunch-club friends. But housewarming, beams, and friends, he saw, were inevitable.

When the day came, nearly six months after the Bitter Site-Selecting War, the two older Raleigh children were packed off to Aunt Elizabeth's in Greenfield. When all settling detail was complete, the Raleighs promised themselves a smaller, more sacred housewarming—all their own, for their own. But first came eager and curious friends.

In the living-room of the new house, on a late August afternoon, there were thirty people—mostly women. They fluttered, admired, envied, and secretly criticized only the merest details. They said: "But, Alice, such marvelous *taste!*" They said: "A-*dor*-able!" And "Oh, the fireplace." And "But the wall-paper is simply perfect!" And "But don't you *love*—?" and always a returning theme, music to Alice's doubly alert ears: "It's a beautiful site, perfectly chosen. You've got the most from it, my dear." Alice Ross Raleigh was in a seventh heaven. The wearying struggle had been well worth this moment of genuine appreciation.

To Jeff, it was an ordeal. He looked anxiously from the nearest window. A fourteenth automobile parked unheard on the driveway. Even the swift crunch of new gravel went unnoticed above the rippling chatter, and the tread of heels upstairs as Alice piloted the current squad of exclaimers-with-delight.

But the doorbell's ring was plain enough, and, as he turned to answer it, Jeff's heart was heavy in his breast. There they were —*five of them*—all come in Pat Morgan's car! Val Williams, Joe Orson, Shorty Cornwall, Ed West, and the burly Pat himself; his friends of links and locker room, his cronies of club and Pullman smoker. On their faces were grins of derision which served to conceal the embarrassment and warmth which lay underneath. These earnest, hard-working, boastful, and solid men were known to Jeff Raleigh as "the boys."

"Us bums welcome here?" boomed Pat Morgan, holding open the screen door as if to run.

"Yes, you bet—any old time at all," said Jeff, shuddery with beam-fears.

The boys filed in. Jeff became garrulous in his effort to avert their shifty attention from the ceiling of the living-room. He spoke in sparse, jerky sentences: "Come out see kitchen. Got something refrigerator. Hey? No— Maybe go upstairs first. Or cellar, perhaps. See oil burner, so forth."

Victims of Jeff's uncertainty, the group swayed this way and that and finally surged for the stairs. But their path upstairs was blocked by Alice and a cluster of bright-laughing friends who were on the way down.

"Say, Alice," called Jeff, frantic in his desire for her to greet his roughnecks cordially. "Here's Pat, and Val, and the boys!"

"Oh," said Alice, with a restrained but welcoming smile. She had been the least bit on her dignity since the Beam Argument. "How do you do, Mr. Morgan, and—and—I don't seem to remember—"

"Shorty," supplied Jeff, jittery with haste. "I mean—Mr. Cornwall. Why, you know old Shorty."

Alice gave Shorty her hand. Shorty said: "Well, by gosh. So you're Mrs. Raleigh, hey? Wonderful place you got here."

"I'm *so* glad you like it, Mr. Cornwall."

Jeff felt as if emery paper wouldn't smooth away his goose flesh. He cast an anxious glance about the room for Pat Morgan. If he could get the boys upstairs, then down the back way to the ice chest, and give them a highball or two, they might actually think they *liked* the beams when inevitably they discovered them. But, when at length Jeff spied Pat, it was already too late.

Pat was standing near the fireplace, his arms locked behind him. His head was tipped back, and his cigar whipped in violent agitation from one side of his mouth to the other. He was scowling blackly at the beams! Near him stood no less a socialite than Mrs. Charles B. Applegate. Pat said something to her without once taking his gaze from the nearest beam. Whatever Pat's withering comment, Mrs. Applegate promptly passed it on to the woman at her side. The message—the libel, the excoriation, the lashing rebuke—traveled around the living-room like fire. There was a concentration of human flesh around Pat Morgan. He stood on a chair and waved a fat arm toward the ceiling. All within a radius of fifteen feet were raptly attentive.

"Yessir!" said Pat, his cigar magically sliding to the opposite corner of his mouth. "They're the genu-wine article. You don't often see 'em quite like this. See the axe marks? Prob'ly done about two hundred years ago with a hewin' axe, with offset handle. Hundred years, anyway—and sound's a nut. Why say! You couldn't drive a modern nail into that old oak. It's hard as iron. No fake antique stuff, that."

There was a rising murmur of corroboration. "That's right, Mr. Morgan." "Those beams were the first thing I noticed." "Set the room off beautifully." "I wonder if Jeff has any left over?" "If he has, I get first crack at 'em."

Pat Morgan climbed down from the chair and flung his cigar butt into the spotless fireplace. His head turned on his short, thick neck. Spotting Jeff, he cried: "Some beam-picker, you are! Where'd you get 'em, anyway? Give my eye teeth for some like 'em."

Jeff gulped and leered at Pat. He plucked at his collar and grinned forlornly at Alice. He turned again to Pat. "Why—uh —shucks—Alice found 'em. Some old place her sister knew about."

"Some wife, Jeff. Some beams. Boy-oh-boy-oh-*boy!*"

A dizzy, steaming peace pervaded Jeff Raleigh. It made his head buzz and his heart soar. He longed to be alone with Alice and his own children. He liked all these people here, even loved some of them—especially Pat Morgan. But he wanted to be alone with his own, own. And that would not be for one more day. On that day, he would tell Alice a grim and dangerous secret that he had sworn never to reveal—not for years, at least.

The next day the Raleighs closed the doors of their erstwhile rented home. They looked back once at the blank, shade-drawn windows. They thought once, quickly and a trifle sadly, of leaving the old place—and they turned their faces happily toward the house on the hill.

At six in the evening baby Charles had gone to sleep in his strange, new room with practically no sounds of indignation. Joan and James, home from Aunt Elizabeth's, raced tirelessly about the rooms and the grounds. James had paused breathlessly in his bike-riding to say admiringly to his father: "Dad, it's the best driveway to ride a bike on I ever saw. You go like a bat out of—" James hesitated, grinned at Jeff, and added, softly "—hell."

Joan had usurped a tool shed attached to the garage. She had carefully removed what tools were there and replaced them with pulled grass, odd ropes and wires, and seventy-five Palomino stallions. The shed looked like the tack room of a dryad. In the sweet, August twilight, she came into the house and drew rein beside Jeff. She amazed him by climbing into his lap and putting her arm around his neck. "Father," she said, "tonight—for the first time, I have learned to love you." Jeff gulped and looked over her head into Alice's eyes.

The Raleighs went to bed in their new home, *en famille.* The children went to sleep on the instant. Jeff and Alice didn't. They lay listening to the reedy incessance of a katydid, their katydid. Their eyes were wide in their very own darkness, on their very own hill. The rustle of night-wind in their white oak filled them with a queer, yearning peace.

Alice had been very careful about commenting on the beams, especially after the turn the housewarming had taken. But she longed to have her husband like them. It was one of two things needed to perfect this all-important moment. "Jeff, darling," she said, leadingly. "I thought Pat Morgan, and Val, and your friends were wonderful. I—I really like them, you know. And—and I picked Pat's cigar butt out of the fireplace with my own fingers, too."

"They're good fellows." The katydid sounded for a few seconds before Jeff added: "You know, dear—you were right about those beams. I like them. Getting used to them, I guess."

Alice's heart thumped. She rose on her elbow, and reached across to Jeff's bed. "Darling, you really do, don't you? And the house site? Don't you like it—*now,* I mean?"

She felt Jeff's shoulder stiffen under her hand. Oh, he *had* to like it—or she'd never, never, never forgive herself. There was no way to change the site, now. "Jeff—*please* say you like it."

He moved, as if writhing. "But Jeff, do you know what? I got a note—she must have written it last night, right after the house-warming—from *Mrs. Charles B. Applegate!* She said: 'The site was chosen with rare intelligence.' "

"All I care is," groaned Jeff, "do *you* like it?"

"But don't you see?" cried Alice, almost in tears. "If you don't like it, I—I c-can't!"

The katydid repeated himself till Alice thought she would go mad. Why did this last, grievous detail have to mar their happiness? "Oh—Jeff," she sobbed, climbing all the way over into his bed. "*Tell* me you like it."

He put his arms around her and held her head tight against his shoulder. He whispered in her ear: "Dearest, I moved that darn line twelve feet nearer the brow of the hill—and that's where our house stands, and you never knew it, and I was afraid to tell you!"

In the Reign of Jeff Raleigh

Two days after his wife's operation for appendicitis, Jeff Raleigh came to her in the hospital bearing anxiously awaited tidings of the new maid of all work. Yes, said Jeff, his expression quieting Alice's fears, Justina Novicky had arrived!

"Oh, Jeff—how wonderful!"

"You said it."

Jeff's heart pounded at the relief in Alice's voice. He took her hand and pressed it to his lips. Justina, he went on to explain, had showed up as planned, an hour after the departure of the former toast-burning, collar-scorching, sailor-chasing incumbent.

And the children? Jeff saw the concern in his beloved's eyes and hastily reassured her. Not only had Justina repaired James' broken ski binding, but she had played at horses-out-West with Joan. Both children had been won at the start. Then, with grace and ease, Justina had sailed into the housework. Not a dish broken. Not a vase toppled. And the steak, concluded Jeff, smacking his lips, was brown outside and red in the middle.

Alice was now so blissfully content that she overlooked a gas pain and sighed: "Thank heaven."

"Yuh, sure," said Jeff. "Now you can have peace of mind. I got things right under control."

Convinced that Justina Novicky, not Jeff, was the one who had things under control, Alice gave him a shrewd glance and hand pat. Bless his heart! A lion's share of credit was essential to his happiness. He wanted to feel indispensable in emergency. Let him!

"Dearest," said Alice, her heart brimming, "as soon as Justina gets into the swing of things, back you go to Maine to finish your precious ice fishing!"

"Guess maybe I'd better stick around a while," Jeff answered thoughtfully. "Wouldn't feel right, running away now."

"But you needed that vacation so much! And my fool appendix spoiled everything for you."

For the twentieth time Alice upbraided herself for taking sick when Jeff was vacationing, and a transfer of maids imminent. The foulest luck imaginable! Under protest the doctor had allowed her a day to prepare. She had managed to reach Jeff, who drove the four-hundred-odd miles home over icy, February roads. He had arrived at dawn, his face gray with anxiety. How nobly he had obeyed her last-minute orders—bundling baby Charles off to Aunt Elizabeth's in Greenfield, running endless errands; and now his last sacrifice, standing by to receive the new maid!

"You've been a perfect tower of strength, Jeff."

"I didn't do much," said Jeff, pleased.

Alice reached for writing materials on her bedside table. "I think I ought to drop Justina a note."

"Oh, yuh, sure, note," said Jeff, giving a slight start. "I'll take it to her."

While Jeff sat meditating, Alice began the first of her daily missives to Justina.

My dear Justina: It was such a relief to hear of your arrival! I'm sure you'd have been pleased to hear Mr. Raleigh's accounts of your cooking and of your winning the children's hearts. But you couldn't possibly be as pleased as I.

I am dreadfully disappointed that I couldn't be at home to welcome you, but we can keep in close touch through Mr. Raleigh. He'll deliver any word you care to send.

There are a few things I must tell you in this first hurried note: Mr. Raleigh's gray suit to the cleaner's Wednesday, his brown one the following Wednesday. Joan should be in bed, light out, at eight-thirty. James at nine. It was so kind of you to repair James' ski binding and to play horse with Joan. Apparently you already understand Joan's passion for horses!

Alice looked up from her writing. "Jeff, dear. I'm going to plan tomorrow's menu. What would you like, special, for supper?"

"Huh?" Jeff blinked his way back to the hospital room. "Supper? Oh—well, let's see—say a meat pie. That recipe Pat Morgan and I got at the Yale Club that time in New York."

"You shall have it! I'll instruct Justina accordingly."

"Swell," said Jeff.

Alice finished her note, blotted it, and handed it to Jeff. He folded it and carefully tucked it in his pocket. Then he kissed Alice good-bye, arranged the time of the next day's visit, and left.

During Alice's convalescence, Jeff came to the hospital at least once every day. After the second week, her brisk energies reviving, Alice grew impatient to return to home and children. Her fingers itched to grasp the domestic reins once more. But Jeff, backed up by the doctor, urged her to stay a few days longer. Appeased by Jeff's reports of domestic serenity and delighted by Justina's notes scrawled on pink stationery, Alice finally gave in.

Apparently Justina was developing into a perfect marvel. Alice reflected that she had not acquired the tall, bright Polish girl without a struggle. She had inherited the right to Justina from Kay Applegate, her dearest friend, who had recently moved to Syracuse. But there had been low, overbidding tactics from a bonded dowager named Mrs. Alexander Vanderpool. Alice wrote a letter to Kay boasting of her triumph. She gloated over Mrs. Vanderpool for two pages and quoted Jeff on Justina for another. Kay's reply arrived the afternoon Alice left the hospital, coming as the crowning joy to her release.

"Kay's so clever," Alice burbled to Jeff as they rolled over the bridge leaving Springfield. "Listen." She unfolded Kay's letter and read: " 'I can still see the Vanderpool simultaneously waving those two wands of snobbery, her lorgnette and her nine-inch cigarette holder. Erk! She's the complete ghoul, my dear—and don't let her within furlongs of our Justina. Oodles of love, Kay.' "

Jeff's response was so negligible that Alice glanced toward him curiously. He seemed preoccupied. "Isn't Kay a scream?" she prompted.

"Certainly is a scream," mumbled Jeff, swinging lackadaisically into the road toward Northerst and home. Three cars passed, throwing slush on the Raleigh sedan windows.

"Jeff, step on it, please! I want to get home for supper!"

"You'll get there, plenty of time."

A cement truck thundered by. It was traveling less than thirty miles an hour.

"Pity's sake, Jeff! I want to see my children!"

Jeff's lean fingers tightened on the wheel. The car spurted—and slowed maddeningly. It was then that Alice Raleigh felt a vague premonition.

"Is there anything wrong with the children? Have you been keeping it from me?"

"Well, I—"

Alice's premonition changed to dread. "What's wrong with them? You've got to tell me!"

"Doggonnit, Alice! Nothing's wrong!"

"But you said—"

Jeff yanked the wheel to the right in time to avoid an onrushing bus. "I didn't say anything! You butted in on me. I was just getting ready to tell you that—"

"Is it about Justina? Is she sick? Did she break something valuable?"

"Alice," Jeff groaned, "I don't know! I never laid eyes on Justina in my life. She never showed up!"

Alice stiffened. Dazedly she lifted a hand to her mouth and bit her gloved knuckles. *"Vanderpool!"*

"Yuh."

"You never told me!"

" 'Fraid you might worry. Have a relapse, or something."

Recovering from the initial shock, Alice pressed Jeff's knee and said: "Oh, you angel! What you must have gone through!"

"Yuh," said Jeff, significantly.

Alice gave him a sharp glance. "Those letters of instruction I wrote Justina—darn her hide! What'd you do with 'em?"

"Buried 'em," confessed Jeff wryly, "in a little grave I kicked in a snowbank, behind the hospital's parking space."

Alice studied her husband acutely. Jeff seemed thoughtful, strained, but far from humbled by his domestic travail. There was even a hint of smugness in his attitude, an air of tentative self-approbation. Quite clearly he was withholding something. Alice began an oblique examination: "That lie you told me about Justina's psychopathic aversion to telephoning! I—I fell for it!"

Jeff had taken an artist's pride in that particular lie. Contrived in desperation, it had come forth a blazing, alabaster white. "Yup, you sure fell for it."

"The letters you brought me from Justina were forgeries, of course."

"That's right. My shop foreman's daughter wrote 'em. The pink stationery was hers. Just the right touch."

Alice snatched another lie from Jeff's inspired galaxy. "You said the washing and ironing was as smooth as if a laundry did it!"

"A laundry did, dear."

A silence ensued. Jeff felt the tension mounting. He drove slowly, thinking hard, and praying for guidance in answering the interrogation which was bound to follow. What, exactly, had he done? How had he managed the children? Where had he found help?

There were certain things which Jeff was loath to reveal. And, concerning the present domestic arrangement, there was at least one factor about which he was himself in doubt.

"I suppose you got a substitute for Justina?" Alice asked.

Jeff braced himself. "Yes. Quite a number of them."

"Good Lord, Jeff! What are you preparing me for? What shall I expect? Is the house still standing? Who've you got there, now? Quit stalling!"

"Well—" Jeff hesitated. He decided to adopt a debonair manner and lead into the thing gradually, appealing to Alice's sympathy before playing his ace.

"Jeff! I asked you who you've got in the house *now?*"

"Not quite sure, dear," said Jeff airily. "Don't know, exactly. But there's a—a couple."

"You know we can't possibly afford a couple!"

"I know, but—" Jeff's attempt to cover his own uneasiness was masterly "—you just wait till you see them!"

"I suppose I'll have to. You're the least bit vague, dear."

"You'd be, too, in my shoes. All I know is the fellow phoned me at the office this morning. Said he'd come. Said they'd have the house ready by seven tonight."

"Oh. I—I understand. Kindly drive a little faster." Alice didn't really understand. Her mind had suddenly seized on another of Jeff's duplicities. "Hah! I see! I see why you were so sticky and solicitous about my staying on at the hospital."

"No, Alice," Jeff meekly corrected, "you don't see. Fact is, so much happened I can hardly remember myself just what was going on then."

"Oh, come, Jeff!" She moved closer to him, hugging his elbow to her side. "Who did you get first, when you found Justina wasn't coming?"

"Violet O'Doul was number one. She was a honey."

"H-m-m. Where'd you locate her?"

Jeff plunged recklessly. "The State Reformatory for Women. Now wait, Alice. *Wait!*"

Jeff's plea was unnecessary. To his astonishment the anticipated verbal guillotine did not fall. He was deeply grateful for the stay. Alice merely said: "Why, you smart man! Who gave you that idea?"

Jeff sighed. "Pat Morgan told me about a fellow whose wife hired a colored girl that stayed seven years. Got her from the Reformatory."

Alice wriggled impatiently. "You're slowing down again."

Jeff spurted till Alice reopened the examination: "I gather," she said, "that Violet was not wholly reformed? Did she drink?"

"Drink? No—not Violet." Jeff was thinking of another. He squirmed in his seat. In the gathering twilight the motion was imperceptible.

"Well?" pressed Alice.

Jeff reached to the dash and switched on his dimmers. Between Holyoke and Mt. Tom Junction, he sketched the background of Violet O'Doul. . . .

Violet was an angular brunette, a little taller than Jeff himself. She was definitely the athletic type. She had been confined for an offense the authorities called Stubborn Child. Her time up, Violet longed to white-wash her past with a chance in a respectable home. Jeff offered her the chance on the spot. She had got along well with James and Joan. True, she worked dinningly, and her voice was something to wake the dead, but it seemed that she was an adequate substitute. Therefore, to reward Pat Morgan for suggesting the source of Violet O'Doul, Jeff had given a poker game. . . .

At mention of poker, Alice felt bound to interrupt. Her quick mind had darted to the emergency-ravaged budget. "Jeff! How much did you lose?"

"Well, let me think," began Jeff. "Oh, yes. I remember now. Val Williams won, and Pat Morgan won a little, and so did Shorty Cornwall—"

"I asked you a question," persisted Alice. "How much did you lose?"

"Fourteen dollars—and Violet O'Doul."

"You mean Violet was at stake?"

"No, dear. But Violet thought so. She thought her virtue was, I guess. She was upstairs in bed. Been asleep for hours, we naturally supposed. But she must have waked up. We—uh—well, we were singing."

Alice covered her ears and said: "Ugh!"

"We were singing 'Frankie and Johnny,'" pursued Jeff, ignoring the slight. "It was about the eleventh or twelfth verse. I forget. But we looked up, and there on the stairs—it was two in the morning—stood Violet. She seemed upset. So I went over to her and said: 'Violet, I'm sorry if we woke you up.'"

"She just stared at me accusingly. Then she stared around the room. Then she said: 'So this is the kind of a place I've come to! Singing rye-bald songs! Gambling! Drinking beer! It's a sink of iniquity! What chance has a girl got to go straight?'

"Then she ran upstairs and locked her bedroom door. In the morning she was gone."

Alice's reception of the Violet incident was heartening to Jeff. She said nothing about his poker loss. She made no further comment on his cigar-smoking cronies, or their nightingaling. She merely squeezed Jeff's arm a little tighter and wheedled: "Dear, you're forgetting your driving again. Please! I'm dying to see that couple you've got waiting for me."

"Oh, sure," sighed Jeff, staring soberly into the twilight, "me, too."

As they passed Mt. Tom Junction, Jeff jockeyed for time to tell the harrowing tale that had led by fateful steps to the engagement of the couple. Alice was showing signs of impatience, but she must hear the full story, lest she mistakenly condemn him. . . .

The morning Violet left, Jeff had brooded darkly on the servant problem while preparing breakfast for his children. He got them off to school and while washing dishes, brooded further. In a cruel light, he saw exactly why the loss of Justina would crush Alice. And he determined then and there to find a servant

—an everlasting one—beside whom Justina Novicky would be a lowly scullery wench.

In the rising mists of inspiration, Jeff had cracked a breakfast plate and scalded a finger in the dish water. But he had also conceived Edward! Edward swirled into his mind carrying a julep and bowing from the waist. Edward was born, mentally, from a union of Jeff's longing to please Alice, movies of the deep South, and half-remembered bourbon advertisements. . . .

"But Jeff," protested Alice, when he had got this far, "I don't *want* an Edward!"

"Alice," Jeff consoled, "you haven't got one."

"You didn't hire one?"

"I'm just beginning to tell you all about it."

With Edward's specifications blithely on his tongue's tip, Jeff had driven straight to the Certified Domestic Employment Agency.

"Brother," growled the employment agency man, after Jeff had limned Edward, "there ain't no Uncle Remus. But you can take your pick of *them!*"

Whirling in the direction of the man's thumb-jerk, Jeff had looked through a door to a dismal corridor, whence came a whiff of creosote. On a bench along one wall, sat the job-seekers. They were four old ladies, the siftings left by a hundred, sharp-shooting housewives.

Their glances lacerated Jeff's heart. He surged with an impulse to hire them all. Surely, in the Raleigh home they would rediscover light. Their ears would tingle afresh to the lilting voices of children—Jeff's children. From James' quick enthusiasms, from Joan's elfin dreams of horses, these dejected spirits would revive.

In his overwhelming sense of obligation to them, Jeff nearly forgot his duty to Alice, home and children. And because he could not bear to raise false hope in any of the withered breasts, he hired the first prospect he interviewed.

She was a Mrs. Leftings, once of Puddleston, England, but

more recently in service in Hartford, Connecticut. Mrs. Leftings exuded an odor of anise. She kept her hands in a black muff, and on the way home talked incessantly.

"My last position," she babbled, "was at Perfesser 'Erbert 'Enderson's, in 'Artford. A lovely 'ome, Mr. Raleigh. Lovely. But the poor perfesser up an' passed aw'y. 'E was along in years. 'Ad to 'ave a great deal of personal attention. It was 'ard, 'ard."

"Sure," Jeff had said, encouragingly. "But at our house, you—"

"The funeral was lovely," persevered Mrs. Leftings. "Never saw such flars, Mr. Raleigh. 'Undreds an' 'undreds of them-there —oh, 'olly'ocks, like. An' Perfesser 'Enderson layin' in 's open casket, like in life."

"We have just the two older children at home while Mrs. Raleigh's in the hospital," Jeff had managed to insert. "James is thirteen, Joan eight. Charles, the baby, is—"

"A biby? Oh, *'ow* I love a little biby!" Mrs. Leftings sniffled, and the anise smell grew strong.

Arriving at the house, Jeff had introduced the children, who were just returned from school.

"My, waht a'nansome little girl," cooed the new servant to Joan. "Come 'ere to Mrs. Leftin's, 'oney girl."

Joan Raleigh stood firm, her delicate nostrils flaring, her feet braced. Her enormous brown eyes rolled, showing the whites, as might those of the stream-lined horse she was impersonating. Mrs. Leftings made a purring noise and held out her arms. Joan shied and pranced.

"Don't be frightened, dearie," pleaded Mrs. Leftings.

Joan, who had never been frightened of anything, minced forward and said: "Hello. Have you ever been out West?"

James asserted himself at this point. He gave his sister a shove, admonished her to quit horsing around, and boldly shook hands with Mrs. Leftings. . . .

Alice Raleigh, by chewing her knuckles, had managed to keep fairly quiet during Jeff's introduction of Mrs. Leftings. She had uttered only a few brisk exclamations; but when it flashed into her mind that Mrs. Leftings might be half of the couple Jeff had so vaguely described, she could restrain herself no longer.

"Did you," she asked fearfully, "give me to understand that this Leftings person is no longer with us?"

"Gone!" said Jeff darkly.

"Could she cook?"

Jeff shuddered. "Creamed codfish. That's all."

"Oh, you poor dears," sympathized Alice. "How awful. Did you fire her? Or did she just leave, like Violet?"

"Both," said Jeff, glancing timorously toward Alice. "She was allergic to horses!"

Alice's jaw dropped. "What on earth are you talking about?"

Jeff leaned forward and switched his headlights full on. He lit a cigarette, inhaled deeply; and, buoyed by Alice's appreciation of his trials, gave her the full account. . . .

As the car rolled onward, nearing home, he told of the night he had entered the house to find Mrs. Leftings sprawled in his arm chair. Wheezing asthmatically, she had bleared at him through the tendrils of her disordered hair. In her vicinity the odor of anise, though powerful, ran a bad second to that of gin.

"Where are the children?" Jeff had cried aghast.

" 'Ow in 'ell should I know?" Mrs. Leftings had whimpered, groping for a handkerchief. "They're out, around, somewheres." She had given a vast gesture, and her arm had flopped back to her lap.

"Mrs. Leftings! I'm afraid you've been drinking!"

"There, there, now. Don't be afraid. I've 'ad a bit of medicine. Right. I was compelled to 'ave it."

"Compelled?"

"You 'eard me! Compelled is waht I said, an' compelled is waht I meant!"

Arising, Mrs. Leftings had made an effort to arrange her

tresses. Then, pointing straight at Jeff, she had accused with stunning irrelevance: "Mr. Raleigh! There's an 'orse in this 'ouse!"

"A—a—a what?"

"I said an *'orse!"* Mrs. Leftings had stridently insisted. "W'en an' 'orse enters an 'ome, out the door goes Lou Leftin's. Why, you asks? Because 'orses gives me hasthma. Always 'as!" Here Mrs. Leftings, reaching to the mantelpiece, had taken a deft gurgle from the bottle which was resting there. "Gin 'elps a bit," she had finished in a strangled tone.

"I'll drive you to the nearest bus stop at once!" Jeff had muttered.

Because of the fact that no horse was visible, Jeff had felt that Mrs. Leftings might be a mental case. Lest harm befall the broken old lady, he left her at the police station where, even against her will, she would be sheltered from the bitter night. . . .

Having heard this much, Alice Raleigh savagely interjected: "You were too easy on her, Jeff!"

"But gosh, honey. You couldn't leave the poor creature to herself, the way she was."

"She left our children, didn't she? She didn't even know where they were! Oh, Jeff!"

"The kids were home when I got back from the police station," Jeff said.

"Were they all right?"

"Yes. Yes, they were. But they were excited, jittery."

The suspense was beginning to tell on Alice. Jeff realized that his time was short. He must hurry. The lights of Northerst were drawing near. Alice grew more and more difficult to put off. She repeatedly demanded a concise statement regarding the couple she was soon to confront. Jeff only wished he could satisfy her on that point. But one or two other things required prior consideration. . . .

On the night of Mrs. Leftings' fall from grace, while preparing bacon and eggs for his children's supper, Jeff had heard a noise like that of an anvil being dropped on a cement floor.

"What's that noise?" Joan had asked in feigned surprise.

"You know darn well what it is," James had blurted. "You might as well tell Dad, too. We'll have to, sometime."

"Well?" Jeff had asked, paling.

"It's just Rosemary stamping her feet in the garage," Joan had casually informed him. "Don't give her a thought, Daddy."

"Mr. Andrus, the farmer," James had explained, "said we could keep her over night for a dollar and twenty-five cents. The whole bunch of us kids chipped in our allowances."

Mrs. Leftings had been right! There *was* a horse! Reeling from the kitchen, Jeff had opened the fire-proof garage door to find himself eye-to-eye with Rosemary. He estimated her weight at twice that of a piano, her height at nine feet. Her hoofs were as large as cornerstones, and she flung them around without regard for human life. From eyes the size of door knobs, she shot Jeff a baleful glance. He recoiled.

"She won't hurt you, Daddy," Joan had soothed, giving Rosemary a loving pat. "Don't you think she's simpully deevine?"

"No!"

"Watch me, Daddy." Joan had moved a box against Rosemary's side elevation, grasped the ropy mane, and hoisted herself aloft.

Blanching, Jeff had gazed at his girl-child sitting far above him in the valley that stretched off behind Rosemary's withers. "Joanie, get down! Get Andrus on the telephone. Get that horse out of here!"

Joan's eyes had clouded. "Father, are you the kind of man that would deeliburately take a littul girl's horse away from her?"

"Doggone right I am!"

"Very well. Then I'll write Mother. I'll tell about Justina not coming. I'll tell about Violet O'Doul. And Mrs. Leftings—who *drank!*"

"You wouldn't! You couldn't do that to Mother!"

"Dad," James had said manfully, "you don't know that girl. She'd do it, just like she says. Better let Rosemary stay to-night."

The next morning, after the children had breakfasted, fed Rosemary, and gone to school, Jeff had phoned farmer Andrus' residence. Mrs. Andrus advised that her husband had spent the night in Boston attending the Sportsman's Show, and she didn't know exactly when he would return. . . .

"Poor, tormented Jeff!" comforted Alice, as they entered Northerst. "You really went through a lot, for my sake, didn't you, dear?"

"I waited till darn near noon for Andrus!" cried Jeff, his voice tinged with a sudden, growing elation. "But by gosh, it was sure worth it!"

Alice roused to Jeff's new tone. "What do you mean, dear?"

He began to speak excitedly, like one describing a magnificent personal exploit. There was a boyish enthusiasm and a marked lack of false modesty. "Well," he caroled, "when Andrus finally came to get Rosemary, he told me about the Sportsman's Show! Seems he'd seen the Guides' fly-casting event in the big indoor pool."

"Yes?" prompted Alice, sensing a revelation.

"Guess who won it, Alice! Just guess! Boy, oh, boy!"

"Who? I don't follow those things, you know."

"Zeke Brackitt!"

Alice's lips went dry. "Zeke Brackitt?" she queried. "I thought he was the guide you had on your ice-fishing trip."

"He was! That's the point. I had to leave him stranded, so he took the opportunity to come down to Boston and enter the fly casting. Alice! Don't you see what a break it was?"

"I—I suppose he was pleased to win, yes," said Alice, alarmed.

"Oh, I don't mean that, at all! I mean it was a break for *us!* For the kids! For everyone!"

"Jeff, do you mean to say—?" Alice's voice died off in a rustling sound.

"That's right!" Jeff rushed on, oblivious to Alice's quaking silence. "I got Zeke on the phone at the Maine Guides' booth at the show. And *was* he glad to hear my voice? He said to me: 'Gol dang it, Mr. Raleigh! You just bet I'll come. Mighty glad to be with you!' You can't imagine how I felt, Alice. Zeke hopped the next train to Springfield. I met him there and brought him home."

So this, thought Alice, dazed, was what Jeff had been so proudly holding back! She had managed to control herself through Violet O'Doul, Mrs. Leftings, and the mythical Edward—but Zeke Brackitt was one too many! What would the neighbors say? And especially Mrs. Vanderpool, who had stolen Justina?

"Jeff," said Alice, desperately hoping, "I simply don't believe it! You didn't really hire a Maine guide for a house servant!"

"You're darn right I did!" exulted Jeff, mistaking Alice's incredulity for admiration. "Just perfect for the children, too! Chance of a lifetime for 'em! Learn all about the outdoors and everything!"

"Who—who listened to Joan's prayers at night?"

"Zeke and I did!"

"Jeff!"

"And do you know what?" Jeff blindly gushed. "Zeke cooked all our meals over the open fire in the living-room. Right on the coals, dearest. Just like camping out! Why, say! The kids were just wild about it!"

Alice felt herself losing her grip. The end was near. "What cooking equipment did he use, Jeff? His own?"

"Nope. Didn't happen to bring it down with him. So he used that white enamel stuff you bought recently. You know."

"I know," choked Alice. "Did it get black?"

"Just woodsmoke, dear. Little woodsmoke never hurt anything. House smells of it, too. Nice."

"Jeff Raleigh!"

"Wait a minute, dear. I want to tell you about the tent Zeke put up. 'Course the snow was deep outside. So he put it up in the living-room. Slickest thing you ever saw. Cut some birch poles out back, and—"

"My little birches!"

"They weren't good for much. Just wire birches, Zeke said. So he got the poles up and used those brown curtains for canvas. Just the right color for a wigwam. The kids—"

"Stop it, Jeff! Stop! I can't stand any more! My brown curtains!'"

Jeff's armor of self-approbation was pierced with dread. "But —Zeke's an authority on those things," he protested feebly as the cold truth dawned.

"Is—is the wigwam still standing in my living-room?"

"No," said Jeff sadly and after a pause added: "Zeke ran out on me four days ago. Haven't seen him since."

"Thank God!" sighed Alice.

"So—so—you don't like Zeke," groaned Jeff, as the car approached the house.

"I hate him!" blazed Alice.

Alice was both repelled and morbidly attracted by the sight of her own front door. When Jeff drew to the curb and stopped, she covered her face with her hands. Jeff had hired a myth, a malefactor, a drunken harridan, and a Maine guide in the order named. Who were the couple? Quite likely they were living in sin. Probably they had escaped from an insane asylum.

Alice felt Jeff's hand on her shoulder. She shrank away, took her hands from her eyes, and glared at him. "Who is the couple in my house? Who are they?"

Jeff looked at her despairingly. If she had hated Zeke Brackitt, how could he answer her? "Alice!"

"I ask you for the last time, Jeff! Who are they?"

"Alice, there's something—"

But Alice had flicked open the car door and jumped out. She started to race up the pebbled walk.

"Don't run like that," wailed Jeff, charging after her. "Don't you know it's bad for you? *Alice!*"

She had gained the front door and streaked through. Jeff followed her into the living-room. He approached her, holding out his arms. But as the door to the kitchen opened, she spun away, showing him her back.

In the kitchen doorway leaned a tall, self-composed man. His gaunt face was pleasantly weathered, his hair cowlicked, and his eyes a tranquil blue.

Alice advanced menacingly upon the man, her chin firm, her cheeks white. "I am Mrs. Raleigh," she announced.

"Pleased to meet you, ma'm," said the man. Looking beyond her to Jeff, the man said: "Howdy, Mr. Raleigh."

"Hello, Zeke," said Jeff hollowly.

Alice gave Jeff a furious glance and returned to Zeke. "Mr. Raleigh gave me to understand that you had left us," she snapped.

"I did, ma'm," said Zeke, coloring, "and I was mighty sorry about it, too. But I came back."

"Evidently," remarked Alice. Slowly recovering her poise, she grimaced at Zeke in the manner she felt befitted a housewife when greeting a woodsman in the parlor. Zeke smiled back in perfect serenity.

"Mr. Raleigh tells me," said Alice, "that we are—indebted to you."

"Thank you, ma'm."

"Not at all, I'm sure. But since we do not wish to carry this indebtedness further, why—" Alice's meaning was ice-clear.

Jeff, standing behind her, gave Zeke a supplicating gesture. Zeke responded nobly. "Well, Mrs. Raleigh," the woodsman said, "seems to me, most any way you're a mind to look at it, that it's Mr. Raleigh we're all indebted to."

Alice's smile was now bleakly fixed. "Very kind of you, I'm sure. I—I see what you mean, of course."

"Take me, for one," slowly continued Zeke. "If 'twan't for Mr. Raleigh's drivin' back down here to take care of you, why, I wouldn't of got a chance to win that fly-castin' event, down to the Boston Show. Nor I wouldn't of got to come up here to help out Mr. Raleigh."

"Obviously not," said Alice.

"And gol dang it, if I hadn't come here to Northerst, I wouldn't of met my wife that night at the movies when she dropped the peanuts."

"That's all very interesting, Mr. Brackitt. But frankly I don't see where—"

"Give him a chance, Alice!" inplored Jeff.

Alice put on a grimly patient look, as Zeke continued: "Well, there ain't much more to it, ma'm. Only my wife got fired from her job, because I come callin' on her nights where she worked for the rich woman. Seems the rich woman didn't allow her to entertain none in the kitchen. So I says to my girl, let's get married an' fool the rich woman. So we got married. And gol dang it, a bang-up Polish weddin' takes about four days. So that's why I run out on—"

"A *Polish* wedding?" Alice breathed.

"Yes ma'm. Justina's folks wanted to do it up right. And gol dang it, they sure did!"

"Justina Novicky!" Alice's hands writhed. She swayed toward Zeke.

"That's her, Mrs. Raleigh. She's out in the kitchen right now. Kind of scared to come in here to face you."

"Oh, Mr. Brackitt! Zeke—" said Alice, waveringly. "I—I must talk to Mr. Raleigh alone for just a moment. Would you mind, terribly?"

"Why no, ma'm," said Zeke, courteously moving toward the kitchen.

"And—and Zeke! Tell Justina I'll see her in a minute. And—be sure to give her my love, too!"

When Zeke had gone, Alice turned to Jeff, who was leaning limply on the banister of the front-hall stairs.

"Jeff! How could you be so cruel? Why didn't you tell me

Zeke had married Justina? Oh, why didn't you tell me?"

Staring foggily, Jeff answered: "So help me, I didn't know who he'd married till this minute. He simply called me this morning and said he wanted to come back, to make up for running out on me. He said he was married, and his wife was a skilled servant and out of a job."

Alice gave the living-room a swift look of estimate. "But—but who's been here the last four days, Jeff?"

"Just—just me."

"But the brown curtains have been washed and put in place!"

"Yes, dear. I—I did it myself. I got the black off the cooking things, too—most of it."

Alice gave the living-room a closer inspection. "You—Jeff! You waxed the floors, too!"

"Yes, dear."

Alice ran to her husband's arms. Weeping in gratitude, she sobbed out a few more questions. Did Zeke intend to work for the Raleighs? No. Due to his casting skill, Zeke was soon to take a job over in Westfield for a line manufacturer. He was to commute, returning each night to Justina.

Suddenly recalling that Jeff could cook only two things, Alice loosened his arms and looked at him in fright. "Have James and Joan been living four days on bacon and eggs?"

"Should say not!" replied Jeff Raleigh, pridefully. "Hot biscuits, roasts, green vegetables, and twice we had apple pie!"

"But you can't—"

"The heck I can't! Zeke Brackitt showed me!"

Just before her two rosy-cheeked children burst through the front door to welcome her, Alice said adoringly to her husband: "I—I think I'll take up fly casting next spring. Zeke's so *darling!*"

FAMILIARITY BREEDS CONTENT

Whatever your literary ambition—be it to achieve immortality, mere independence, or both—you can be sure that the commonplace is the richest mine of story material you will ever find. Journey the world over, if you must and if you can, but you will probably return to Elm Street, or Hogan's Alley, or wherever, and write at least some stories about the Joneses and the Smiths and the Browns. These stories of the familiar comprise the most central tradition in all fiction, from Chaucer to Sinclair Lewis, from the Parables to Proust, whether the treatment is comic, tragic, romantic, or satiric. They do not, of course, comprise *all* the traditions of fiction, as the selections in this book attest. But the point for the beginner is that he, or any one writer, has under his nose all the material necessary for immortal fiction. He has lived on the earth a number of years; he has certainly known longing and frustration, anticipation and success, and he has probably known something of fear and hope and failure, of love and death. "It is not," writes Miss Mirrieless, "lack of experience which handicaps any writer. What it is, is the purblindness which prevents his seeing, or his seeing into, the experiences he has had."

There is another thing to remember about the familiar: What is commonplace to you, is certain to be exotic to many others. If you are in college, say, remember that for every one of you, there are many people your age who are not, and a good many of them wish that they were. Almost always your material has this multiple appeal; anyone who has been to college will receive pleasure in reading your story because of the pleasure inherent in recognition of the familiar. And so in the outside world. Conversely, if you have never lived on Elm Street, you are curious about those who do. Everybody likes to get behind the scenes and discover exactly how you run a railroad locomotive, or a hotel, or a garage business, or a college. And everybody who does those things for a living delights to read about his own experiences.

In brief, this chapter boils down to advice quoted earlier: *Write about what you know.* This is not to say that you shouldn't exercise your imagination, or that you should be afraid of venturing into the unknown. But the unknown will have to be known to you before you venture to write a story about it. Fletcher Pratt is fond of saying that the greatest obstacle to his literary career was the first story he ever wrote, which was about an invasion of the island of Madagascar by legions of octopuses. Mr. Pratt had never been within thousands of miles of Madagascar nor ever seen an octopus, yet the story sold the first time out. That sale was a misfortune, Mr. Pratt avers, because it gave him the false idea that the less you knew about the material the better. It took a long and painful apprenticeship, and a hatful of rejection slips, to teach him that a writer must know what he is writing about. Even fantasy must adhere at least to its own logic, must stay within the logical limits of the material. The fantasies of Robert Nathan are excellent examples here. If it is necessary to sail a boat on wheels down the highways of the country, as in *The Enchanted Voyage,* the special navigational problems set up by the fantasy must be dealt with and solved in terms of ordinary sailing. You had, that is, better be a sailor before you write that book. There is, certainly, interior evidence that either Nathan is a sailor himself, or that he called one in as consultant. A publisher once told me, in discussing a manuscript he had rejected: "I hated to turn that novel down, but I don't trust its author. Too many simple little details are wrong. I don't think he thoroughly knows what he's writing about, and *authors must know!*"

Yes, *authors must know.* Knowledge is the prime condition of authorship, whether you write for the pulps, the slicks, the trade journals, or the reviews. That is why instructors and critics keep telling beginners to *write about what you know.*

But it is admittedly difficult to find—or, rather, to see—stories in commonplace material. And the further warning must be repeated that any story has to be a story, not simply an exposition of how a household runs, or of what happens mechanically when you advance the throttle of a steam locomotive. Mr. Ware makes it all seem a little deceptively easy, perhaps, when he says " 'In the Reign of Jeff Raleigh' is the story of the Raleigh household while Alice is in the hospital with appendicitis, and Jeff is at home, in charge." It is that, of course, but it is also the story of a very special set of circumstances and characters: the general situation fitted with specific people and episodes. It is the filling in of the skeletal outlines with the flesh and blood of specific people and events which makes the actual stories. Let the reader try his hand at working out two or three story ideas about his own family. You have had dozens of experiences which have included several members of your family—your high-school graduation, a family vacation (Mother wanted to go to the seashore, Father to the mountains); a too violent attachment for your years to a member of the opposite sex; your return from a camping trip or from boarding-school; a business deal which worried your father; a fight with neighbors over the real or imagined damage your dog has caused; a childhood prank which nearly precipitated catastrophic consequences; your sister's (brother's) beau (girl) whom you couldn't stand; Mother's new hair-do; Aunt Minnie's impending visit—the possibilities are endless and familiar to all of us. Study the three Raleigh stories reprinted here, and try to work out one of your own.

Here are some guiding suggestions for this exercise:

1. Use members of your own family, but heighten certain traits to establish definiteness of character.
2. Make these traits have direct bearing on the story.
3. Exaggerate the clash of family interests—Mother likes bridge, Father likes fishing, Junior likes automobiles, Sister likes romantic novels. Or different attitudes toward some general thing—music, for example.
4. Select dramatic yet familiar family experiences—the move to a new and bigger house; the acquisition of a pet (an eccentric uncle has sent the family a Newfoundland puppy); an engagement; a marriage; a birth (twins, maybe); a lost child; a runaway child; lost ration books; a fire.

USE AND RE-USE

There is another reason for reprinting as many as three stories about the same family. Readers are interested in stories, and they are interested in people. They like to read about familiar friends. Many writers have succeeded in enthralling large audiences almost indefinitely with the adventures of the same people. In today's magazines, for example, we find Sally Benson and her Junior Miss; Guy Gilpatrick and his incorrigible Muster Glencannon; Rose Francken and her young marrieds; Bill Upson and his indefatigible tractor salesman, Alexander Botts; Arthur Train and his loveable lawyer, Mr. Tutt; and Mr. Ware's other series about the one-eyed poacher, Uncle Jeff Coongate. The list could be greatly prolonged.

And not only can you use the same characters, but you can often use almost the same situations. One writer for popular magazines worked out what he considered to be four fundamental situations, each with its own group of characters. There was a college story, a reporter's story, a young married story, and a ranch story. From these four sources of material, he wrote and sold scores of stories in a few years.

Some say there are only a dozen or so story situations. It is idle to try to count them. What is important is that there are an infinite number of variations possible in each situation. The writer mentioned above, for example, wrote twenty-odd stories from the same fundamental situation. He achieved his variations in part by telling almost the same story from varying points of view, in part by showing the different meanings of the same episode to different characters, and in part by shifting the situation so that it applied to different people in different settings and circumstances.

We believe that it is good advice for beginners with professional ambitions to attempt to write some stories about the same group of people. Do not, of course, confine your activity to a single set of people for too long, because you should range far during your apprentice years in order to discover what it is you can do best. On the other hand, concentration does teach much, especially about technique. And if you do succeed in establishing a series, the professional rewards are great. It's one thing to be in demand as a writer; it's even better to be in demand as the writer of specific stories, though there are admitted risks here—it is possible for an author to become so closely identified with a certain character that readers demand from him stories about that character and no other. That, however, is a professional hazard not faced by the beginner! After he has sold a couple of dozen stories about the same people, he can then begin to weigh the values involved.

VI

THE WRITER COMMENTS

SINGLE TRAIT

Uncle Jeff Coongate, the one-eyed poacher of the north-woods hamlet of Privilege, is a character with a single trait. To wit, he is against game wardens. He is a composite of several amiable outlaws whom the writer knew personally. Of course, besides his hatred for game laws and their enforcers, he has other traits, such as a fondness for whiskey. But his conflict with game wardens is perpetual and is the motivation for approximately thirty stories in which the old gentleman has played the leading part, sometimes for better, but usually for worse.

It is illuminating, if not alarming, to trace the origins of the general form and pattern of the one-eyed poacher stories. They appeared in *Esquire,* and in *Outdoors,* both of which are very modern magazines. Yet Uncle Jeff Coongate plainly was abroad in Sherwood Forest four or five hundred years ago in the guise of Robin Hood. The one-eyed poacher shoots deer belonging to the State. Robin Hood shot stags belonging to the King. Uncle Jeff uses a rifle, the great archer his long bow and cloth yard shaft—which, aside from superficial matters of speech, dress and age, is the only essential difference between the two loveable rogues.

Both Robin and Jeff have a single trait, or perhaps more accurately a common purpose, in that they are poachers. The writer is only fractionally indebted to Robin, for he must acknowledge other portions of gratitude to Bret Harte, the author of "The Outcasts of Poker Flat," and the creator of Mr. John Oakhurst, gambler. Mr. Oakhurst was a refinement of the loveable rogue—a man outside the law, but with a heart of gold and a certain majesty. Later influences blended into the character of Mr. Coongate through the writer's studious acquaintance with Jeff Peters and Andy Tucker, O. Henry's two con men, who sold Indian remedy made of water and coloring matter, or stock in non-existent companies and institutions, and were constantly uneasy about the police.

Still later, but still as probable an influence, on the shape and form of Uncle Jeff Coongate, come the stories of Scattergood Baines, by Clarence Budington Kelland; and those of the immortal Mr. Glencannon, by Guy Gilpatric. Scattergood, of course, as his name implies, is on the fair side of the law. But he is single-trait. Mr. Glencannon, more complex and devious, is also single-trait in his uproarious fidelity to a brand of whiskey called Duggan's Dew. Introduce Glencannon to a bottle of Duggan's, and a story rolls. Expose Uncle Jeff Coongate to a game warden, and trouble begins.

Primarily for its illustration of the loveable rogue, or single-trait story, Mr. Bailey selected "Jeff Coongate's Perfect Crime." He also felt that the story might have a further interest in its structure, concerning which the writer has only this to say: For ten or fifteen previous Coongate stories, Uncle Jeff had been striving through three or four thousand words per story to evade the law and stay out of jail. Perhaps the "Perfect Crime" illustrates how a new or different use may be made from an old formula or old material.

The writer does not wish to imply that there is anything either new or different about this story—except as it varied in one essential way from the other stories about the same character. The writer, tired of his character's desire to escape jail, simply thought it would liven things if he could invent a situation whereby Uncle Jeff might logically wish to get *into* jail. By an ironic oversight in his elaborate planning, the one-eyed poacher failed even in this possibly more worthy enterprise, as the last lines of the story disclose.

THE STORY

Jeff Coongate's Perfect Crime

LATE in October, the year of the great drought, Uncle Jeff Coongate found himself in a deserted trapper's cabin far up the Mopang River. He had poled up-river in his brand-new canoe on a nice pitch of water. But in the weeks he had cruised the country in search of beaver sign, the water had lowered until the mere thought of putting his new canoe down-stream among the jagged rocks saddened the one-eyed poacher. He was a good thirty miles from Privilege, and of that distance twenty miles was river. Not only was he feeling his age, but bad luck had dogged him without a let-up for several months. He had located no beaver, and he was now a long, long way from the settlements where his old clients would buy venison or moose meat for cash, and no questions asked.

Sitting on a cold stone in front of the cabin one morning, Uncle Jeff was brooding over the prospects for a hard winter, when a small buck came nosing from the sere and yellowed beeches. His professional instincts suddenly keening, Jeff glanced hastily about for signs of game wardens, picked up his rifle, and shot the buck through the heart. But even the unexpected presence of venison in his dooryard did not mend his spirits, for he had aimed for the neck, and as he dressed out the buck, he muttered gloomily: "I can't even shoot where I point no more."

He rolled the paunch in the hide, carried it into the woods and hid it, and hung the carcass on the extended ridgepole of the cabin. The fresh venison, hanging there in plain sight, made Uncle Jeff uneasy. "A man can't rest good with you danglin' front of his door," he addressed the swinging deer. "Better I lug you back in the woods, an' spring you up on a maple saplin'."

It was this general line of thinking which led Uncle Jeff to the perfect solution of all his problems.

Three weeks ago, Warden Tom Corn had observed him loading his canoe at the public landing in Privilege. Now, with crystal clarity, Uncle Jeff remembered their conversation.

"I see you got some beaver traps there, Jeff," young Tom had said.

"Who said they was beaver traps?" Uncle Jeff had bridled.

"The season opens November first—not before."

"I know when the season opens."

"That's fine, Jeff."

"Besides, you can't prove these here are for beaver."

"You must be going a long way, old timer."

"How do you know where I'm goin'?"

"I don't—but it's four weeks to trappin' season. A man can go miles an' miles in that length of time."

"Aw—go 'way an' leave me be."

At the time, Uncle Jeff had been extremely twitchy. In righteous indignation, he had shown Tom Corn his hunting and trapping licenses; and he had paddled across the lake actually feeling holy—but looking over his shoulder now and then, just in case. He was virtually certain that sooner or later Tom Corn would follow him. Always, if he remained in one place very long, a game warden happened in on him for a look around. He hoped, now, that there would be no exception.

If only Tom Corn would step out of the woods and see that venison on the ridgepole! It would solve everything! Uncle Jeff could leave his new canoe in the trapper's cabin and come after it in the spring. The warden would arrest him and take him down-river in *his* canoe. At Mopang he would come up before Judge Beeswater, and the judge would find him guilty and fine him. Since he couldn't pay his fine, and wouldn't even if he could, he would take the ninety-day jail sentence! What better place for an old man to winter than in jail? Why, it was mighty near home to him. It was warm and comfortable there in his own old cell. Zack Bourne and Steve Ireland would pay him a visit now and then and keep him in tobacco. There would be pleasant, lazy days talking with Ed Post, the turnkey.

Uncle Jeff looked up-river and down. Hopefully he peered into the woods, mumbling: "Come on out, young Tom Corn. You got me this time, boy. Many's the old doe I've head-lighted in closed time under your nose, but this trip, boy, you got me by the short hair. Yessir, there's the evidence danglin' from the ridge. I shot that buck. I confess, son, an' I'm a-willin' to atone fer my crimes an' square myself in the eyes of the law."

But there was no Tom Corn in sight that day, or for several more. "Dang it to hell," Uncle Jeff groused, on the fifth day. "You might know a warden would allus be in the wrong place. Here young Tom could make a big name for hisself, capturin' single-handed the greatest poacher ever this country heard tell of, and he never appears on the scene at all. He better hurry, or I'll have the evidence all et up."

When the old man dreamed of the actual working out of his scheme, he was deeply contented. He could see it all so plainly: his new canoe safe in the cabin, and himself resting comfortably in the bow of Tom Corn's, which would grate and rip on the saw-toothed rocks. He would lie back in peace, gaze admiringly on the fading fall foliage, and smoke his pipe, while Tom Corn pushed and sweated. Every now and then, he would say: "Take a rest, boy. You'll tear your guts out. We got lots of time. Now, jest side in here to Forty Brook, will you? An' dodge up a way and fetch me a drink of that nice cool water. The river's still kind of warmish for my taste. There's a good fellow."

On Chancery Portage, the warden would have to lug the canoe and outfit all alone, and Jeff would walk happily along behind, encouraging him in his work. "She a little heavy for you, son?

I'd put her across for you, only, that is, for my lumbago. Allus seems to come on me bad, right about here."

Uncle Jeff's one eye blinked in his anticipation of the meals they would eat. He was not certain whether the law would allow them both to feed from the evidence itself, but he was fairly sure that Tom Corn shouldn't, in any case. So, while Tom Corn gnawed away on fried salt pork, he, Thomas Jefferson Coongate, would eat tender, juicy, loin steak. He would say: "Warden Corn, fry me another hunk of that. Your responsibility for your prisoner demands thet you feed him good an' care for him. That first hunk wa'nt cooked well enough. Leave the next one on the fire longer. You salted her kind of skimpsy, too."

For days, Uncle Jeff had let these heavenly scenes roll in great soft clouds through his mind. He had worked out countless delectable angles. In case of rain, for example, the warden would be obliged to let Uncle Jeff sleep under the canoe: "Tom, you wouldn't want to see an old man take a chill, would you, boy? No, 'course you wouldn't. Mighty decent of you, too. Old Jeff Coongate won't forget. Now, if you don't mind, leave me have your raincoat for a pillow, will you? Ground's mighty hard."

One afternoon, when he was in the midst of imaginary objections to the way Tom Corn made tea, the young warden actually appeared, stepping softly from a clump of shoulder-high spruces.

"Howdy, Jeff," greeted the warden.

Uncle Jeff, startled, let out a squawk of surprise, but quickly recovered. He hung his head in dramatic shame, while, with a guilty-looking hand, he indicated the half-eaten buck.

"I give up," he said. "Tom—you got the goods on me, at last."

"Any beaver, old timer?"

"Not a dang one, not even any sign."

"Mind if I look around a bit, Jeff?"

"Sure, help yourself—but first, tell me this: If you catch a man poachin', you're obleeged to take him in, ain't you?"

"You ought to know."

"Just what I thought: It's ninety days for deer, ain't it?"

"That's maximum."

"Well—how'd you find the river, comin' up?"

"Low—darn hard goin'."

"Hurt your canoe any?"

"Sure. Looks like it had smallpox, what with all the canoe glue on the bottom. I'll have to recanvas her, sure."

"She'll get us down, all right, though, won't she?" asked Jeff, but Tom Corn had entered the cabin and did not reply.

Jeff followed him in and asked: "Well, find anything?"

"Nope. When'd you kill the deer?"

Jeff sighed and renewed his expression of tragic guilt. "Well, sir—I was settin' here one morning, an' out he stepped. I don't know what come over me. Things jest kind of went black. When they cleared up, the buck was dead, an' my rifle hot in my hands."

"You didn't dog him with hounds?"

"No, didn't have no hounds."

"You didn't shoot him in water, or at night, over a jack-light?"

"No, Tom—no, I just shot him—murdered him in cold blood, you might say."

"Was it a Sunday?"

"No, 'twas last Thursday mornin', Tom. I'll swear to it. I'll sign the confession, if you jest ask me. Now you cook us up a meal, and then we better git started, don't you figure? We could camp on the pine bluff tonight. What say you fry us a couple of slabs of the loin, Tom?"

"All right."

"I knowed you was a good sport at heart, boy. There ain't no use wastin' good meat, law nor no law. That's how I look at it. We might's well be pratickle."

"Sure."

"Well, you won't have no trouble takin' me down, Tom. You can take my rifle an' all my ca'tridges, if it'll make you rest easy."

"I wouldn't want to do that, that I know of."

"Well, son, it sure does me good to get this fiendish crime off my conscience. My sins has weighed mighty heavy on me these days. When I looked down into that poor little deer's eyes, I damn near cried."

"Why?"

"To think what I done."

"Why, what had you done?"

"Killed a deer. May the good Lord forgive me."

Tom Corn began slicing salt pork to try out in the pan. "Uncle Jeff," he said, quietly, "you killed a legal deer."

"What?" The one-eyed poacher went crimson to the roots of his thinning hair. Slowly he reached up his hand and scratched the back of his neck: "I—*what?*" he repated, in a shocked tone.

"You killed a deer legally."

Uncle Jeff sat down and rested his chin in his hands: "Jeepers, Tom," he moaned. "I don't see how I done it!"

"Well, maybe it just happened, Jeff."

"I swear before God it wa'nt intentional!"

"You've got a license because I saw it back in Privilege. It's open season, legal open season—"

"I never even give it a thought," muttered Uncle Jeff, his eye rolling.

"And you didn't shoot it on Sunday."

"So—so you ain't a-goin' to take me in, Tom?"

"Nothin' to take you for, old timer."

"An' I got to ram my new canoe down through them hellish rocks!"

"I guess that's about it."

"There ain't a thing you could dig up to hold me on, Tom?"

"Not a thing."

The old man's hands slid up along his temples, his fingers twisting in his hair. From the caverns of his despair, he mourned: "The way of the transgressor is hard, mighty hard. Only—there's jest one thing."

"What's that, Uncle Jeff?"

"Don't you never tell it 'round that Jeff Coongate shot a legal deer."

CONFLICT

The basis of all fiction is conflict. Therefore, start a conflict, and you start a story. More specifically, in Mr. Ware's words, "Expose Glencannon to a bottle of Duggan's, and a story rolls. Expose Uncle Jeff Coongate to a game warden, and trouble begins."

In the Glencannon stories, the conflict is usually between thirst and capacity, both prodigious, leading in turn to conflict between law and disorder, which is to say between law and Mr. Glencannon. In the Coongate series, the conflict is usually between Uncle Jeff's determination to shoot a deer illegally and Tom Corn's determination to put him in jail if he does.

Conflict begins when somebody wants something, and somebody or something stands in the way. In other words, it generates spontaneously when desire approaches obstacle. To paraphrase what Mr. Ware says several times, the bigger the conflict, the bigger the story. This is not to imply that good stories cannot be made from what is actually trivial in the long span of human history; the fate of a child's whim can be as important in a given story as the fate of an empire to its peoples in another. What is important about conflict is its importance at the time to the people involved. How strong is the desire, how big is the obstacle? How may both be made more important to the people involved? Sooner or later, any story in the process of composition should be held up against these questions.

Because stories are about human beings, desire must be embodied. Often the obstacle is also embodied, though not always. In "Weather Prophet," for example, the obstacle is the storm, "dreadfully impersonal" as Mr. Ware describes it in his preface. The storm, however, works in conjunction with another obstacle which *is* embodied, namely, the doctor's stubborn self-confidence. Often, desire and obstacle are embodied wholly in the same person. In "A Place to Cry," Rush Atwood's desire is to escape the emotional consequence of his experience; the obstacle is the fact of the experience itself within him. In "Some Have to Get Hurt," the desire is release from the hold of alcohol, the obstacle, the habit of alcohol.

TRAITS

Desire and embodied obstacle are shown through the traits which a writer gives his characters. In a story of simple conflict, the characters will be those with single traits. The policeman pursuing Glencannon, Tom Corn tracking down Uncle Jeff, are both fully characterized for the story's purpose by the mere fact of their uniforms. They are very broad symbols, with no need of complexity or subtlety. So also Glencannon and Uncle Jeff; their desires are simple, direct, completely understood.

The single-trait story is a simple story about opposites, about single desires against single obstacles. It is a story greatly to be recommended to beginners because of that simplicity. It has been said elsewhere that the only way to learn to write stories is to try to write them. "But I have terrible trouble thinking up a plot," wails the student. Well, anybody can think up a story about two people with opposite, single traits; anybody, at least, can start such a story. All you need do is put them in a scene. Hunter and hunted. The possessor and the covetous one. The rich and the poor. The high-born and the low-born. The list of opposites is endless, and each pair contains the nucleus of an infinite number of stories.

Where conflicts are intricate or complex, or where the writer's aim is to make serious or ironic comment, and to make it realistically, it is necessary to equip characters with many traits. The single-trait story is suitable for broad humor and satire, fantasy, fable, and certain kinds of specialized writing such as detective and "Western" fiction. No reader seriously takes the single-trait character as a realistic representation of a whole person; it is only a portion of a person, an embodiment of a broad, rather than a deep, idea.

In complex fiction, however, there is a place for the single-trait character, and that is in the minor personages of a story. Here, fiction and the stage use the same method. Talkative servants, henchmen of the villain, "types," dowagers, and so on, almost always show a single trait as their contribution to the play. In this book, Joan Raleigh is such a character; her single trait is her "elfin love of horses."

The single trait is not to be confused with a dominating trait.

Fictional people are, to repeat, embodiments of their author's ideas; consequently, all fictional people must stand for something, must represent something, or they have no reason for being. In life, it is often difficult to know what many people do stand for, and often people themselves don't know, or stand for things quite opposite to what they think and say they stand for—an idea, incidentally, at the back of many and many a story. Analyze any of the principal characters in this book, except Uncle Jeff Coongate, and you will discover that they have a dominating trait, or set of traits, together with other, subsidiary traits. The dominating trait of Web Rivers, for example, is affection for his father, but many other traits are brought out in the course of the story: his desire for self-deception in the circumstance; his woodsman's and riverman's skills; his associative memory; even a hint of the district's racial problem together with a boy's normal interest in girls ("Web, you keep clear of them young squaws, boy, or you'll hate the smell of sweet-grass the rest of your life."); all of these add up to his touching goodness of character.

HOW MANY—AND WHAT—TRAITS?

The number and kind of traits you give a character depend on how you want the reader to feel about him. Here, the problem may be referred to experience. If you see someone perform an act against the public safety, you make a quick, definite judgment of his character. A car, wildly speeding down Main Street, in defiance of the rights and safety of others, rouses your anger, which is immediately focused on the driver. "That man ought to be thrown in jail, and kept there!" you mutter through clenched teeth. That is one reaction based on simple evidence. But suppose you discover that he has his wife with him, and that they are, as the newspapers put it, "racing the stork to the hospital." Immediately your judgment is revised, if not actually reversed, especially if you've ever been in the situation yourself. You smile, and accept the driver's frenzy and law-breaking as quite proper to the circumstance, and even wish him luck. Going one step further, if you know him to be a nervous, worrying sort of man, your sympathy for him is greatly increased.

But suppose the driver hits somebody? Your reaction is much more complex, though it still may be tinged with sympathy. "Well, the poor fellow certainly had no right driving like that under any circumstances, though I can't say I altogether blame him. I'd probably drive that way myself." Or how would you feel if the victim were a close friend of yours? Or your child?

It is thus in stories. How the reader feels about a character depends on how much he knows about him, and how that knowledge pertains to the circumstances of the story. This is not to say, of course, that all of a character's traits should be given the reader in one lump early in the story. Many stories depend for their effect on the withholding of a trait. "Some Have to Get Hurt," for example, suspends full information about the narrator until the end, which is what gives the story its point. And Jeff Raleigh, for another example, is actually more determined to have his house built in the location he has picked for it than the reader can suspect; it is the suspension of that information which allows for the unexpected turn at the end of "The House That Jeff Built." Indeed, a great many stories achieve their effect by causing the very opposite of character or event from that which the reader anticipates. In "Angler, Beware!" you read along, secure in the belief that Sue's antipathy to fishing is one of the certainties of this world, only to discover that it isn't. Traits, therefore, may both affirm or contradict early impressions.

If the motivations of a story seem weak, if the reasons why somebody does something or fails to do something are not clear, an examination of the traits you have given the characters may reveal the trouble. I recall a story that was causing its writer much difficulty. The problem was to lead a gentle old man, the essence of kindness, toward an act which could be construed, if not as murder, certainly as manslaughter. At that point, the writer was blocked. The story mainly concerned the consequences of the act, innocent enough in intention, but appalling to the old man's conscience.

The problem was solved through the use of the old man's dominating trait of kindness, and the introduction of a single-trait character who was altogether and exclusively cruel. The old man was a guide by profession, and when the sportsman he was guiding wantonly continued to slaughter game-birds that were out of season, the guide reported him to the game warden, an act which in itself exemplified his kindness. In retaliation, the sportsman deliberately killed the old man's favorite dog by running over it with his car. The guide, who was also a taxidermist, stuffed the dog and placed it at the exact spot on the road where the sportsman had run it down. In trying to kill it a second time, the sportsman ran off the road and killed himself. The old man's intention was simply to assert to the sportsman that his devilish cruelty had not achieved the end he thought it had. The story from then on recounts the turmoil in the old man's mind and the irrational acts he committed in an attempt to salve his conscience; the idea behind the story was that of homicide that would be justifiable to everyone except him who had caused it, but the writer could not see how a kind and gentle character could be led to the act. The traits of both characters, used logically, were what did it.

To repeat, the writer controls the reader's judgment of character by the number and kind of traits the characters show. To play a little further with the idea of the sportsman in the story just sketched, the reader's reaction to acts of wanton cruelty is simple and immediate: he condemns the person who commits them, and a strong desire to destroy the destroyer arises in him. But suppose the acts of cruelty were to be traced back to some forgotten experience, perhaps some horrid perversion forced upon the child by a stupid and brutal father; suppose you understood that behind the cruelty there were motives for which the character could not be held totally responsible because they were compulsions operating below the level of consciousness? Now, your condemnation still stands, but it is tempered with some sympathy. The act itself is still intolerable, of course, and its repetition must be prevented, but part of the responsibility for the act has been shifted to someone outside the story. Consequently, your first instinct, to destroy the destroyer, has been modified, perhaps to some such sentiment as: "Put him in an institution, or send him to a psychoanalyst. He can't help himself, but at the same time society must be protected against him." Your sentiment is what the law's is in regard to murder committed by one judged insane, or in regard to what the law calls "justifiable homicide."

RASCALS

Human beings are full of marvelous inconsistencies. We make laws to protect ourselves against rascals, then we turn about and make heroes of rascals who defy the laws! Perhaps this particular inconsistency rests on two dimly perceived truths. One, that laws can be, in relation to special circumstances and individuals, quite unjust, and that to break them is a virtue. Two, that we are all to some degree still untamed, anarchic, chafed by restraint. We have voluntarily placed ourselves under the law, for we accept the general necessity for so doing, but often, in the secret recesses of the heart, we yearn to drop respectability, to take up long bow or rifle, blackjack or bottle, and sally forth on gaudy, defiant adventure. Fortunately for society and for literature, most of us are content to indulge our yearnings vicariously in the adventures of literary rascals.

Certain it is that the rascal is a fixture in fiction. Certain it is that rogues are lovable, and disreputability has charm. Carl Sandburg sings a song from *The American Songbag* called "The Good Boy": [1]

> I have led a good life, full of peace and quiet,
> I shall have an old age full of rum and riot;
> I have been a good boy, wed to peace and study,
> I shall have an old age, ribald, coarse, and bloody.
>
> I have never cut throats, even when I yearned to,
> Never sang dirty songs that my fancy turned to;
> I have been a nice boy, and done what was expected,
> I shall be an old bum, loved but unrespected.

Which period of that man's life would you choose to read or write about?

Creating a literary rascal is an exercise in tone and in the use of traits. Although readers possess an enormous adaptability, and are, on the whole, extremely charitable, the writer must be careful not to alienate sympathy. A rascal must be lovable, not brutal; amusing, not disgusting in his law-breaking, and there must be clear reasons of character or circumstance for the law-breaking, reasons which will strike a note of sympathetic understanding in the reader. For example, my own hobbies are shooting and fishing, and I have, therefore, very strong feelings against breakers of game laws. Nevertheless, I accept Uncle Jeff as a lovable character because I am somewhat sympathetic to his attitude despite my own opposite one. There was a time when the fish and game were communally free for the taking at any opportunity, and although I clearly recognize the necessity of laws for the preservation of our natural resources if we are to enjoy

[1] From *Read 'em and Weep: The Songs You Forgot to Remember,* by Sigmund Spaeth. Copyright, 1926, by Sigmund Spaeth.

them at all, yet I also recognize the laws as an infringement on ancient rights. Perhaps another reason for my charity is that I recognize that a deer is meat and income to Uncle Jeff, but only sport to me. Nevertheless, depending on the tone and emphasis of the story, I am as often delighted to watch Tom Corn get his man and to leave Uncle Jeff once more behind the bars of the Mopang jail. As he himself discerns in this story, it is a pretty good place for him.

VII

THE WRITER COMMENTS

THE MYSTERY OF OLD NOTES

One reason for the inclusion of "Weather Prophet" is that it originated from an incomprehensible note the writer found, among other notes, in a forgotten file. Some of the notes are ridiculous, some solemn, and all of them must have had a purpose in that they were supposed to remind the writer of a story idea he had once thought tolerable. As Mr. Bailey has pointed out, it is often helpful to write down the chance observation. Something may come of it. Something may not. But months, or years, after the writing, the notes often are bewildering or amusing.

Here are some items as they were first written on odd pieces of paper at the time when they seemed important:

> She didn't marry him for his money; she married him to escape poverty, and there is a difference.

From this note, years after its writing, came a short story about a girl who married to escape poverty and fell in love afterwards with another man:

> A man walking out of a tavern, facing the viewpoint of the unintoxicated world, squaring himself with himself by pulling his hatbrim forward over his eyes and stepping from an unexpected curb. Such a man can stumble and keep his dignity, for he is briefly immune from judgment and the law of gravity.

So far, this note has produced nothing, not even the recollection of its origin.

"*Theedths.*" This one word, which is not in the dictionary, was a reminder to use a character that lisped in some story long since forgotten. Presumably, the character was trying to pronounce the word "seeds."

When the wind blows in the summer the grass looks like fur on the long fields, and the leaves of the trees look like sparks in the sun.

Part of that descriptive bit was used in a novel called *Watchman's Duty,* in which some people passed a field in the summertime.

The difference between being afraid and being frightened is a time difference, and even when you are in a place where fear is a long thing, a matter of hours, you can lose it completely now and then by examining it.

That note has been turning up for years and is still homeless.

Here is a list of odd titles, apparently written in some forgotten mood of irony or hilarity: "The Poker Game in the Parsonage"; "Mother's Day at Minsky's"; "The Machine Shoppe"; "The Air-Conditioned Cathedral"; "Breath in the Afternoon."

With one exception, these titles have not appeared over any story. The exception is "Breath in the Afternoon," which became the title of one of the Coongate stories.

Jeff Raleigh enjoyed the radio in secret because his wife was very musical and detested the programs he usually selected. When Jeff was alone, he dialed a Negro chorus, if he could. Then he would join mightily with the voices, thrilled at the beauty of his own. He sang frequent duets with an electrically transcribed Paul Robeson, and he liked especially the way they sang 'Water Boy' together.

This note is the origin of all the Jeff Raleigh stories, now twenty-six in number.

He looked once at the girl and decided not to eat the onion.

Nothing of a literary nature has yet come from the decision of this unknown character, but it was probably noted as a device for boy meeting girl.

"Weather or No." From this watery pun, by devious processes, came "Weather Prophet," which proves, if nothing else, that notes can lead anywhere.

As I hope these prefaces show, the origins of any story are complex and multiple; of this story, the writer now remembers mainly the labor of writing and straining for a certain effect, the rewriting, and the miserable feeling that he had conceived a fine story and missed it, somehow, in the execution.

The writer admits, or confesses, that he sat down deliberately to write as excellent a story as he could, with no thought of any market and with plenty of time on his hands. The idea of the story is old and dependable—human beings against elements greater than themselves. The story of Dr. Musgrave is an experiment in tragedy which illustrates by devices of time and space an act, or action, which is far removed from the narrator, yet presumably close to the reader. "Some Have to Get Hurt," in another chapter, also illustrates a treatment of off-stage action, but not, the writer feels, with a simplicity or precision equal to the last journey of Dr. Musgrave in "Weather Prophet."

In the northern wilderness, particularly in winter and particularly over frozen lakes, the weather is dangerous, uncertain, and dreadfully impersonal. The weather is so much greater than the conceit of him who attempts to judge it that it often kills the judge. And if the judge is on an errand of mercy, the weather doesn't care; nor does it care whether those it kills are good or bad. This impersonal and oblivious quality of the elements is forever tempting as a theme for fiction.

A device for heightening the effect of tragedy in "Weather Prophet" was to have the doctor's mission that of bringing a new life into the world. The weather didn't acknowledge that—even that. A second device was to make the doctor himself the weather prophet, another fact which the veering wind didn't pause to consider.

The narrator of the tale, and the guide, Steve Ireland, are mere instruments, used only to open up the doctor's character. Why didn't they accompany the doctor on his fearful trip? Why didn't the doctor take a compass? Why didn't he make allowance for the possibility of the wind's changing? All these questions are logical, and the manner in which they are answered illustrates some of the machinery of plausibility.

THE STORY

Weather Prophet

ONCE I came up in February because I had to see how the lake country looked under snow. Steve Ireland met me at Mopang, and we started for Privilege in the pung, with a northeaster building steadily behind us. Steve yelled into his turned-up collar: "Travel eight hundred miles to spend one day in a blizzard."

"Maybe it'll clear."

"Doc Musgrave says it'll hold northeast for two days. He don't often miss."

Whenever Steve mentioned Dr. Delirious Musgrave, there was a note in his voice of troubled fascination. I had always wanted to meet the doctor. His personality seemed to weigh on Steve's mind. I wanted to hear Steve talk about him now, but a quickened bitterness of the storm made talk an effort.

We were crossing the wake of an old burn where the blown snow towered around us, and the wind struck sharp. When at length we came into the shelter of the spruces, the wind seemed far away. You could hear it roaring in the branches, and the snow swept down like spilled veils, but the storm was at arm's length, momentarily.

Steve lifted his chin above his collar, and said: "He claims the day he does he'll die."

"Does what?" I asked, my wits half numbed.

"Figures wrong on the weather."

"Oh, Doc Musgrave?"

"Yuh," said Steve, resettling his chin.

We put a blanket on old Chub in the Privilege stable, fed him his oats, and floundered up the hill above the lake to Steve's cabin. It was nice inside. You could smell peeled spruce, oakum chinking, and wood smoke. The wind sent the fine snow hissing against the windows, reminding us of our comfort within.

"This time of year," Steve said, as he primed the pump, "there ain't much doin', only ice fishin'."

"I don't mind. I got to dreaming about winter on the lake, and had to come and see."

"You're seein' it, all right. You better stay over a few days."

"I can't do it. I'll have to go in the morning."

I opened the bottom draft of the stove, and the fire woke up and made the chimney roar. "Maybe if the storm holds, I'll be snowbound."

"He claimed it would," Steve said. A gust rattled the stovepipe in its guy wires, and Steve added: "Listen to that."

We ate fried salt pork, pickerel, and tea. Steve inquired for all my friends he had guided. I asked about Uncle Jeff Coongate, Neilly Winslow, the Iron Duke, and Jim Scantling. Steve said they were all smart, and let it go at that, but when I mentioned Peter Deadwater, the Indian, he perked up.

"Say! Peter's wife's goin' to have a kid."

"Honest?"

"Fact, so help me. Talk about a happy Injun."

"I thought Peter and Sadie couldn't have any kids."

"Well," Steve said, "they thought there wa'nt no hope, an' so'd everyone. They been wantin' one twelve years."

"When's the baby due?"

"Peter figures apple-blossom time. He's been poundin' ash, an' got a cradle built, an' a basket, an' a doe-skin suit with pants to it, soft as silk. It's a caution, the way that Injun works. Changed his whole character. He ain't touched a drop of lemon extrac' nor essence of pep'mint, not for five-six months. Just works, an' tends Sadie, an' lays plans for that kid."

"That's wonderful, Steve."

"It's the Lord's mercy. Let's wash the dishes."

We cleaned up and got out the ice-fishing equipment. We were ready to start for the lake, when Steve spotted a gap in the chinking. A fine spray of snow had blasted through, building a hard white mound on the floor. Steve got a mallet and caulking iron and closed the gap with a twist of oakum. "Some storm, to find a hole that small," he said.

"Steve, didn't you say you drove Doc Musgrave's buggy for him when you were little?"

"Yuh. We was good friends in them days."

"Aren't you now?"

"It's mighty queer, but he don't care for me now, me nor anyone at all."

A moment later we were out in the blizzard, toting our fishing gear down to the lake. I was more than ever determined to meet the doctor some day; but now his prophecy of weather was of direct concern. We chiseled our holes in the lee of Genius Island, but shelter was scant. The snow gave visible shape to the turbulence in the sky, and my forehead ached with cold.

The tip-ups were active, but we couldn't hook a trout. "They're slapping it with their tails," Steve said. "You can watch 'em do it, if you lay still over a hole."

I tried it, shading my eyes with my hands. Down there in the deep clear water, you could see the togue swimming along slowly in single file. They would bump the bait with their noses and, as they swam by, bat it with their tails.

"Can you see 'em?" Steve asked.

He was kneeling on the opposite side of the hole, facing me. I glanced toward him, but the answer froze. Just behind Steve, and to one side of him, stood Peter Deadwater, the Indian. He was wearing snowshoes—the long, narrow Cree model for open travel. Suspended from a thong in his left hand were two lake trout of about six pounds. Steve saw my astonished expression and turned.

"You ghost," he said to the Indian.

"No." Peter made an up-and-down motion with his free hand.

"Heard us chiseling," Steve explained to me; and the Indian grunted.

I stood up and brushed off the snow. "Hear good news, Peter," I said. "Congratulations."

Peter grunted again.

"How things with Sadie?" Steve asked.

Peter shrugged. While we took up our sets, he stood perfectly still in the exact spot where we had first seen him. Steve kept glancing at him curiously, and, when we were ready to go, said: "Peter. You come my cabin. Get warm. Tea. Pickerel chowder."

Peter declined with a headshake and held out one of the lake trout, saying: "Namaycush."

"Come help eat," Steve said, taking the trout.

"I go home. Sadie hot. Crazy talk."

Steve looked quickly at me. "He means Sadie's sick." Then he turned to Peter. "How long Sadie hot? How long talk crazy?"

"Morning."

"This morning?"

Peter Deadwater nodded, his eyes vacant.

"She got pain some place?"

Peter touched his forehead, then put his hand down over his stomach, groaned, and stared at Steve.

"You go home. Take trout to Sadie. I get doctor. See?"

Peter moved away a few steps, turned on his long webs, and came back. "Doctor cross lake to Injun Village in storm?"

"Yes."

"Tell him open water Leadmine Point. Spring-hole. Tell him very danger spring-hole."

"I know," Steve said. "I tell him."

Peter started off, the snow blowing shoulder high around him. Ten steps and he had vanished. It was six miles, due southwest across the lake to the Indian Village. In the falling dark, even with the northeast gale full on his back, it would be a bitter journey.

Steve and I hid our tackle on Genius Island and went straight in to Privilege. I had to stop behind a shed at the public landing to get out of the wind for a minute. I thought my forehead was frozen, but it wasn't. Steve drew off a mitten and blew on his knuckles. "You're goin' to get a hell of a start," he said. "Doc Musgrave talks like he wasn't there at all."

"What? How do you mean?"

The shed trembled in a gust. In the dark you could still see the snow-shapes racing. Steve said: "Well, he don't say 'I done this,' nor 'I done that.' You'll think he's talkin' about someone else that ain't anywheres around. Once, when I was a kid, he told me why. Thought I'd forget, p'raps, but I didn't. He told me it was his other self he is talkin' about—the man he might of been, he said. But all the time it's really him, because he ain't no one else. But you got to talk to him like he was."

"Are you going to drive him across the lake tonight?"

Steve put on his mitten. "You can't work a horse on the lake. Four bad reefs in the ice between Genius Island and Caribou Rock. He'll go on snowshoes."

In the back room of Sam Lurch's barber shop in Privilege, we found Dr. Musgrave. He was a man in his early fifties. He sat on the wood-box, a bottle between his knees, apparently entranced by the gleaming nickel stove-rail. The air in the room was hot and foul, but Musgrave wore a heavy sheepskin coat. The lamplight showed the birthmark which spread from his right temple over his entire right cheek to his jaw. His upward glance was too swift for me to see his eyes. With no sign of recognition for Steve, whom he had known since boyhood, he resumed his staring at the nickel rail. Steve had told me what to expect, but no warning could have prepared me for talking face to face with a man who not only dreamed he wasn't there, but demanded that others honor his unreality.

"Well," Steve said to him, "he said it would hold northeast for two days."

"Yes," said Musgrave. "He is an authority on the weather, as well as on rum, axe wounds, and obstetrics."

Outside, the wind rose shrieking. You could hear the hard snow batter the walls like shot. As if at this corroboration of his prophecy, Musgrave grinned and leaned closer to the stove.

When the gust had spent itself, Steve said: "Would he cross the lake tonight to tend a sick woman in the Injun Village?"

After a long silence, Musgrave said: "He would think hard during such a trip—think himself into a stupor."

To see the man actually sitting there, yet talking of himself as if he were absent, gave me the shivers.

"He would have his coat collar up," he went on, "and his face wrapped to the eyes. He would keep the wind dead fair on his back, and—"

Steve moved toward the doctor nervously. "He would want to keep the wind heavy on his right shoulder. That would bear him inside of the open spring-hole off Leadmine Point."

Dr. Musgrave took a small drink from the bottle, replaced it between his knees, and, as if Steve had not spoken, resumed:

"—his thoughts would keep him company, and he would hum. His humming, and the cadence of his steps, would make him forget the night."

"But," said Steve, his voice rising, "he would want to keep his mind on that spring-hole. If the wind backs into the north, it would veer the doctor off course. He would walk right into *open water* in the dark."

"He stated that the wind would hold northeast," said Musgrave, complacently. "And it will."

"Even so, he'll pass within two hundred yards of the spring-hole!" Steve took a radium-dialed compass from his pocket and held it out to Musgrave in his open palm. "The snow is blowing so he won't even see his feet," he went on, his voice growing unsteady. "Wouldn't he take this?"

"Does a prophet need a compass?"

The man on the wood-box seemed to ignore our presence as well as his own, and, while we humored his strange conceit, the purpose of our visit had been obscured. When I could bear the suspense no longer, I began speaking to him, unnaturally, in the third person: "Is he equipped to take a six-months baby from the wife of Peter Deadwater? While the men discuss the weather, the Indian's woman lies out of her head with fever."

"He had performed Caesareans in this country under strange conditions," Musgrave answered, "and with strange instruments. Once he cauterized an amputation with a heated abutment spike. And he did a transfusion with the quill of a goose."

"But the Indian woman has been delirious since morning," I cried. "The man with Steve Ireland thinks it may be emergency."

"Ah, yes, no doubt," replied Musgrave, blandly, "but the doctor hates cold—cold and terror, they are the same." He picked up the rum bottle and held it to the light. As near as I could judge, he had drunk half the contents. He removed the cork, took another swallow, and said: "Northeast for two days."

"Maybe the Indian's woman will die," I said, "and they are all here talking."

"Maybe," said Musgrave rising.

In the act of buttoning his coat collar to the throat, he turned toward us, and I saw him full face in the light. I knew why Steve Ireland both feared and pitied him. Above the doctor's straight, merciless mouth, were the eyes of a child; and I saw in these features the evidence of a man divided. You looked into his wide child's eyes and pitied. You remembered his mouth, and shrank from him.

Steve went to him, begging: "Would the doctor please take a friend for company tonight? The friend that used to drive the buggy for him?"

"No."

Musgrave jerked his snowshoes from a peg and kneeled to tie their lampwick lashings. Whether Steve was driven by a superstition about putting on snowshoes indoors, or by his dread that the wind would shift, I do not know. But when Musgrave stood up, Steve clutched him by the shoulders and shook him, saying: "If he walks into that spring-hole, *both* of him will go under the ice together—the one he is and that other one, too!"

For an instant, as Steve backed away, the child part dominated Musgrave's face. He seemed touched that anyone should go to such lengths to warn him away from danger; and, in the only natural sentence I heard him speak, he said: "That's all right, Stevie— I'll be there in two hours."

He put on the pack which I assumed contained his instrument bag, and we followed him out into the blizzard. At the lake shore, he said: "He will go on from here alone." He hesitated for just a moment, then turned away and walked off in the dark.

For two or three minutes after he had vanished, we stood looking out over the howling blackness of the lake. Then we turned wearily up the hill to Steve's cabin.

The warmth, the smell of broiling trout, and the leaky kettle's hiss could not remove the spell of Dr. Musgrave. Steve kept glancing at the black windows. It was as if he thought he might actually see the wind's direction.

"Steve," I said, "how wide is that spring-hole?"

"Better than a quarter-mile, when last I saw it."

After we had eaten, I lay in my bunk; but, despite my snowburned face and eyes, there was no drowsiness. And there was none for Steve. He looked at his watch, and said: "It's thirty-eight minutes, now."

"Where would he be, about?"

"Mouth of Hardwood Cove."

Presently, as if Musgrave were with us in the cabin, we began to talk his way. To Steve Ireland, whom I had known fourteen years, I said: "The men lay in comfort wondering if the wind would change."

Steve got up, opened the door, and looked out into the whirlpools of the sky. He had to use his strength to close it, and the cold wind drove in a spray of snow and tore the ammunition-company calendar from its hook. "One of the men knows the wind is changing," he said.

"Where would he be now?"

Steve answered so quickly that I knew he was with Musgrave almost step for step: "Forty-three minutes—off Bear Trap Landing."

"They thought of how, in summer, they had paddled often across the six miles to Peter Deadwater's shack."

Steve got out his compass and set it on the table. He looked again at his watch. "The men couldn't rest good."

"No," I said. "They were thinking of the other man, counting on the wind to hold him on course, and the wind veering him toward the open water, and the Indian waiting, and his wife hot and crazy talking."

"For Chris' sake!" Steve cried. "I'm goin' outside and see for certain!"

When Steve came in again, his face looked numb. His hair, powdered white with snow, made him seem prematurely old. He went to the stove and sat on the deacon seat, his back to the warmth. He kept looking at his watch, while the snow melted, glistening in his hair.

"Well?" I said.

"The wind's due north—changed, with never a lull to warn him."

Steve got a lumberman's blue-print map of the lake and spread it on the bench beside him. With a pencil he drew a straight line due southwest from Privilege six miles to the Indian Village on the far shore. Along that line he marked various points and the times he estimated it would take Musgrave to pass them at a speed of three miles per hour. Hardwood Cove, 38 mins. Bear Trap Landing, 43 mins.

At Caribou Rock, an hour and five mins., Steve drew a gradual curve on the map. The curve bore left—southward, as the wind veered into the north. A mile south of Caribou Rock, he drew in the spring-hole off Leadmine Point. Then he looked at his watch again, and said: "Munson Reef—an hour and twelve minutes."

"My God, Steve! How many, many times we fished that spring-hole in hot weather when the trout were deep!"

Steve made a dot on the penciled line which curved and then straightened toward the open water. He sat tense, his watch under his eyes, his pencil poised.

"Sometimes," Steve said, "when we was makin' calls away out somewheres away from the villages, he was mighty nice. He was kind. He would tell me to stop the buggy by a field of daisies, or hockweed. Them things made him happy. If he saw a doe deer on the lake shore, that would make him happy, too, or a loon callin'. It was the same with insects, any livin' thing, or anything that was pretty to look at. He could explain them things. I thought the world was flat, till he told me why it ain't. He said I was the only one he could talk to, or that could talk to him. I was eleven years old, then. . . ." Steve's pencil point touched the map as he checked the time. "Little Mopang Bar—hour an' eighteen minutes."

"Steve! How close is he to it—now?"

"Seven minutes."

Steve brushed his hand over his damp hair and wiped the wet palm on his thigh. "It was when I got older that he changed toward me. But I guess he thought 'twas me that changed. He wouldn't talk to me no more, nor he didn't want me 'round. He said people was no good after they stopped bein' children. But *he* was good, them times with me, when I was a boy. There wa'nt a thing he wouldn't do for people that was ailin'. But outside of for that, he wouldn't go near no one."

Steve got up from the bench, took off a stove lid and stirred the fire. A furious wind-blast drew back down the stovepipe, and the fine ash rose in the room.

"Big Mopang Bar," Steve said, "hour and twenty-three minutes."

"That leaves him three minutes."

"Two. . . . I wonder how Peter's woman's makin' out?"

"But he knows the lake, Steve! Maybe, when he got out there alone, with the storm and the darkness—maybe he remembered what you said and kept the wind heavy on his right shoulder. That would save him. He would pass Leadmine Point inside the spring-hole."

Steve looked intently at his watch. I saw his lips move as he checked over the last minutes. Then he stopped counting. He was so quiet it was as if he had stopped breathing. After a long time, he folded the map, put the watch back in his pocket, and stood up.

"Well," he said, "I liked him, just the same. It's like I was with him out there tonight, right beside him the whole way, till he drowned. Only nothin' I could do to help him, like watchin' a blind man walk off a cliff, an' your voice gone."

"Steve, I can't believe it!"

"That's 'cause you don't want to, an' I don't neither."

Steve crossed to the table and turned down the lamp. He stood there with the dim light on his face, until I had stretched out under my blankets. "All set?" he said.

"Sure—maybe he made it all right."

"Maybe." Steve blew out the lamp and we lay in the dark, listening to the long-drawn fury of the storm.

Morning broke clear with a light north wind. Steve had the bacon frying. The cabin was warm, and bright sunlight streamed through the windows. I looked out and saw the lake stretching white and lovely below us. That view, so peaceful now, so immaculate, made the night seem unreal.

"Steve, how do you feel this morning?"

"Frisky," he said. "That was bad last night."

Yet in Steve's voice there was uncertainty. I felt it, perhaps in his very cheerfulness. When we had eaten and were on our way down to the stable, Steve said: "Would it trouble you if I got

Jim Scantling to drive you to Mopang this mornin'? I want to cross the lake."

"No, Steve, of course not. I'd stay and go with you, if I could."

"Well, I just got an awful hankerin' to make it across," Steve explained.

Jim and Steve hooked up, and old Chub's breath blew white in the cold. We climbed to the seat, and I reached down to shake hands with Steve. "Let me know about things, will you?" I asked.

"Sure. I'll write you a letter. So-long."

I looked around once to see Steve striking off across the white-glaring lake toward the Indian Village.

Dere frend,

I seen from his tracks right where it begun to change on him near Caribou Rock. I followed the curve of them until I dassent go no closer the open water, where his tracks run off I seen one of his mittens layin' on the ice where he tried to claw back on but that is all so I swung back and went to the Peter Deadwater shack and the priest was there. Peter's woman was dead and the baby was dead.

Well my good frend I must close now as there is a diver coming from Eastport to dive for him and I am to lay a boom on the ice for him to work off of, but they will never find him as the currents will draw him under, as ever your frend Steve Ireland.

P.S. I told Peter how we tried to get the doctor to him and he said all right.

NOTES AND DIVIDENDS

In Chapter IV, I touched on the value of having some notes before you when you sit down to begin a story. As Mr. Ware shows in his preface, notes jotted down at random may lead anywhere or nowhere. A proportion of them, however, leads somewhere, and the writer is advised to have faith in the old law of physics that no energy is totally lost. Some will be, of course, but on the whole, investment of time in note-making is likely to pay the writer more later dividends than anything else he can do when he is not directly engaged in composing stories.

Take notes on everything: chance conversations; reading; on the emotions or ideas generated when you witness a play or even a movie; on music; on hobbies; on close friends and total strangers. This is not to advise that you dramatically interrupt a bridge game by whipping out a note-book and jotting down on the spot some chance remark your partner has made that seems to you fraught with significance. To do a thing like that is to act with silly self-consciousness. What is recommended is the formation of the journal habit; keep a good-sized note-book in your room and write in it every day, at odd hours and at regular times as well, and not always with an eye toward any particular story. Try to preserve in your mind what seems to you interesting, shocking, or amusing until you can write it down in the privacy of your own retreat.

Gregariousness is probably the writer's greatest single handicap. Writing is a lonely business, and large amounts of solitude are essential not only for the conception of stories but for their gestation as well. If you make a covenant with yourself to keep a journal in which you will write every day a minimum number of words—say, five hundred—no matter what you write, you will at least remove yourself for a time from the drains on your spiritual energy which one's fellows, however pleasant and stimulating their society, always exact. You will have time in which to think a thing through, to catch up with the day and with yourself, and to make a record of the day's inner experiences. Those records may preserve something that will later nourish a story as yet unconceived. The journal habit will also increase your overall skill as a writer, for constant, regular writing produces both ease and heightened perception. By itself, the keeping of a journal will not make you a story-writer; only the writing of stories can accomplish that. But it will shorten the period of your apprenticeship by increasing your familiarity with the basic tools of your trade and by making you think. Furthermore, every writer has his black days, when he says to himself, "Dear God, there is *nothing* to write about! My mind is a vacuum!" Often, the contents of a journal, when perused by its writer, will fill the vacuum to overflowing.

OFF-STAGE

A great many potentially good stories are abandoned before their time because their writers too easily give up the struggle against various technical problems, particularly plausibility. Suppose that the basic idea for "Weather Prophet" had crystallized in your mind, but that it had never occurred to you to have the action take place off-stage. You had decided to adopt Mr. Ware's method of telling the story through a first person narrator, but you were going to give the climactic scene direct presentation.

On the surface, the scene has fine possibilities. The three characters start out across the lake, carrying on the argument begun in the barber shop. Each step they take increases the suspense. The doctor keeps plodding his stubborn way toward peril; Steve and the narrator keep urging him away from it, expostulating, trying to make him stop to look at the compass in the flare of a match. The doctor refuses. He plods on. And on. And—on. Suddenly, Steve and the narrator know that he isn't there any more!

Uh-huh. And where are Steve and the narrator? How, in that swirling wind and snow could they tell they'd reached the water-hole unless they too fell in? Then where would the story be? And why, if they are as sure of the peril as the reader must be, did they not physically restrain the doctor from plodding to certain death?

It's all too implausible, you sigh. And you let it go, consoling your conscience with the easy thought that you didn't really have a story here after all.

The problem of staging is one with the problem of perspective and point of view, which is discussed in Chapter X. There is much mystery to the writing of stories, and neither Mr. Ware nor I can exactly tell you how he came to hit upon the device of off-stage action to solve this story's problem of plausibility. But implicit in the fact that he did is the fact that many of the most knotty problems that stand in the way of plausibility can be solved. The solution has its basis in technical study and analysis and their application to specific problems. The student should study these technical devices and try to put them into practice in order to make them his own when the need arises. Examine, therefore, the off-stage action in "Weather Prophet" and "Some Have to Get Hurt," and try to write a story employing the device.

Mr. Ware's use of off-stage action in "Weather Prophet" seems to me no less than a technical *tour de force.* He has managed to make the action utterly vivid even though the narrator is some four miles away. The map, watch, pencil, and compass are extremely well-chosen instruments; through their use the reader is placed both in the cabin and out on the lake. He suffers with Steve and the narrator, and also with them he is plodding along beside Dr. Musgrave on his journey to death, not only the doctor's death, but that of Peter's wife and child as well. Finally, the scene is given one last, graphic touch in Steve's letter: ". . . where his tracks run off I seen one of his mittens layin' on the ice where he tried to claw back on. . . ."

The off-stage action in "Some Have to Get Hurt" is of a different kind. There, the narrator openly embarks on an imaginative re-creation of his own. It is instructive to study closely the precise mechanisms of his embarkation. I mention one of them in another context in Chapter VIII: "Actually, since I had lifted him from the canoe, the boy had said little. But in this other way he had said so much! He set your imagination on fire, and you knew that the things you imagined were true to the lives of the father, the mother, and the boy." These flights of the narrator's fancy are further prepared for in many places: "What struck me now was the depths of this boy's understanding." "My mind started racing again, only this time it wasn't so much imagination. The story seemed to pour out of the boy's eyes."

"You didn't need to know more than that. You had the whole scene, the mother sitting under a tree near the picnic basket, and the father teaching the boy how to use a fishing rod." And so on. These preparatory passages render plausible to the story what would be implausible standing alone.

"Getting away with murder," the uninitiated call this sort of thing. It is not that at all, of course. It is the conscious application of what Mr. Ware calls "the machinery of plausibility" to specific fictional problems. And unless the writer knows about that machinery and can use it, he is often going to be balked in his attempts to carry conviction to the reader.

VIII

THE WRITER COMMENTS

A CONFESSION OF INFLUENCE

Mr. Bailey optimistically urges the writer to show, as nearly as may be by actual quotation and illustration, how other writers have influenced the writing of these and other stories. The story selected as the clearest example of influence is "Some Have to Get Hurt," which appeared originally in *McCall's.*

At the outset, the writer balked at the teacher's request to expose himself through a confession of influence. Possibly the writer wished to be considered original in all his thoughts and compositions. But such originality is impossible, and to deny having been influenced is absurd.

For some reason it is considered exciting to detect a person in the act or state of being changed by another person. Yet quite clearly such changes or influences are at work on everyone during every waking hour. Every individual is being influenced practically all of the time. Maybe the things which influence a person reveal something extra about that person and, therefore, satisfy a natural if not particularly noble curiosity.

Beginning writers and accomplished writers are alike advised to read. Why is this, if not to learn? And when the learning is applied to one's own writing, then one most surely has been influenced. This influence, I believe, is for the good, and so is even downright imitation —as exercise, practice, desire to emulate, and most of all, transition.

By influence our points of view change little by little, our vocabularies grow, our tastes and receptivities alter in ways frequently so subtle as to baffle analysis. But presumably, if all the data were available concerning the life experience or influence of an individual, you could pluck the poor fellow apart second by second, contact by contact, influence by influence, and by a process of addition and percentages show him just what and who have made him what he is this instant, for better or for worse. Happily for human privacy, the psychologists have not yet been able to develop any truly accurate measuring apparatus for all the ingredients of human personality and character.

There is left still a little mystery, and maybe this is why one writer's influence on another continues to be a topic of conversation and a subject for scholarly essays. When a writer puts his thoughts and emotions into type in a certain way, certain influences are at once detectable. But whether it be Boswell and Johnson, or Anderson and the early Hemingway, it is presumed that the actual mechanics of influence are similar. One hears, sees, feels, smells, tastes, and these are all the senses in our possession. In various combinations, these senses are at work all the time. Through them comes all our experience, and our experience is influence. How, then, could an individual avoid influence except by complete separation from his senses, which is to say death?

When Stephen Crane got his idea for his short story, "The Blue Hotel," he got it through his senses, which were extraordinarily alive. What happened inside of Crane after the idea first entered his mind and pointed itself against all his previous experience, is beyond my power to decipher. But when the idea came out of Crane and landed in words on paper, it was set forth in such a way that it fell with the ring of truth on the ears of a great many people, including me. Just how hard it struck, I will presently confess, but first "The Blue Hotel" must briefly be described.

In a Nebraska hotel during a blizzard, five men are passing the time playing cards. It is to be remembered that the card game is for fun. No money whatsoever is involved. One of the men is a Swede, and the Swede accuses a character named Johnny of cheating. Johnny defends his honor by administering a severe beating to the Swede. Because of his drubbing, the Swede leaves the hotel in a dark and melancholy mood. He goes to a saloon, gets drunk, and insults a professional gambler. The gambler has nothing to do with the story at all except to kill the Swede in self-defense. The gambler gets a year in jail. The ending of Crane's story is quoted below:

"Fun or not," said the Easterner, "Johnnie was cheating. I saw him. I know it. I saw him. And I refused to stand up and be a man. I let the

Swede fight it out alone. And you—you were simply puffing around the place and wanting to fight. And then old Scully himself! We are all in it! This poor gambler isn't even a noun. He is a kind of an adverb. Every sin is the result of a collaboration. We, five of us, have collaborated in the murder of this Swede. Usually there are from a dozen to forty women really involved in every murder, but in this case it seems to be only five men—you, I, Johnnie, old Scully; and that fool of an unfortunate gambler came merely as a culmination, the apex of a human movement, and gets all the punishment."

The cowboy, injured and rebellious, cried out blindly into this fog of mysterious theory: "Well, I didn't do anythin', did I?"

"The fog of mysterious theory" must have condensed at some time or other in my mind. I cannot remember when I first read "The Blue Hotel," but it was roughly twenty years ago that I first felt something in my mind, or my ear, for Stephen Crane's writing. Something must have registered very deeply, for in a short novel of my own, published twenty years after the experience of reading Crane, a certain passage appears. This passage is the comment of an interested bystander concerning a young man whom a night watchman has just shot off a fire escape. The young man lies bleeding on the cement sidewalk in the glare of searchlights, and the bystander, himself an accidental contributor to the circumstance, says this: "We're all responsible—the whole of us, and we have killed this boy. We don't know why we killed him, or who he is, or anything about him. We just shot him dead, that's all."

There, straight from "The Blue Hotel," reappears the suggestion that sin is the result of a collaboration; that the young man's death has come—in Stephen Crane's words—as a culmination, or the apex of a human movement. There is evidence, too, that the sound of Crane's words had an effect on the sound of my own.

Crane's unusual combinations of words—unusual in a way to make them very effective—made me want to imitate him the first time I ever read any of his work, which was some years before I began writing. Here are a few samples by Crane, culled haphazardly from his work, and used here by way of illustrating his influence: "The barroom door engulfed them with a gleeful motion."

In describing the barroom's atmosphere, Crane says: "There was an uproar of fraternal feeling."

Crane refers to a cloud as being fat. In his Civil War novel, *The*

Red Badge of Courage, Crane's hero sees the sun setting through the smoke over a battle-field. Crane refers to the sun as a thin, red wafer. He gave great character to sound, form, and color. His imagery was sharp and original. When a man in a cold rage begins talking, Crane says the words slid from his lips as if they had struck against ice.

Crane's marvelously keen perceptions, letting light into his total experience, are, of course, responsible. He excited my imagination, and made me want to absorb some of his quality and apply it to my own writing. Evidence that I tried, consciously, is sprinkled through a novel of mine called *Rider in the Sun.* Here are some directly quoted samples of Crane's influence:

> The stream spoke among stones in a small, careless way. . . . Remote tendrils of music came from young frogs in the swampland. . . . He heard in the night sounds the litany of spring. . . . He knew that a single accident could tumble him wantonly into hell. . . . He did not know the meanings of the men's words, but the sound was immense, like the gossip of emperors. . . . The old lady's sewing basket was Gorgon-headed with washed stockings. . . . His whisper was like sand sliding off a shovel. . . .

The novel from which these phrases are quoted appeared ten years ago. Since that time, presumably, I had either squirmed out from Crane's influence, or blended it unrecognizably with other influences into a style which could be called my own. But with irritable amazement, I find a line in the story of this chapter—"Some Have to Get Hurt." The line is as follows: ". . . some cheerful doors swung open, and a man rushed out on the sidewalk, hailing them with an avalanche of cordiality." It is both interesting and slightly embarrassing to compare that line with two of the above-mentioned by Crane, to wit: "The barroom doors engulfed them with a gleeful motion," and "There was an uproar of fraternal feeling."

The Crane influence in "Some Have to Get Hurt" is all the more amusing, because the story is included, partially at least, as an illustration of the influence of Ernest Hemingway! This confession proves nothing, if not that any writer is a combination, or result, of a lot of other writers! A possible partial exception may be William Shakespeare, the greatest phrase-maker of them all. If anyone really influenced him, he was able to smother the evidence under his own robe of originality. It has often dismayingly seemed to me that Shakespeare wrote it first, that he wrote it the right way, and that if you are going to be influenced by him you are therefore obliged to write it down in his words and use quotation marks.

For example, there doesn't seem to be any righter way to describe the tattered sails of a fleet of ships than to say, as Shakespeare said in *Othello,* that the sails are "lean, rent and beggared by the strumpet wind." I once took the liberty of applying exactly the same description to a wheat field which had been despoiled by wind and drought, but I had to use quotation marks or be forever branded.

Word-choices, word-combinations, metaphor, sentence-structure—style effect in general—are but one of the signs of influence. Often far more important to one's writing is the other author's effect on one's point of view, or entire philosophy. Today you might get an idea for a story and write it as you felt it at the time. Tomorrow you might read something by, say, Ernest Hemingway, which would so affect you that you would write the story in a profoundly different way. "Some Have to Get Hurt" is a clear example of this type of influence. It came about in this way:

For a number of years, as managing editor of two outdoor magazines, it was my duty to write stories on hunting, fishing, and camping. The policy of the magazines called for first person narratives, and there were certain standard yarns that invariably met the readers' demands. The death or recovery of a dog was surefire. So were fishing stories involving father and son. The father-son fishing story was invariably best when the son caught the largest fish. I had written literally hundreds of such stories, and the formula had become tiresome and empty. One day, toward presstime, during a moment of procrastination, I wondered what would happen to the old fishing-story formula—sweetness, light, sentiment, and success—if you charged it with tragedy. What would happen to the formula if Ernest Hemingway got hold of it? His stories of fishing and hunting, and fathers and sons, are superbly faithful, and his use of the first person unparalleled. "Some Have to Get Hurt" is a result, then, of boredom with an overworked magazine formula, and the influence of Ernest Hemingway, Stephen Crane, all the other authors I have ever read, and everything that ever happened to me from birth to the last period in the last line of the story.

THE STORY

Some Have to Get Hurt

You know how it is at a prize-fight when the fighters are hitting each other hard. You can feel the blows hurting the fighters, but the blows can't hurt you. You're not fighting. It's the same at the theater. If there's a tragedy being enacted on the stage, you can feel it, but you can't get hurt except outside on your own street, in your own life. In the theater you're immune, and you're plenty safe. It's a swell feeling.

It was something like that the afternoon the squall broke over the lake. In my cabin on the shore I had a ringside seat. Before the spindrift shut out the view, I had convinced myself that the black speck off Munson Island was just a floating log, and not someone out there in a canoe in trouble, so there was nothing to worry about. My own canoe was tied to its rack. It couldn't blow loose. The power of the wind and the violence of the lake couldn't scare me, because they couldn't hurt me. They were part of the setting. So was the weird, shrieking wind-call of the loon.

The storm passed as quickly as it had come. The sky brightened. An unearthly stillness settled over the lake and the forest. And then, a little way off shore, foundering in the heavy swells, I saw the canoe. So perhaps you are not safe unless those near you in your element are safe too. While they live, and while you live, there's obligation. I went down to the canoe feeling sick, knowing that the speck off Munson Island had not been a log, and knowing I was about an hour behind a tragedy.

In the canoe, which I dragged ashore, I found a fish, a whiskey bottle, and a boy. Water taken in over the gunwales had apparently revived the fish. It was still alive. The bottle was uncorked and empty. But you wouldn't have thought twice about the fish and the bottle. You would have thought only of the boy.

He was about twelve years old. He didn't quite know where he was, or what had happened. He just stared like a sleepwalker, clinging to the canoe as if he thought it might perform a last, terrible gyration before annihilating him. I lifted him out and stood him on the beach.

"What happened?" I said. "Who was with you?"

His lips worked, but he couldn't speak. I kneeled beside him, and while he stared over my shoulder toward the lake, I rubbed the small of his back. His eyes had the look of twilight. You knew he was full of blurred memories. Something about him seemed to reach out. You wanted to see what his eyes had seen, and feel what his heart had felt. You wanted to share the weight that seemed to be crushing him. You knew this boy had been in something bigger than a storm on a lake.

"You're safe, now," I told him. "You're all right. What's your name? Can you tell me your name?"

He answered almost inaudibly: "Chris—Christopher Blake." Then he smiled and added: "I'm Barney Blake's son."

He said this with a pride and sweetness that warmed you all the way through. You liked the boy's father, even without knowing him. Just from the tone of the son's voice, you formed a good picture of the father.

"Was your father with you today?" I asked.

"Yes."

"Where is your father, now?"

The boy's lips were all fixed to answer when, suddenly, the fish began thrashing in the water in the bottom of the canoe. It startled me, because I'd forgotten all about the fish. But the sound did something more than that to the boy. He stiffened, and memory came up darkly in his eyes, like an omen of returning dread. He pointed toward the fish, and said: "Kill him. Please kill him. Kill him dead."

It was a strange thing for him to say, and he said it in a strange, dull voice. I was curious. I hesitated a moment, then picked up a piece of driftwood, stepped to the canoe, and tapped the fish on the head.

"There you are," I said. "That's a handsome bass. He's just about ready for the frying pan."

"Hit him again!" the boy cried out. His voice wasn't dull, now. It was wild. "Hit him some more? Smash him to pieces!"

I was astonished and a little bit unnerved. Brutality didn't belong in this boy. "What's the matter, Chris? I can't hit him again. He's dead. Can't you see that? He's dead."

The boy stumbled forward, and I caught him in my arms. "My father is dead, too," he wept. "My father—my father—"

"Your father, Chris? What makes you say that? What happened to him?"

He pressed his face against my chest, and his fingers twisted in my shirt. "I saw him sinking and drowning. I want him to be alive again. My father, oh, my father. It was because of the bass and the candy. Oh, that candy! I couldn't seem to help it. It was my fault."

I didn't say any more. I carried the boy up the path to my cabin and tucked him into a bunk. Pretty soon I would take him down to the village, but he seemed now to be deranged from shock. His reference to the candy and the bass didn't make any sense. They just seemed to come out of his agony.

He had quieted down a little. I felt him watching me while I whittled some tinder and started a fire in the stove. I made tea and brought it over to him. He followed every move with his twilight eyes.

Some eyes! They told so much that you didn't need to ask many questions. They shone out of the dark corner where he lay in the bunk, and they strung you so tight your imagination hummed. It was exciting just to watch him look around sizing things up and getting his bearings. He saw my traps and snowshoes hung from the rafters for the summer. Then he saw my fishing rod, and said: "It's a Landseer, isn't it?"

"That's right. How did you know? Not many people would recognize a Landseer."

He smiled, and his eyes filled with gladness. "My father knew about rods, and fishing, and everything. He showed me all about them, ever since I was little. Oh, boy. We certainly went a lot of places together."

When he talked this way about his father, you felt as if you'd inherited joy. It was easy to see the boy and his father together. You couldn't help seeing them. You followed them 'way back on one of their camping trips and heard them talking, like this:

"Dad, can I clean the fish and cook them, all myself?"

"Sure you can."

"And build the fire, too? And light it, and everything?"

"You bet. Be careful with the axe."

Then, in your mind, you saw the smoke of their fire and their white tent in a clearing. Pretty quick you saw night coming down around them, and the boy lying close to his father, and both of them staring up into the night sky.

"Dad, how high are the stars?"

"Millions and millions of miles. No one can imagine the distances to stars."

"Is Mother looking at the stars?"

"I'm pretty sure she is."

"I wonder what she's thinking about."

"I guess she's thinking about us."

"Why, Dad?"

"Because we're thinking about her. When you love people, you think about them, especially at night."

Suddenly, out of the starlight, a voice seemed to say: "If it could always be like this!" Maybe the boy said it, maybe the father. Maybe the mother said it. But maybe you just said it your own self, because when there is this kind of beauty, you want it to last forever, and all the while you know there's a shadow and a trouble waiting to spoil it. . . .

Actually, since I had lifted him from the canoe, the boy had said little. But in this other way he said so much! He set your imagination on fire, and you knew that the things you imagined were true to the lives of the father, the mother, and the boy.

Now, in the cabin, his thoughts had jumped an incredible distance from Landseer rods and fishing.

"Why does everyone have to die?" he said.

"I can't tell you, Chris. I don't know."

"My father didn't know, and my mother didn't, either. I used to ask them, but they didn't know."

"There's some things no one knows."

He lay thinking for a moment, then asked: "Do you think it hurts very much to drown?"

"No Chris. I don't think so."

"Do people really have wonderful dreams when they're drowning?"

"I think they do. I think it's really true."

He was lying on his back, staring up at the rafters. All of a sudden his eyes filled with tears, and his throat began to work. "I wish I knew what my father dreamed," he said.

I couldn't say anything at all for a while after that. I went over and looked out the window, wondering just how it had happened, wondering about the bass and the candy, and what they had to do with it, and why the boy blamed himself. The lake was dead calm, peaceful in the sunset, but all I could see was the accident happening, and afterwards the boy lying alone in the canoe, the blown spray climbing around him, the waves high and white, and the canoe blowing wild.

I turned away from the window and started to put some wood in the stove. The boy was lying still, his eyes closed. I thought he was asleep, so I didn't touch the stove for fear of waking him. Instead, I got my bottle of whiskey from the shelf where it had stood untouched for three years. It wasn't a problem to me any more—the whiskey, I mean. But right now there was a hollow in me that a drink would fill. I took a little and put the bottle back. When I turned around, the boy was up on one elbow, his eyes shining and happy.

"I know what my father dreamed," he said. "I know, now! He dreamed of not wanting a drink!"

So that was the trouble waiting to spoil their happiness! I stood there as if my moccasins were nailed to the floor. I had clean forgotten the empty bottle in the canoe, and because of what I already knew of the boy's father, I couldn't believe that it had a bearing on the accident. I was to find out that it had—but not in the way you would naturally think.

What struck me now was the depth of this boy's understanding. He wanted to think of his father's having a last dream, and he wanted his father's dream to be beautiful. He knew, somehow, that to a man who is trying to stop drinking, a dream of not wanting a drink is beautiful.

I came over and sat on the bunk by his side. "Maybe that's what he dreamed," I said. "I used to dream that dream, once."

"But not any more?"

"No, not for a long time. It came true up here."

It was getting dark in the cabin, but you could still see the curiosity in his eyes. After a time he said: "Do people have to get hurt before they stop?"

"Some of them do, but it isn't their fault. It's the way they're made."

"My father said that. He said it to my mother one night in their room. I woke up and heard them talking. There was a chocolate bar beside my pillow. He always put one there when he came home late."

My mind started racing again, only this time it wasn't so much imagination. The story seemed to pour out of the boy's eyes. He kept referring to the night he had overheard his father and mother, and he gave hints of how he had first learned about his father's trouble, sticking in a name or a detail once in a while.

From his voice and eyes you knew so much about his father and mother that you could almost hear them talking.

Now, out of some old corner of his memory, the boy said: "I caught a trout that day. It was a swell day by the brook. My mother had sandwiches, and we were all together."

"What day was that, Chris?" I asked him.

"The day Doc Morrison came up from the brook to see us, and my father said, 'No, thanks, Doc.' "

You didn't need to know any more than that. You had the whole scene, the mother sitting under a tree near the picnic basket and the father teaching the boy how to use a fishing rod. Orioles sang in the elms, and the brook talked among the stones of its bed. They were all happy there together, and there was no cloud until Doc Morrison waded toward them from the brook where he, too, had been fishing.

You knew all about Doc Morrison. He was like the other lucky ones—jolly, good-natured, big, and red-faced. He was full of friendship and compliments. Maybe he visited the family once a week, but he would greet them always as though he hadn't laid eyes on them in years.

"Ah! My dear girl, you're lovely as ever!" he'd say to the mother, and to the father: "Barney Blake! Barney, old pal, old pal. Certainly glad to stumble onto you folks. And little Chris, too. Some boy. Yes, sir! Tops!"

Maybe it was right then that Doc Morrison took a flask out of his fishing coat and waved it like a banner. The father and mother looked at each other, and the boy wondered why they looked that way.

"No, Doc—no, thanks," the father said.

"What's this, Barney, old pal? What's this you say to me?"

"No, thanks, Doc."

"Ah! So you can take it, or leave it alone, eh?"

The father glanced quickly at the mother, and then he said to Doc Morrison: "I wish it was as simple as that."

So Doc Morrison's face got round, and serious, and full of understanding. He put his flask away. "I'm terribly sorry it's that way, Barney," he said. "All those other times I thought we were having fun together. But I didn't know how it was. I'm sorry."

Then, on that day by the brook bank, after Doc Morrison had gone, you saw the mother turn gay, and sparkling, as if a danger had moved back. You saw the boy looking curiously from his mother to his father, mystified by his father's danger because it was invisible, and troubled because he could not help his father by means of fists or a flung stone. . . .

While this part of the story had been coming from the boy I had been sitting beside him in the dark. I stood up now and lit the lamp and stirred up the fire in the stove.

"Do you think you could eat a little something, Chris?"

"Yes."

"Afterwards, I guess we better go on down-lake to the village. Don't you think so, Chris?"

"Yes."

He had been dreading that trip, and so had I. He had been thinking how he would telephone to his mother, and what he would say, and the way her voice would sound after he told her.

I cut some bacon and put it in the frying pan. Pretty soon after the bacon began to sizzle, the boy got up from the bunk and walked over to the stove. He sat down on a bench I had hewed out of a spruce log. He drew up his knees and locked his elbows over them, resting his chin on his crossed arms. The lamplight carved dark hollows under his eyes, and sharpened the points of his cheek bones. He was watching me, but his mind was a long way off.

"I didn't eat the chocolate bar that night," he said. "If I wanted it, and didn't eat it, I would feel the way my father felt. He came almost home with me that night. But he let go of my hand, and went back in the rain to see Jake and those other men in a place down town."

He was referring again to the night he had listened to his

father and mother talking. You didn't have to take much for granted. He said enough, in that strange way he had. He said it all. . . .

You could see the boy and his father walking toward home in the rain. Maybe his father had stopped at a tavern—stopped just for a minute—and when he was like this, Chris was happy. There would be affection in the father's voice and the warm lift of life and confidence. His thoughts would come fast and beautifully worded, and Chris would know he could ask his father anything.

"Why did you marry Mother, Dad?"

"I fell in love with her."

"What is love like, anyway?"

"It's like having the answer to all the questions you ask yourself when you're looking at the stars. It's as if you looked into a person's eyes and asked her 'Why?' and she said to you, 'I am the answer. I am your reason for being alive and on this earth. Stop searching. You have found me, and I have found you.' "

As they walked along on the wet street of the town, the boy must have been wondering if he, too, would fall in love, and what the person would look like. And it must have been while he was wondering that some cheerful doors swung open, and a man rushed out on the sidewalk, hailing them with an avalanche of cordiality.

"Hi, Barney! Saw you through the window. Where have you been hiding these days? Come on inside out of the rain. Some great fellows in here I want you to meet."

You knew that Barney Blake drew people to him. They approached, as if to warm themselves in his warmth. But now, while the man expanded his welcome, you knew that Barney Blake was struggling. You knew that his hand closed hard over his son's hand, as he said to the man: "I guess I'd better not, Jake. Thanks a lot."

"Just one."

"I've already had one."

"One more, Barney."

"Not now, Jake. Maybe some other time. Maybe a little later."

So Jake stepped back to the doors, holding them open for an instant as he went through. There was a glimpse of a bright room and a row of pleasant men arranged at a bar. Heads turned. Faces gleamed. Inviting arms shot upward, and just before the doors swung shut, a voice called: "Hi, Barney! Where you going? What's the matter?"

As they turned into their own street, Chris must have believed for a little while that his father had won a victory, and that he, Chris, had in some way helped him. But his father was quiet. He wouldn't talk any more about love, and Chris stopped trying to make him.

Then, in the rainy dark in front of their house, Barney Blake suddenly and unexplainably let go his hold on the boy's hand.

"Go ahead into the house, Chris. Tell Mother, I'll be along. Tell her I—"

"Where are you going, Dad?"

"Down town again."

"I thought you weren't going to do that."

"I thought so, too."

"I don't see why you have to go, Dad."

"I don't, either."

You saw them standing there, both of them bewildered. You saw the father's arm creep out hungrily and hug the boy around the shoulders. That was Barney Blake trying to tell his son that he loved him, that he didn't want to go back, but couldn't help going and didn't know why.

So Chris went on into the house and told his mother. You knew what she was like. She was already facing it straight. She was one of the cool, steady kind that would say: "Let's wait a while, dear. Supper isn't quite ready, anyway. Have you done all your homework?"

"Why don't you call him up, Mother?"

"No. I guess not. I guess I won't do that."

"Why? He's at that place by the hotel—the Shamrock."

"I think he'd rather I didn't call him."

"But we ought to help him! Something's wrong with him!"

"We are helping him—every single second."

"But how, Mother?"

"By loving him and believing in him during these times when he has lost faith in himself."

A long time later that night Chris woke up and heard his father and mother talking in their bedroom next to his. The rain had stopped, and their voices were lonely and frightened in the still night.

"Oh, Barney, how did it happen? Why did they let Jake drive the car when he was like that?"

"It might have happened anyway. The road was slippery. He couldn't make the turn."

"Was he hurt badly?"

"Yes."

"Are you sure you're not hurt, Barney?"

"I wish I was hurt. I wish I was hurt in some way that would make me stop. Why am I one of those who has to get hurt? Why can't I be like the other ones?"

"Barney, don't talk like that! I'm so frightened when you say that. You can't be hurt. I won't let you be hurt. I love you."

It must have been right after they stopped talking that Chris' hand touched the chocolate bar his father had left beside his pillow. He unwrapped the candy, put it to his lips, and then snatched it back. He lay in the dark stillness trying to multiply his longing for the candy. He multiplied by a hundred, a thousand, and a million. He wanted to feel as his father must have felt that time on the brook bank when he said to Doc Morrison: "No, Doc—no, thanks. . . ."

You know how it is when someone you love is dead. You think of the last time you saw him, and what he said, and what you said.

I guess the boy had been trying to stay away from that last moment when he saw his father in the water, but now, as we cleaned up the supper dishes in the cabin, he was getting closer to it. Perhaps he was thinking of what he would say to his mother on the telephone when we got down to the village at the foot of the lake.

"Well, Chris," I said to him. "How do you feel?"

"All right."

"I guess we better get going. What do you think?"

"I guess we better."

I got him an old jacket. It came down to his knees, and his hands disappeared in the sleeves. When I blew out the lamp he moved over close to me, and we walked down to the lake together and got in my canoe. He sat in the bow, facing me, the moonlight glowing over him, and his eyes on me every instant.

I kept close to shore, still-paddling the way the Indians do. The boy was quiet for a long time. Then, suddenly, when we were sliding past Caribou Point, he began telling me about the accident. Maybe he wanted to get it all straight in his mind for his mother, or maybe he wanted to talk it out with me because of my understanding of his father's trouble. His story came out in little bursts, and just once in a while I asked him a question.

"We always had a candy agreement on our trips," he said. "It was my idea. I thought it was a swell one, too."

"How did it work, Chris?"

"Dad said a boy ought not to eat too much candy between meals. So I agreed to eat a piece just only when I caught a fish."

They had got to Red Jackson's camps on the lake at three that afternoon, two hours before the squall. A little wind had already sprung up, but the black cloud was low down in the horizon to the northwest. They unpacked in the camp, and the boy's father took a drink of whiskey and left the bottle on the table when they went to their canoe at the wharf.

"I saw a fish swirl down there," Chris went on, "but the chocolate bars were up in the camp. Dad went to get them, and when he came back he brought the bottle with him. I guess he wanted it a million times more than I wanted the candy. Was he bad? Was my father bad because he wanted it?"

"No, Chris," I told him. "You never want to think of it like that. He was good. I know he was good."

The boy moved a little in the canoe, and some ripples spread out over the lake in the moonlight. He began talking again, his voice was young and clear.

"After we were on the lake, I thought of a plan to help my father. He took some more whiskey, and then it was time to tell him the plan. I said from now on he would get a drink out of the bottle only when I caught a fish. It was just like me with the chocolate bars. I told my father how we were both in it together, and I thought it would help him, because I didn't think there were many fish around, with the wind blowing so hard."

But pretty quick the boy and his father had come in their canoe into the lee of Munson Island. The wind quit roaring around them. The black cloud had climbed up hiding the sun, but they couldn't see the cloud. It was coming up fast behind the island, and the loons were shrieking their crazy, wild, storm-call.

"All of a sudden," Chris went on, "a white perch jumped, and I was afraid I would catch him, but I got the fly away from him in time. There was a whole school of perch, and I wanted them, but I didn't catch any. They were wonderful ones, huge ones. But I could see their fins come out of water when they started for my fly, and I'd pull the fly up quick and miss them.

"Once or twice, when I almost caught one, I saw my father reaching behind him. He was doing something with the bottle. I guess he was getting ready, so he could have a drink when I caught a perch. But I didn't dare look at him much. I had to keep missing those perch; they were wonderful ones, too, but I didn't even catch one, and I guess my father thought I wasn't fishing very well. When the perch all went away into deep water, I looked at my father, and he had the strangest expression on his face. He was smiling, but his eyes were—they were—"

"They were what, Chris?" I asked him.

"Well, they were wonderful, but not happy. I never saw him look that way. I never saw anyone look that way."

Now, listening to the boy, you suddenly knew something that he didn't know. You knew what had happened inside his father. You knew that Barney Blake realized exactly what his son was trying to do. Barney Blake must have added it all up, right then—all the misery and heartbreak, all the chances he had taken with the two people who loved him most and had faith in him when he didn't have any in himself. He added it up and told himself the right answer in that instant when he saw his son giving up everything he loved in order to help him.

A few minutes after the perch had disappeared, Chris raised the big bass near some lily pads on the point of Munson Island. Just beyond the point in the open lake the waves were running white and wild, but they didn't notice it especially.

You saw them there together, each intent on the other, thinking of the other, the father with that strange look on his face, and the boy tense, fearful that he would catch the bass. You felt as Chris must have felt when the big bass came to his fly. You knew how he wanted the bass, with all his hot, boy-longing. And when he snatched his fly away, his father said: "Cast again, Chris."

Chris cast again. He cast deliberately in the wrong spot, and his father said, "That isn't where he was, Chris. He was over near the lily pads. Go ahead and catch him."

"Heck, Dad. He won't come again. He was only a little one, anyway."

"He's a beauty, Chris. I never saw a better one anywhere. Go ahead and cast near the lily pads. It's all right, Chris. I want you to have him."

So Chris, not knowing what had already happened to his father, gave in to his own hot, boy-longing and hooked the bass. When the canoe came around the point into the open lake, the wind hit them with a cold, quick pressure. Barney Blake couldn't hold the canoe into it, but he wanted Chris to have the bass.

It may have taken Chris ten minutes to play the bass on his light rod out there in the wind, and when his father slipped the net under the fish and flopped him into the canoe, the squall was nearly on them. But Barney Blake knew they could ride out the squall lying down in the canoe. Right now, he had something he wanted to say to his son, but he didn't get a chance to say it. All he said was: "Chris! That's a wonderful bass! Look at him, Chris! I want you to be glad you caught him. Are you glad, Chris?"

Then Chris looked miserably at his father and said: "I guess you won a drink, Dad!"

When Barney Blake reached around to get the bottle, a big wave heaved under the canoe, and the landing net rolled off the gunwale. He grabbed for the net, and another wave pitched against the canoe. He lost his balance and went overboard.

It all happened in a second, and it changed everything. He came up and caught the gunwale with his hands. Chris grabbed him by the arm, and his father said: "Don't do that! We'll upset her. Lie down, Chris. There's going to be a big wind."

"Get back in, Dad! Can't you get in?"

Barney Blake tried to climb in over the gunwale, but it was hard with the big waves knocking the canoe around. He might have done it, but he didn't want to take the chance. He couldn't hold onto the gunwale much longer, either. His weight tipped the canoe in the combers, and one of them crashed in over the gunwale, drenching the boy. Barney Blake was afraid that he might swamp the canoe.

"Chris, listen to me. Lie down flat and don't move. You'll ride it out all right."

"Dad! What are you going to do?"

Barney Blake knew what he was going to do, and he did it. He did what every man would want to think of himself as doing. He did what a man would always hope to do and dream of doing. He let his fingers slide off the gunwale, and the canoe blew free in the gale. In a second, the canoe was twenty yards away.

"Lie flat!" he yelled once more. "Don't move!"

Chris peeked over the gunwale and saw a huge wave break over his father. He saw his father come up swimming, saw him make a downward motion with his hand. Chris saw his father's lips move. He knew his father was telling him again to lie down, but he couldn't hear anything but the roaring of the wind and the crashing of the seas around him. Then the blown spray came up off the lake like a white curtain, covering his father, and that was all Chris knew or remembered till he got ashore on the beach in front of my cabin. . . .

Now, in this still, moonlit night, as I was paddling the boy down to the village, it was hard to imagine there had ever been a storm. The islands looked lonely, part of another world, and a thin mist lay along one shore. Only when you looked at the boy's face did you remember the storm and what it had done to him. Telling about it had hurt him, and he was crying softly.

"I wish I hadn't caught that darn bass," he said. "I wanted to help my father, but I guess I didn't help him at all."

I looked away at the lights of the village for a time. Then I said: "Chris, let me tell you something. He knew what you were doing when you began missing those perch. He knew why you were doing it, and that's what helped him. He wasn't going to take a drink after you caught that bass. He had already taken his last drink, and he knew it. He was just going to show you the empty bottle. He'd poured it out in the lake. That's what he was doing when you saw him reaching around, while you were missing the perch."

"Do you think so?" the boy asked.

"I know it. The bottle I found in your canoe was uncorked and empty."

We didn't talk any more till we got to the canoe landing at the village. But I was thinking how it is that some have to get hurt, and how it must have hurt Barney Blake when he was watching his son out there in the lee of Munson Island. And I thought how bad it was that this good man, his father, had to get hurt so hard it killed him, and how in that last moment he didn't even think once about himself, but just about his son.

At the canoe landing, Chris said: "I haven't got any money to telephone. Have you got any?"

"Sure. Don't worry about that."

"It might cost a dollar."

"That's all right."

We went up to the store where the old men were sitting. They had probably started their talk about today's storm, but now they were telling about storms that had happened forty years ago. Chris stood just outside the telephone booth, facing the door, while I put in the call for him. They had trouble getting the call through. I guess some poles had blown down.

But while I was waiting, I saw something happen that made my knees shake. I was watching the boy when suddenly his face turned ash white. He swayed, and took a half-step forward. Out of the whiteness of his face his eyes burned like a dark, blue flame, and all the old men in the store got still. I knew who the boy was looking at. It couldn't have been but one person.

My voice must have sounded crazy, like someone yelling in a library, when I said to the operator: "Never mind. Let it go. Just let it go."

They were standing looking at each other, the father in the doorway of the store and the boy by the telephone booth. They were white-faced and frightened, each thinking he had killed the other, each thinking he was maybe dead himself and in heaven with the other. They never said a word—not a word. Maybe they didn't think it was real. Maybe each was waiting for the other to vanish. Then, suddenly, the father, Barney Blake, walked slowly and kissed his son on the mouth, the way his mother would have kissed him.

The boy kept reaching out for his father and feeling of him, the long sleeves of that old jacket bothering him, because he couldn't get his hands outside where he could touch his father.

"Hi, Dad," he said, in a thin voice. He had to know if it was real, if his father was real, and if he was real.

"Hello, Chris."

"Are you okay, Dad?"

"Yes. Are you all right?"

"Sure, Dad. I'm all right."

Before I went back up lake to my cabin that night I found out how it happened; how Jim Blanket, the Indian, had sighted them in trouble off the point of Munson Island; how old Jim had gone in the Forest Patrol boat, holding her straight down-wind when the spindrift hid everything from view, and how he had come sliding through it almost straight to the boy's father struggling in the water. Barney Blake was almost done in, and old Jim had taken him back to the Forest Service camp on the mainland. Afterwards they had gone in the boat hunting for the boy, but they hadn't seen his canoe on the beach by my cabin, because they had come onto that shore a half-mile below.

So I went back up lake that night in that wonderful calm moonlight feeling pretty good. But I wished I had got hurt like Barney Blake. I wished I could have got hurt just a little sooner, before it busted up my family. My own son would be about two years older than Chris was. I wondered what he looked like now. I hadn't seen him for three years, and I wondered if he was a swell kid, like Chris. I wondered if it was all right now for me to go back again and start over, and if they would want me. And I wondered if my son had ever wanted to help me, the way Chris wanted to help his father. I guess he had wanted to, all right.

THE TEACHER COMMENTS

THE SEDULOUS APE

Mr. Ware's statement that, "Every individual is being influenced practically all the time," is certainly true. Human beings are such complexes of intricate causes and effects that beside them the most profound fictional character is as simple as stone. And of all human beings, artists and craftsmen are the most complex because not only do they share the common unconscious susceptibility to influence, but they actually seek it!

How much one should seek to be influenced, I am not prepared to say. The history of literary scholarship, as Mr. Ware points out, establishes that most writers are influenced a great deal by other writers, and in that fact is an important moral for the aspiring young. One remembers Stevenson's advice to play "the sedulous ape," his own confession of deliberate imitation as the best preparation for literary art. And anybody who has had anything to do with young writers in our own times knows very well the enormous influence exerted by our leading contemporaries and near-contemporaries: Hemingway, Lewis, Anderson, Crane, James, Dos Passos, Huxley, Eliot, and a dozen others.

It is a knotty problem. If one becomes too consciously concerned with manner, he is likely to become too oblivious of matter, or to clothe his matter in a style that critics call precious. On the other hand, no one has in himself more than a fraction of the resources of the language, and he must seek constantly to improve his expression by studying the word texture of better writers.

If it should come to a clear-cut issue between matter and manner, there can be, it seems to me, no choice; you must concern yourself primarily with matter, though I am well aware that successful literary careers have been built on little else than an exquisite use of the language, and also that the finest matter can be corrupted by poverty of manner.

But the problem, of course, never does come to a clear-cut, two-valued issue, and although it is always a temptation for any teacher of writing to expound at great length on the general subject of "style," I am going to resist the temptation and dismiss the subject with the following advice: Cultivate your enthusiasms for your favorite writers; study them, revel in their felicities of expression, imitate them—but at the same time, also be yourself. And above all, remember, always: *The story's the thing!*

FLATTERY AND THEFT

"Imitation is the sincerest form of flattery," the adage tells us. True. But there is a difference between imitation and downright theft. Literary theft, as ugly as any other kind, and punishable by law, is called plagiarism. Sometimes, the line between flattery and theft is a fine one, almost undiscernible to the literary novice. The best advice is to follow your conscience, just as you would about your roommate's clothes or other belongings. Even in the most casual college relationships, there is a difference between stealing and borrowing a shirt, or a watch, or anything of value. Mr. Ware's preface to this chapter tells what influence and imitation are. Plagiarism, to offer a short and incomplete definition, is quoting without quotation marks. It is also stealing ideas, though here the problem sometimes becomes very complex. If any reader is in doubt, he is advised to look up the subject in an encyclopedia or handbook of college composition. He is also referred to the "Funny Coincidence Department" of *The New Yorker,* whose editors have been hawk-eyed in detecting and exposing illegitimate literary "borrowing." To repeat, then: Follow your conscience, and when in doubt use quotation marks or some other form of acknowledgment.

ENDINGS—HAPPY OR UNHAPPY?

"Some Have to Get Hurt" is a story full of interesting and important technical matters. First, however, I wish to dispose of an objection to the story raised by one of my students: "But the ending," she wailed, "why it's so trite, so cliché. But then, of course, what else can you do if you write for the popular magazines? You have to have happy endings, don't you?"

No, you don't. Is this, for example, really a story with a "happy ending"? Whose story is it? Think it over. The boy is happy and so is his father. But what about the narrator? What *is* the story, what is it *about?* It is the story of the narrator's personal tragedy, and there simply wouldn't have been any story if the father had not turned up at the end.

Next, my student's question in itself betrays a state of mind quite as trite as any general magazine practices she imagines the editors follow. A great many otherwise intelligent young people interested in writing are convinced that good fiction can tell us but one thing: life is a bitter defeat, and human beings are grotesque travesties of what they're supposed to be.

Nonsense! Look about you. Or jot down the names of the first fifty people that come to mind and consider them. Some of them, maybe, are horrid, and some are good, gentle souls undeservedly beaten by life. They are both good story material. Some others exhibit the highest human qualities of kindness, tolerance, understanding, fortitude, sacrifice, heroism (did you read the newspapers during the war?) and downright nobility, and live in concord with God and man, and they, too, are good story material. But most of these fifty will show in varying degrees good and bad qualities, happy and disastrous experiences. And they are the best story material. An easy pessimism is quite as unrealistic as an easy optimism.

There is, perhaps, another reason why young writers emphasize the sordid and macabre in their first fiction. It seems to them easier to gain immediate dramatic effects by dealing with the doleful. This is, however, a confusion of fictional values; if there is one kind of amateur story ending now triter than "they lived happily ever after," it is "they all fell down dead, pronto." Young people, as somebody said, tend to over-emphasize the literary values of death and adultery.

For these and other reasons, I generally advise beginning writers to try to write stories of accomplishment rather than of defeat. It is harder and it teaches more, because the writer's reliance is on himself and not merely on his material. More important, when the time comes for him to make a deep and genuine protest against the crassness of the world, he will be better equipped to make it effectively. Critics have pointed out that *Babbitt* is superior as a novel to *Mainstreet* not because it has less anger in it, but because the novelist came nearer to winning his struggle with anger, transmuting it from polemic to fiction. So with the short-story writer: He must learn first to write stories, not mere delineations of nasty characters. Fiction, of course, could not exist without nasty characters, and the constant imminence of defeat in optimistic fiction certainly requires some more realistic stories in which the defeat actually occurs. But let us have some balance, and let us remember that when youth wallows in misery it is usually not being perceptive and courageous and emancipated, but is merely following the line of least resistance.

Editors print pessimistic stories in the popular magazines. The most depressing story I ever read anywhere was written by Paul Gallico and appeared in *The Saturday Evening Post* for July 13, 1940. Look it up. And Mr. Ware himself has published a first-person story in which the hero-narrator actually dies! Most such stories I notice, are written by practiced writers who have learned how to make actual stories out of their material. "We'll buy any kind of convincing story," a fiction editor told me recently when we were discussing this matter. "But nine out of ten of the unhappy stories by beginning writers are simply trite tripe." "What about the other kind?" I asked. She grinned. "Only eight out of ten are as bad for the same reasons." I suppose the big point is that it takes little ingenuity to set a character on the road to hell, and let him get there, but that it takes a lot of ingenuity to start him off and save him. It's the exercise of that ingenuity that teaches you more than anything else about fictional technique.

On the other hand, I do not wish to press my advice too far. You can only write the stories that are in you, or that your widening and deepening perceptions lead you toward. If you are genuinely moved by the world's injustice, of which there is certainly plenty, if you have been genuinely hurt by people or yourself, it would be equally foolish to put on rose-colored spectacles. I have raised all this pother only because it seems to me, and to many editors and other teachers, that young people insist on looking at life, in Mark Twain's words, "as through a glass eye, darkly."

TALK

In Chapter II, we said that people reveal themselves in four ways: by what they say, think, and do, and what other people say, think, and do about them. Of these four, talk, or dialogue, is by far the most important and the most difficult. It can, and frequently does, embrace the other three ways simultaneously, as in stories made up entirely of monologue or dialogue, and as in monologues on the stage.

The problem of talk is very much like the problem of fact, in that the writer's aim is to achieve truth of representation. Dialogue in good fiction is highly selective, not merely transcriptive. Human beings are constantly making a vast number of noises with the mouth—words, grunts, lip smackings, burps, hisses, growls, and jabber—only a very few of which are of use to the story writer. Of all these, words themselves must be carefully selected.

While the listening habit should be assiduously cultivated, while one must constantly strive to catch the rhythms and emphases of living speech, nevertheless what appears on the printed page is never more than a small fraction of the total words a character in real life debouches from his lips. As proof, I offer the early experience of a now successful writer. He had been told to study dialogue, and since he knew shorthand, he determined to make a really exhaustive study of the subject. For a period of weeks he listened carefully to the conversations of strangers and recorded them verbatim—at the corner store, in the subway, along the street, at parties, at the beach, in offices, in short, wherever his pleasure or his business took him. When he had compiled a vast number of such notes, he transcribed them on the typewriter and proceeded to analyze the results.

He discovered that the topics of human conversation fall into two general categories. The first comprises about eighty per cent of the words we speak, and in turn breaks down into three subcategories. First, in order of occurrence, is conversation governed by the general tone of indignation ("Who does he think he is, anyway?"); second, that governed by boasting ("And then I said to him, I said: 'Oh, well maybe you don't know who I am!,' and believe me, that shut him right up!"); and the third, hypochondria ("Did you hear about my operation?"). Only the remaining twenty per cent of our conversation, that which is on special, focused topics in special circumstances, can be of value to the writer. People are always griping, or boasting, or enjoying their ill health, and rarely is there special significance in such noise.

(Lately I have heard of another survey of actual speech which discovered that seventy-five per cent of men's talk is about women, and seventy-five per cent of women's talk is about men. The discerning will immediately see that the two surveys verify each other, for the second shows, in different words, about the same proportion of indignation, boasting, and even hypochondria!)

Mr. Ware mentions Hemingway as an influence on this story, and that is why, at this point, I have brought up the subject of dialogue. Nobody has ever written such dialogue as Hemingway's, whose characters seem to talk with all the authority of actual, human speech. His influence has been enormous and certainly salutary insofar as imitation of his dialogue is concerned. No one should neglect to read and study this author's short stories as models of effective dialogue.

It has been objected that Hemingway's conscious limiting of all tags of dialogue to the austere "he said," is in itself a kind of affectation, and perhaps it is. Nevertheless the principle is sound. Economy is one of the great canons of all writing, and you achieve economy in dialogue by investing speech itself with its own qualities. For crude example, here is a sentence from an undergraduate story: "Oh, Bill," she gushed admiringly, "I think you're just wonderful."

The weakness is that the adverb is implicit in what she says, and so, also is the verb. Furthermore, if there are but two people engaged in the dialogue, any identifying verb at all is unnecessary. Better than "said," or any synonym here, would be a gesture of some kind, something like the following, perhaps: "Oh, Bill—" Her hands reached to his lapels, and she pulled him toward her. "I—I think you're just wonderful!"

For another warning, do not dilute dialogue by combining it with too much action in the same sentence:

> "What say, Harry," Dick said, stretching his long legs indolently before him as he settled back on the sofa, and reaching lazily into the cigarette box on the end table, striking a match on his thumb nail, touching it to the cigarette, then flicking the dead match carelessly toward the fireplace as he blew out a great cloud of smoke, "what about calling up Janice?"

With these points in mind read any of the stories in this book, particularly "Some Have to Get Hurt" and "Miss Laurie Will Be Late Tonight." Notice how, most of the time, adverbial description of dialogue is unnecessary because the dialogue itself carries its own quality of speech in the very words spoken, and how most of the action or description accompanying a speech is placed in separate sentences.

For a further warning, be careful that your dialogue does not fall into a pattern in which the conversational football is passed back and forth from one character to another in a series of set speeches. This is a common fault in amateur fiction and comes from too great absorption on the part of the writer in what his characters are saying. If there has been tremendous emotional intensity generated between the two characters, you may for a little while succeed in carrying the story by means of alternating paragraphs of dialogue. The great danger, however, is that the characters lose their identity as people, becoming mere mouths from which words issue; the reader, consequently, loses interest in them as his illusion of them as flesh and blood people evaporates. Seeing is believing; so, but to a lesser degree, are hearing, smelling, touching, and tasting. These other four are effective, but depend very greatly on seeing.

Again, you are referred to the stories. Notice how short are the paragraphs of dialogue, how broken up by gesture and other action, by feeling, by the interruption of one speaker by another. Now check your own story for sequences of solid talk. Break them up; keep your characters constantly in your reader's eye; keep them moving.

THE THINGS UNSAID

Fiction has been called the art of not saying things. More positively, fiction is always attempting to say a great deal more than the mere words it uses. Call it implication, suggestion, over-meanings. This attempt to widen the ripples on the waters of the consciousness is especially noticeable in dialogue.

Mr. Ware makes most interesting use of it in "Some Have to Get Hurt." Look at the paragraph on page 234, "Actually, since I had lifted him from the canoe, the boy had said little. But in this other way he had said so much! He set your imagination on fire, and you knew that the things you imagined were true to the lives of the father, the mother, and the boy." There, what has not been said allows the reader to understand the implications of the story, and permits as well the narrator to tell the story within a story which is completely necessary to the main story. This is an effective but complex device.

On page 246 of the same story, there is a sentence which, without specifically mentioning any of them, shows a host of virtues in the boy. The sentence is five words long—"It might cost a dollar"—and it tells us more effectively than any amount of exposition ever could a whole bookful of information about his character and that of his parents. It shows his qualities of consideration, responsibility, politeness, self-reliance. The sentence is an excellent example of characterization through speech and of the way people in fiction must create themselves. "By their words ye shall know them," is perhaps the most important single rule of fictional characterization.

Look also at the character of Tuck in "Miss Laurie Will Be Late Tonight." In this story, much of Tuck's characterization is accomplished through what may be called interior monologue, but what he says in dialogue with the various other characters is of equal importance. Taken together, they are the sum of what Tuck is—he has, that is, revealed himself to us through his words. Of course, there is subsidiary importance in what he does, and what the other people do and think about him; notice, however, that what other people do and think about him is contained almost entirely in spoken words, although there is importance in the way those words are spoken, in the descriptions given the various speeches.

THE SOUND OF WORDS

"We've lost almost everything," he said. "Beetsugar went to pot on the market almost ten years ago. It killed Father. The last five years have seen even the remnants of the fortune dwindle, until now there is just enough for Mother to get by on.

"I had to leave school a year ago," he continued. Now he spoke with bitterness. She saw the furrow deepen on his brow, his lips were thin. "Went down to our beetsugar farms in southern Colorado, but there's little I could do there, God knows," he snorted. "It's way past doing anything about. Why—" he was incredulous—"we couldn't even get enough labor for our farms! They'd much rather be on relief!" he rasped.

"Mirabel felt the surge of the nameless frenzy of his frustration. She could think of nothing to say. But there in that terrible sad flash of time she knew—she *knew* she knew—she wanted to *do* something."

These three paragraphs, quoted consecutively, are from a pretentious story by a person who, at the time of composition, was exceedingly inexperienced in the writing of fiction. What is wrong with the writing is very largely a matter of sheer sound. There is something thin and astonishingly ludicrous about the word "beetsugar" suddenly shrilling at you after the slow, sad cadence of the first sentence. Then, the ineptness of the writer's synonyms for "said" partly explain, perhaps, why Hemingway never uses anything else. "'. . . but there's little I could do, God knows,' he snorted," and "They'd much rather be on relief," he rasped. Did he "snort" and "rasp" those two sentences? *Could* he? Could you? And consider the over-writing in the third paragraph. A boy and a girl have just met, gone for a walk, and are telling each other about themselves. Where is there evident any "nameless frenzy of his frustration"? Nowhere, save in the writer's mind—he admitted later that he was obsessed with Thomas Wolfe, an example, by the way, of influence and imitation carried to silly extremes. And the writer's ear should have warned him away from the jingly doggerel of the final sentence, as well as from the beautiful but meaningless phrase "the terrible sad flash of time."

How to cultivate a fastidious ear is a problem worth a large part of the lifetime of any writer. It is done partly through reading, partly through writing, and partly through the exercise of whatever aesthetic gifts you may be blessed with. Copious reading of good poetry certainly helps. More valuable is long, assiduous practice in the writing of verse, particularly of such traditional forms as the sonnet and Spenserian stanza, where the necessities to fit sense, meter, and sound together combine to force upon the writer a most valuable discipline in the use of words. Then, you should read deeply and analytically in the classics of our language—yes, the Bible and Shakespeare, as well as standard authors of all centuries, and our own good contemporaries. And you should also *listen*—to recordings of poets reading their own poems, to good speakers, to good radio plays, to recordings from stage dramas. "The ear," wrote Archibald MacLeish, "is already half poet." A publisher once told me that he was always most eager to look at the manuscript of a poet's first novel; a poet, he said, is in love with words, and prose writers ought to be also.

THE NUMBER OF WORDS

A famous composition teacher used to hand back, without reading them, the first papers submitted by his class. His instructions were:

"Count the number of adjectives and adverbs in your papers, and cut out half of them." When that had been done, and the papers resubmitted, he again returned them, still without reading them. "Now, cut half the remainder," he told the class, "and then I shall read and grade your papers."

Often, of course, a noun or a verb absolutely requires modification or qualification; there could not be communication of any subtlety without modifiers and qualifiers. Nevertheless, the teacher was forcing upon his students a most valuable lesson and exercises in effective writing. Nouns and verbs are the strength, the meat, of language; most of the time we want their flavor straight, not diluted. Yet it is easy to fall into the habit of giving nearly every noun its adjective, every verb its adverb. The beginner especially must guard against this tendency, which comes, probably, from unconscious timidity, tentativeness, and inexperience. There is also the mistaken notion that modifiers in general create a richness and depth to writing that nouns and verbs by themselves cannot achieve. As a principle, this is plain wrong. Unless there are special necessities for the modification of specific nouns or verbs, modifiers are but a dilution, an adulteration, a weariness to the reader.

> In the early morning, the fresh, cool dew was a soothing benediction to her bare, hot, tired, aching feet as she walked dejectedly across the grassy lawn, totally oblivious of the clear, sweet melodies of the awakening and happy birds.

For all this read: "The dew was a benediction to her feet as she walked across the lawn, oblivious of the awakening birds."

Other things being equal—and they always are in the absence of information to the contrary—birds do wake up in the early morning, and hence the first phrase of the sentence is superfluous. As a condition of its being dew, dew is fresh and cool. A benediction is soothing anyway, and if it is soothing to the feet, the feet would have to be bare to feel it, and also hot, tired, and aching in order that they may be soothed instead of being tickled. Next, lawns *are* grassy—see Webster. If she was oblivious, she was totally so, because that's what the word means when it stands alone. When birds wake up, the ordinary evidence of their awakening is song, and, with some exceptions unnecessary to remark, their song gives an impression of happiness and is automatically clear, sweet, and melodious, because those are qualities people accept as inherent in birdsong. Finally, since she is oblivious to birdsong, and her feet hurt, she is extremely likely to be dejected in her walk. Maybe by the time she reaches the other side of the lawn she will cheer up, but that belongs in another sentence.

Thus, we have cut out one adverbial phrase, one conjunction, one preposition, one article, one noun, two adverbs, and eleven adjectives, reducing the sentence from forty to nineteen words. By so doing, we have lost nothing but gained much. Of course, unless you are a very bad writer indeed, you won't be able to maintain this rate of reduction in your own work, but the principle is one to follow at all times! Economy achieves not only brevity, but also compression, which is the hallmark of good writing.

IX

THE WRITER COMMENTS

SEND ME A LOVE STORY

Greater even than for the story of high adventure, the father-and-son story, or the dog story, is the editor's demand for stories of young love. Old love is also splendid, but young love leads the field. It is universal in its appeal—and very hard to write about. The opportunities for spoiling love stories are superabundant. Walking the tight wire between sentiment and sentimentality, the writer makes one misstep. Just one is fatal, for the reader laughs when he was meant to cry. It is a shame that anything so sweet can turn so quickly sour or curdle with so little jostling.

"Miss Laurie Will Be Late Tonight" is a love story which started out to be something quite different. Many stories, unless they are air-tight to begin with, seem predestined to change. A few of the reasons for this are that the writer himself changes, that the story develops wide of its source, or that another or new story, breaks off from the original, much as in the process of making cells. "Miss Laurie" is an example.

The idea back of this story came from a query in the writer's notebook which read: "How does a man feel when he goes through an old routine for the last time?" The note was undated, but was probably two or three years old. The origin of the note itself has escaped, but the question it asked was provocative, and the writer asked it inwardly of himself and of imaginary persons in various occupations or professions. A surgeon performing a last operation? An actor making his last bow? A retiring professor addressing his last class? These were discarded as being too obvious or too dramatic, the professions as too frequently chosen to write about.

Wouldn't it be fine to make a story out of a man in a very ordinary profession or occupation going through his last routine? There is something tantalizing about the idea of a broken habit. What would be the man's thoughts? Would he be glad, happy, careful, careless? In the very lastness itself there seemed to be interest, as there is in any act of finality.

Because the opportunity was at hand, the writer chose a garage man for his character and went to work in a garage. At the time, the war was uppermost in people's minds. It seemed indecent to write anything or do anything, or even exist at all, without acknowledging and considering the fact and reality of the war. Thus the war affected the writing of this story, as it has affected so many, many others, so many writers, and so many editors. Tuck Roberts was the fiction name of the garage man, and the war intensified every thought and emotion that went through him when he closed up his garage for the last time before he left for the Army. The story itself moves and breathes in the topicality of the war. Yet similar effects could be created, I believe, through the mere lastness of Tuck's nightly garage routine. The fact that he was going to war simply added finality through the possibility of his death.

The writer had no intention of making this a love story until, on the garage bulletin board, as part of his work, he studied the lists of cars in and cars out. The cars were listed not by registration number or make and model, but by the name of the owner. Thus the record of the ins and outs among the live-storage customers was a list of names, sometimes with predictions as to when the owner was expected to return. The title and the love interest in "Miss Laurie" came straight off the garage bulletin board in the following note, under cars out: "Miss Blank will be late tonight."

The writer will never know whether his original, straight story would have been better. The announcement that Miss Blank would be late bringing her car in was irresistible. The writer's story became in an instant a love story, and his curiosity as to Miss Blank's whereabouts, background, past and future, knew no bounds. The actual Miss Blank, for fictional reasons, vanished from this earth and became "Miss Laurie." Tuck Roberts, the garage man, could well enough be waiting and working for a last glimpse of Miss Laurie before he closed up shop and went to war. Thus would Tuck's final routine of sweeping, storing cars for the night, disconnecting air hoses, locking gas pumps, and shutting off the air compressor take on poignancy and meaning. The original skeleton idea of last-time routine is now enlarged to include human beings *within* the routine, where at first it was merely manual. This seemed an excellent chance to write a touching love story. The result is "Miss Laurie Will Be Late Tonight."

Mr. Bailey asks me to say something more about fidelity to background, using "Miss Laurie" as an example. Obviously, in order to treat in detail the final night routine of Tuck Roberts, the writer was obliged to find out what the routine was. In order to do so, as stated above, he—the writer—worked for a time in a garage. The background of "Miss Laurie," then, is faithful in all detail, and the atmosphere is correct. But let the writer add that he, like many another, fell into an ancient and horrible trap. He became so excited by his garage job, that he very nearly smothered his story with atmosphere and was at last sorrowfully compelled by his writer's conscience to destroy several waste-baskets full of wonderful atmosphere, including works of art on the beveling of valves, the fitting of bearings, and the caster and camber angles of front wheels, as adjusted by a device called the "Bean Front End Machine."

Miss Laurie Will Be Late Tonight

It was about nine that evening in winter when the tall pilot from Westover Field came to my garage to pick up his car. Now, like always when I saw the pilot walking toward me, everything got keener. This pilot did something to you. His eyes were set deep in his head, and they made you think about distance and horizons. He had spent nine thousand hours in the sky. Maybe from looking so long at clouds and stars he had got hold of some kind of knowledge that you couldn't find on earth.

I lifted the elevating door, drove his car out, and gave it a last touch with the cleaning cloth.

"There you are, Captain," I said. "She's all set."

"Will she take me out to the Coast?"

"The Coast?" I was surprised.

"Yes," he said. "I've been transferred. I'm leaving right now."

You'd have thought he was just going down to Springfield to see the Ice Carnival instead of starting on a three-thousand mile trip. He was sure pretty casual about it, but I felt sorry when I realized that if I ever saw him again it would be a lucky accident. There were sure being some big changes made these days. I had one coming to myself, and the thought of it made me feel closer to the pilot than before.

I tapped the hood of his car with my knuckles and said: "She'll take you to the Coast easy. That's my last ring-and-valve job, so I made it the best."

"Your last one?" asked the pilot.

"That's right." I looked at his uniform and grinned. "I passed my physical like a breeze," I told him. "I'm going to Fort Devens tomorrow. I'm in it, too."

"You enlisted?"

"Sure I did."

"What about your garage?"

"Closing it up—except for my live-storage customers. Old Man Burke'll take care of them. Only a few left, anyway. People are saving tires and repairs."

The pilot nodded. He came over near me, and we stood together in the open doorway looking into the garage. My push broom leaned against the wall near a pile of dirt I'd gathered to throw out. Beyond, to the left, were the two hydraulic lifts, the fast battery charger, and the greasing set-up—all in swell shape. In the back room you could see lights reflecting from the polished windshields and fenders of cars in dead storage. For the hundredth time I noticed the blown bulb in the center line of overhead lights, and for the hundredth time in as many nights I told myself I'd put in a new one, but didn't.

I could feel the pilot's eyes on me. He seemed kind of quiet and thoughtful, like when people say good-bye for the last time. He said: "It's been nice doing business with you. You've run a good place. How long have you owned it?"

"Seven years."

"Seven years," said the pilot, "and this is your last night on duty." His voice was so low you could hardly hear him. "How will it seem to you?"

The pilot had something extra, all right. He saw into your mind. He asked you the very question you hadn't quite dared to ask yourself, as if he had guessed the secret thing you would miss most—and for me, that secret was Miss Laurie, who had stored her car in my place for more than a year.

There were a lot of things I'd remember in the months or years ahead of me, but I wouldn't miss them. I'd remember the white gleam of enamel on the casings of the motor analyzers; the thoughts that always crowded into me when I swept the dead flower petals from the undertaker's hearse; and the hiss of the valves operating the greasing lifts. Sure! All these and more—but they were nothing compared to Miss Laurie.

I had been trying not to think about Miss Laurie, but I couldn't help it now. Today, about four, when I had brought her car to her door, she had said: "Why, Tuck! You look so solemn. What's the matter?"

Nothing was the matter, except that I wanted to remember all of her forever. I wanted to get the sound of her voice fastened in my ears and the look of her high-boned face written in my eyes. I wanted to tell her this, but it wasn't in the cards, so I said: "Everything's okay, Miss Laurie."

While we were driving back to the garage, where she was to drop me off, she kept looking at my hands holding the wheel, and I worried about how they looked, with cracks in the knuckles, and my nails thick and broken from fussing around inside of engines. But at the garage she said, "Thanks, Tuck," as if I had done her a favor, when all the time she was doing me one just by being alive.

No one knew how I felt about her, least of all Miss Laurie. She was studying at the college for some kind of a degree, Master of Arts, I think. So it was plenty good enough for me just to sit beside her on the seat of her coupé, and see the copper lights in her hair, and exchange a few sentences with her that didn't mean anything, except to me.

Once when she was sick I sent her some roses, but didn't enclose a card for fear she'd think I was out of place. Next time I saw her she was wearing one of the roses in her hair. It looked red as fire against the whiteness of her forehead. I was so excited and surprised I could hardly talk.

"That's pretty, Miss Laurie," I managed to say. "That flower in your hair, I mean."

Her fingers touched my arm for a second, like a bird lighting on a limb. She took them away, but I could still feel them there. She looked down at my hands so long I wanted to hide them, and then she said: "Oh, thanks, Tuck. Someone sent me a whole dozen roses. I don't know who it was. I've been wondering."

"I wouldn't know."

"I must have a secret admirer."

"I guess you must have."

"It's all very mysterious and romantic."

"Yes, it sure is."

All of a sudden she turned her eyes up to mine, took the rose from her hair, and tossed it to me. I stood there after she had gone, holding the rose, feeling weak and strong by turns, and my heart big.

Right now I tried to tear my thoughts away from Miss Laurie. I didn't want the pilot to see that deep into me. But the memories began to jump out of the shadows. I could see Miss Laurie's face framed in the dark fur collar of her coat; her gloves lying on the seat of her car, holding the shape of her fingers; and the times I'd picked up the gloves and held them as if her hands were still inside.

She seemed so near, and yet so far. We lived in the same town, but in different worlds. Did she notice the little extra things I did for her? Did she have the faintest idea I did them because I loved her? Sometimes I thought she knew. But I was mostly afraid she would find out, and at the same time afraid she wouldn't.

I hadn't answered the pilot's question yet. He had asked how it would seem to go through the night routine for the last time. I really didn't know, so I just said: "Well, it's like this: tonight will be the same as any other night."

"No," he answered in that low, thinking voice. "Last nights are always different, even when you do the same old things."

He wrote out a check for the work I'd done for him, shook hands with me, and got into his car. As he drove down the cement apron to the street, he looked back at me and raised his hand in a slow-motion salute. "So-long, Tuck. I'll be thinking of you," he called, and was gone, and I never saw him again.

I dropped the elevating door and walked into the shop office through the small door. It was like the pilot had cast a spell over the place and over me. All my nerves seemed to rise up on tiptoe. He sure must have left a lot of places for the last time. He knew what it did to a man, all right. Things were the same—only different—even to the familiar night-sounds like the humming of the air compressor, the ventilator creaking in the wind, and the ticking of the time-clock.

I cut the switches on the four gas pumps and through the shop office window watched the four globes go dark. How many thousands of gallons had I fed from those pumps? How many miles did they represent and in what directions? I could hear the echoes of a thousand travelers' voices: "Fill her up. Check the oil. Twenty-eight pounds all around."

Before, I never thought twice about those words; but now they seemed to mean the destination of a race of restless people. It made me feel like singing. No matter where you were tomorrow, you couldn't be lonely with your memory full of ballast like that.

Without realizing it, I began to look around for more ballast. I lifted the memo pad from its hook by the cash register and glanced at the day's notations written by Old Man Burke, who had gone off duty at six. Old Man Burke called each car by its owner's name, and that way made his notes into wisecracks.

1. Wash Mr. Foss.
2. Mrs. Johnson won't start.
3. Dent in Mrs. Bemis. Not responsible.
4. Karowski's clutch slipping. The life he leads.
5. Give the Reverend Ward two quarts of alcohol. Ought to hold him for a spell.

I smiled, thinking of the fun old Man Burke got out of being disrespectful. But when I turned the page and read the next and last note, I could feel the smile changing to a different kind. My heart skipped like an engine with a stuck valve. Was the tall pilot some kind of prophet? No, that couldn't be. But he had made me feel that something big was going to happen to me, and this was it. The note was the promise of a perfect ending to my life of yesterday, and a perfect beginning to the new way of tomorrow. I read the words aloud, and I loved the sound and the meaning of them:

Miss Laurie will be late tonight.

Unless my live-storage customers notified the garage to the contrary, it was understood that I wouldn't stay open for them after midnight. Tonight, my last night, Miss Laurie was the only one who had notified. Old Man Burke must have taken the message while I was out buying parts for the pilot's car. I wanted to thank someone or something. I wanted to thank Miss Laurie, because my last duty would be to drive her home. How would it be in that little minute that always went so fast while she gathered up her purse and books from the seat? What would she say?

"Good night, Tuck. Thanks ever so much for staying open."

"That's all right, Miss Laurie."

She'd hesitate a second and look over at my hands on the wheel. Then: "Will you bring my car tomorrow about four?"

"Well, no. Old Man Burke'll bring it. I'm in the Army."

I couldn't make it any better than that, even in my imagination. It wouldn't go any farther. I'd watch her go up the steps to her apartment. She'd open the door, and it would close behind her. She'd disappear into her world, and I'd be left alone in mine. I'd drive her car back to the garage and store it on the Number One lift, forward near the door. I'd lock up for the last time and walk home along the empty, hollow-sounding street. My last memory would be of her. I couldn't have dreamed of a better break than that.

Now, because of tomorrow, and the spell of the pilot, but

mostly because of Miss Laurie, all the routine night-jobs seemed exciting to me, little jobs like fixing the furnace fire, wiping off the bulk oil pumps, and disconnecting the two air hoses.

While I was outside coiling the hoses, I noticed a man standing in front of the tavern next door. It was pretty dark in the street, but I recognized the man. He was Doc Bennett, and he was swaying a little, like always. In the days before he began hitting the stuff hard, Doc Bennett stored his two custom-built jobs in my place and gave me all his repair business. There wasn't much left of him now, only dignity. But a lot of people in our town owed their lives and their children's lives to Doc.

I put the two coiled hoses inside and walked out to where he was standing on the curb, trying to get his bearings.

"Hello, Doc," I said. "It's a cold night."

He turned to me and bowed, and his old, pale eyes recognized me in the darkness. "Good evening, Tuck. Yes, it's very cold."

My beach wagon that I used for odd jobs stood in the alley between the garage and the tavern. "Jump in, Doc," I said. "I'll give you a ride home."

He lived in a rooming house six blocks from the garage. I helped him up the icy steps, and he grabbed my hand and held it. "You don't forget your friends, do you?" he said.

"I try not to, Doc."

Someone had told him I was leaving for Fort Devens. "I shall miss you," he said. "I want to wish you God-speed."

"Sure, Doc. Thanks. You were swell to me when you had it."

He grabbed my hand again and hung on tight. "When I had it," he said, like an echo. "Well, in a way, I'm still helping your business. I brought some of your customers into the world. Did you know that?"

I'd never realized it, but I saw how it was likely. "You did, Doc? Who?"

"Let me think: there's that young Amherst student, Charles Atwood; and Ed Johnson's wife—Blanchard, her name was. And then that lovely Miss Laurie. Louise Laurie."

"Miss Laurie?" I said, gripping his hand hard. "Honest, Doc? Miss Laurie, that's studying for a degree at the college?"

"Yes."

I wanted to stay there a long time with Doc Bennett asking him questions about Miss Laurie and her family, things I could never find out by myself. It seemed wonderful, and strange, and somehow sad that this old, burnt-out man had brought Miss Laurie into the world. He was so old and tired, and she was so young, and beautiful, and full of life.

"Look, Doc," I said. "Any time you feel like a ride home, you just step into the garage and tell Old Man Burke. He'll see you don't walk. I'll leave a standing order—for the duration."

"The duration," he said. "It won't be long," and he swayed in through the door.

On the way back to the garage I realized that he didn't mean the war so much as himself. He didn't want to live any more. I parked the beach wagon in the alley and walked across the apron by the gas pumps. I saw the blue light shining like a dead eye through the stained-glass window of the funeral home next door. We used to laugh about the garage being centrally located between a saloon and a mortician's, but it didn't seem funny tonight. I remembered a time when Doc Bennett had said he wanted nothing but a colon engraved on his tombstone. He said a colon was a punctuation mark indicating that a lot had been left unsaid, unthought, and undone. I guess Doc knew a lot about death to make a statement like that. But he knew a lot about life, too. He had saved lives and made lives. He had made my life when he brought Miss Laurie into the world.

I went into the shop and looked over the check list of the cars out and in. Old Man Burke had it fixed accurately. The red tabs indicated cars out, and there were only three—Mr. Ayer, the County Treasurer; Professor Hartley, who taught English Literature at the college; and Miss Laurie.

It was dim and quiet in the garage. There weren't any sounds but the singing in my ears, my footsteps on the cement floor, and the ticking of the time-clock that no one punched any more. I looked up and noticed the blown bulb in the center line of lights again, and I said to myself once more: I ought to put in a new one. But I didn't. I just let it go, like a hundred other times.

Every now and then between jobs I'd go into the office, take the memo pad from its hook, and read the last note all over again just to make sure. The words were there, all right. *Miss Laurie will be late tonight.*

Will it be any different this last time, I asked myself? What will I say, and what will she answer? Why is she late tonight? Is she out with some guy from up at the college? What right have I got to wonder, even to my own self? It's just that I want to talk to her about the thoughts I've been having and the questions I've been asking myself about yesterday and tomorrow. I want to leave her some kind of souvenir of myself and take away with me a souvenir of her.

I was standing there by the cash register holding the memo pad when Mr. Ayer drove up outside and honked his horn. I dropped the pad and felt in my unionall's pocket to make sure my key was there. I sprang the lock on the shop office door as I went out. The elevating door was locked from the inside.

"Hello, Tuck," Mr. Ayer said. "Do you mind driving tonight? I'm tired."

"Sure," I said. "Okay."

He moved over, and I climbed in behind the wheel. We drove up Main Street and turned left on South where he lived. He began to explain why he was tired, and his voice sounded blue.

"I've been up at the Court House organizing the report center for air-raid alarms. Been there since eight o'clock this morning."

"You're sure doing plenty," I said. "And your own job on top of that."

He was quiet for a time before he answered: "I've got to do something to feel worthwhile. The Army doesn't want me."

"But in this war everyone's in the Army, and no fooling."

That seemed to cheer him up. He sat straighter in the seat,

and his voice brightened. "It would do your heart good to see them coöperating," he said. "The ones that work hardest at their regular jobs are most willing to take the tough tricks at the signal lights at night. Take Louise Laurie, for instance; works all day long studying for her Master's degree, and—"

"Did you say Miss Laurie? Louise Laurie?"

"Yes."

"Is she on duty at the report center?"

"Yes."

"So that's why she'll be late tonight."

"She'll be late, all right," Mr. Ayer said. "She's on four hours—ten till two. You're not staying open for her, are you?"

"Oh, I don't mind hanging around."

We had stopped in front of his house. The motor was idling, and I could feel him looking at me. After a while he said: "Well, Tuck—you're going to Fort Devens."

"Sure. Tomorrow morning."

He was feeling blue again. He got out of his car and stood with one foot on the running board. He was a swell, quiet guy. He had tried half a dozen times to enlist, but every time they turned him down because of his heart.

"I'll miss you," he said. "It won't be the same. We'll all miss you."

He took his foot off the running board, then reached in and shook hands with me. "So-long," he said, and turned away up the walk to his house.

On the way back to the garage I felt proud and kind of lonely to know that Mr. Ayer would miss me. Doc Bennett had said he would miss me, too. Would Miss Laurie? I didn't know, but somehow I wanted her to. I thought of all the good people who came to the garage, and how most of them seemed to have a place in Miss Laurie's world. Doc Bennett knew her family and all about her since she'd been born. Mr. Ayer worked with her at the report center. What was her world like, anyway? What did people talk about in places where she felt at home? I never figured I'd get even a glimpse of Miss Laurie's world, but I did, and it changed everything.

Professor Hartley's car was waiting on the apron when I drove up. I saw the twin tail-lights, and the headlights focused sharp on the elevating door. His motor was running, and the cold white vapor foaming out of the exhaust. I pulled up alongside and jumped out of Mr. Ayer's car.

"Sorry to keep you waiting, Professor," I said.

He had a thin, wonderful face. He was wearing a fur cap like teamsters used to wear and a wool scarf around his neck. He seemed happy and eager about something.

"I forgot to notify you I'd be a bit late," he said. "I've been out on the bridge spotting airplanes—ten to midnight shift."

"That's all right, Professor. There's one more car to come in, anyway. Was it cold out there?"

I parked Mr. Ayer's car in the garage near the wash-stand, then came out and got into Professor Hartley's car to drive him home. We started, and he told me he had heard a big plane going over high. He had reported it over the phone in the bridge pylon to Army Flash. You could feel the pride in his voice. He was an old man, but he was in there doing his stuff like the rest.

"The plane was doubtless from Westover Field," he said, "but we are instructed to report everything."

When I drew up in front of the professor's house, he reached over with his long, bony hand and switched off the ignition. "This is a special night, Tuck. You're leaving us. Come in a minute. We'll have a glass of sherry—a ceremonial."

I started to say no, but he was already out of the car and backing up the porch steps, moving his arms as if to draw me after him. It was the first time I had ever been inside the professor's living-room. It sort of got to me, and for a second I couldn't figure out why. It was a gentle kind of room, and you knew there had been a lot of thinking and conversation in it. You could smell pipe smoke, and a leather smell from the bindings of books. There was a fireplace with logs smouldering, and a pine table covered with books and papers. I looked down and read the title of one of the books: *English Literature in the Eighteenth Century.* Was Miss Laurie's subject literature? Did she read books like this?

The professor took off his fur cap, scarf, and overcoat. He motioned toward an easy chair, and said: "Sit down, Tuck. I'll pour some sherry."

I only half heard him. The dim light in the room was like a mist, and things seemed to move toward me from the mist. I only half saw the professor as he opened a cabinet and got out glasses and a decanter. He must have thought I was in a trance, but I wasn't. I was in Miss Laurie's world for the first time, and I could feel it folding around me.

"Here you are, Tuck," the professor said.

I took the filled glass and said "Thanks"—but in my mind I was saying: This is her world. I'm a little way in. I just stepped through the door into a place where she would belong. I can see her and feel her all around me here.

"Here's to you, Tuck," the professor said, raising his glass. "Here's to the day of your return. We all look forward to that day."

"Thanks," I said. "And—thanks for asking me in here."

"Ah! You like this room?"

"Yes, sir. I do. I love it!"

I had never felt so near Miss Laurie. I saw her in the room, her lips apart as she concentrated on a book. I saw the clean, white curve of her throat, and her hand going up slowly to touch her hair. Her voice came whispering to me from the mistiness of the room. What was she saying? She wanted something, and I didn't know what it was. There was a longing and a curiosity in her eyes. She came over close to me and looked down at the backs of my hands. . . .

Suddenly I wanted to go back quick to the garage and wait for her there alone. I wanted to be alone with my thoughts of her and of her world. It seemed wrong that anyone should be looking at me when I was thinking of her—even this kind old professor who had the shadows of wisdom in his sunken eyes.

"Tuck! You're not going so soon!"

"Yes, sir. I must go back now. There's one more car out. And thank you again for asking me in, sir. It's another good thing to remember."

He followed me half-way down the porch steps, then shook hands with me, and he was still waving when I turned the corner at the end of his street.

It was quarter of one when I got to the garage and backed the professor's car in beside Mr. Ayer's. I drove the beach wagon into a space by the far wall, and that left room for Miss Laurie's car on the Number One lift, forward.

I had never known it to be so still in the garage. The wind had died, and the ventilator didn't creak at all. You could just hear the time-clock, and then, when the motor in the professor's car began to cool and contract, you could hear the sudden snap of a loose baffle-plate in the muffler.

I tried to find things to do to make the time go faster. I soaked up chamois cloths that were already good and moist and tested the valves on the air compressor that I knew were already closed tight. Twice I saw headlights fan bright across the walls, and both times I rushed out—but it was only some night-owl turning around on the apron.

I went to the sink and washed my hands, dried them on a clean towel, and rubbed salve on the cracked places. Then I went to the shop office and took down the memo pad. I tore off a blank sheet and wrote a note to Old Man Burke: "Give Doc Bennett a ride home any time he wants it for as long as he wants it." But after doing all these things, the minute hand on the time-clock had moved only ten or twelve jumps.

I don't know what it was that made me remember a test they had given us years ago in high school. It just popped into my head as a good way to make the time pass. It was one of those psychological tests where they give you a word and ask you to write down other words it suggests. Supposing the key word was night. You'd write down dark, or black, or stars, or fear, or ghosts, or whatever.

I dreamed I was sitting at my old desk back in school, but it was really my desk in the shop office, and the key word was Louise Laurie. I closed my eyes tight and wrote whatever came—feeling my way along the paper with Old Man Burke's stub of a pencil.

So I didn't even see the lights of Miss Laurie's car. And I didn't hear a sound. I just opened my eyes and looked straight into hers. She was staring at me through the office window, her face close to the glass, and one gloved hand resting against the sash. She couldn't possibly have seen what I had written, but she knew it was about her. She knew from my eyes and from the way my hand went down to cover the paper—and in her expression I saw some kind of longing that half troubled me, and made me still.

I stuffed the sheet of paper in my unionall pocket and opened the shop door. "Hello, Miss Laurie."

"Hello, Tuck. You were kind to stay open so late for me."

She stepped to one side to let me pass, and I could feel her eyes following me. I got behind the wheel of her car, and she waited while I slid the seat back to make room for my legs. Then she got in beside me, and we started.

"I thought you were asleep when I looked in the window," she said. "But then I saw you writing, with your eyes closed. What did you write?"

"Nothing."

I drove a block, and another block, and all my thoughts and feelings seemed dammed up inside me, and there was no way of breaking the dam. There was frost on the windshield, and the soft hum of the heater fan, and the scent of her hair filled the car and flowed into my nostrils. This was our last ride together, and I hadn't said anything, and in five minutes we would be at her door. I felt choked with things I didn't dare say, and no time to say them.

"Tuck, aren't your hands cold without any gloves?"

"No."

Another block, and another, and I stopped the car beside her house. Here was the last minute that always went so fast—only this time she didn't gather up her things, but sat looking at me. I held the wheel tight, waiting.

"I guess I shouldn't have asked you to stay open tonight," she said. "It's your last night, isn't it?"

"Yes."

"I'm awfully sorry I was late."

"That's all right."

"But you're angry, Tuck—aren't you?"

"No."

"Then why are you so quiet?"

I tightened my hands still harder on the wheel, turned my head half toward her, and said: "I've been wondering about that myself. I guess I'm quiet because there's so much I want to say."

The heater fan hummed for a long time. She was looking straight into my eyes, then down at my hands. "What do you want to say, Tuck?"

"I'm glad you were late, tonight, Miss Laurie."

"Glad? Why are you glad?"

It was now or never. I had to tell her, even if she laughed at me, even if she hated me. I couldn't look at her when I said it. I made myself think of Professor Hartley's living-room. It kind of pulled me back a little way into her world and gave me the courage to tell her. "I'm glad you were late because you'll be the last one I'll remember. But maybe you would be, anyway."

I saw her eyes grow dark and wide. Her gloved hand moved a little toward me on the seat. The panel light gleamed white on her throat and showed me the strange, haunting expression on her face. She looked as if she had discovered something and didn't know whether it was true.

"You wanted me to be late?" she said. "You want me to be in your memory?"

"Yes."

"Why, Tuck?"

"Because it makes a perfect ending to yesterday and a perfect beginning for tomorrow."

Her hand moved a little closer on the seat, and the doubting, puzzled look came over her face again. "You—you really care that much for me, Tuck?"

"Yes."

"How long have you felt this way about me?"

"Over a year. Sometimes I thought I couldn't hide it. Sometimes I thought you could see it in my eyes. When you left your gloves in the car, I'd pick them up and hold them, as if your hands were inside."

"Did you? Did you really?"

"Yes."

I was all braced for her to laugh, or to say something cool and far away. But she didn't. She seemed happy because of what I had told her—happy, and quiet, and wondering. She put her fingers up slowly and touched my sleeve, and said: "My hand's inside, now."

I reached down and held her hand in mine. She drew her hand away, and took off her glove, and I kissed the tips of her fingers, one by one. I thought maybe I was dreaming. I thought it couldn't be true and that there was a trick somewhere. Then her voice came again:

"Did you send me those roses when I was sick last fall?"

"Yes."

"Why didn't you enclose a card?"

"I was afraid you'd think I was out of line."

"Why, Tuck? Why did you think that?"

"Because I run a garage, and you're a scholar."

She looked past me through the window and out into the cold, still starlight. "Tuck," she said, "is there any difference?"

There was a difference, but now, for a little while, it was either gone, or it didn't matter. We were just two people, close to each other in the night, and I didn't dare look beyond that.

She turned toward me, moving closer to me on the seat. She took both my hands and held them in hers, looking down at them, smiling in some strange secret way, her lips moving as if she were whispering to herself. I didn't understand how she could be so kind, so gentle, and so natural. I kept waiting for it to turn the wrong way and drop me flat, back where I had started.

"I want to tell you something," she said, all the while staring at my hands. "I want to tell you something good that you have done for me. I love your hands, and when they touch me I am real. When you talk to me and tell me what I mean to you, I am real. I am not in a library any more, reading words that were written two hundred years ago. I'm real, Tuck—I am a person, and I am needed. Do you know what I am saying?"

"No, I don't think I do, Miss Laurie—not quite. Only it makes me happy when you talk like that."

"Will you do something for me?"

"Yes. Anything."

She pressed her shoulder against me, tipped her head back, her eyes half closed, and said: "Put your arms around me and hold me."

I did, and her face looked happy, like a child's face when the child is asleep and dreaming of being always safe. I kissed her, and she pressed herself closer to me, then opened her eyes—and I saw the doubt again and the uncertain curiosity.

"Tuck, do you really feel that way about me? Will this, will tonight, will I, mean something in your tomorrow?"

"Yes."

"Tell me again."

I thought suddenly of the sheet of note-paper in my unionall pocket. I reached around with my left hand and fished it out and gave it to her.

"There. That's what I was writing when you came to the garage. It's just a few words and things that came into my head when I thought about you with my eyes closed, and let the pencil go along on its own."

She took the paper, leaned forward, and held it under the dash-light. With her head bowed, her hair swung forward, half hiding her face. After she had read, she put her hands up to her eyes, and I saw her shoulders shaking, and I figured the trick had been sprung on me at last.

"Go ahead," I said. "Go ahead and have a good laugh."

Her shoulders kept right on shaking, and I thinned myself away from her on the seat. "So it's funny, is it?" I said. "I ought to have known."

She brought her head up fast, looking at me as if I had struck her. "No! No! It isn't funny. It's beautiful," she said. She wasn't laughing. She was crying.

She hugged the paper against her, then spread it out under the light and read it again, and I read it again over her shoulder:

> 'Louise Laurie: sweet, sunlight, alone, love, hidden in me to take away, hope, peace, my darling, forever, the last time with her, to remember, to carry, to think, to dream about wherever I am.'

I still felt hollow and frightened from the feeling that she had been laughing at me. I had to make sure, just the way she had to make sure that I loved her.

"So you weren't really laughing," I said. "It didn't seem funny to you, after all."

"No. It's serious, and it's beautiful."

"Why are you crying?"

"Oh, I don't know, Tuck. I guess because I had been feeling helpless and useless, not meaning anything to anyone. And then, tonight, you come along—someone that does things, and you give me your love. You think your love isn't good enough for me, don't you?"

"Yes."

She nodded, smiling as if she thought I didn't understand what I was saying. She reached up her long, strong arms, and pulled my head down to hers, and whispered: "It's too good, Tuck. It's perfect. It's unselfish. And any woman who wouldn't be proud of it, to have and to hold, is shallow and cruel."

I held my face against her hair, and said: "Even if there's no future in it?"

"Even if there's no future in it, and who knows about that?"

Her arms loosened and slid down slowly to her lap, and I knew it was good-bye. She drew a long, tired breath, and gathered up her purse and her books, and put the sheet of note-paper in her coat pocket. "That's mine, Tuck," she said.

"It sure is."

She lifted her head back, kissed me once more, and said: "Good-bye, my darling."

The words rose up in my throat and caught, and I had to tear them loose for her: "Good-bye, my darling."

She got out of the car, walked to her front door, and stood there in the darkness, waiting for me to go. I put the car in gear, and let in the clutch. I never looked back, but I know she stood there till I was out of sight. I didn't have to look back. I could see the pale shape of her face in the night, written in my eyes for good. . . .

I parked Miss Laurie's car on the Number One lift and stood there for a while, looking at it. I wondered who would ride beside her on the seat. "Who will listen to her laughter?" I asked myself. "Who will feel the warmth of her lips and the pressure of her shoulder? Who will wake up in the night, remembering her eyes and touch of her hands? Why, I will!" I said it aloud in the empty, reëchoing garage. "I will, Tuck Roberts!"

I stood there looking around the garage, my heart singing and happy. I never felt so strong, or so happy, or so sure. I heard myself laughing, and it sounded pretty swell. I walked all around the place looking at things and touching them with my hands that Miss Laurie loved. Some hands, I thought! Some wonderful hands! Do something with 'em, Tuck! Quick!

So I went to the supply closet, got out a new bulb, and screwed it in the place of the blown one that I'd never got around to changing. The base of the bulb made contact in the socket, and it lighted bright in my eyes. "There," I said. "There—I'll just make everything perfect tonight, just the way Miss Laurie made everything perfect for me."

I turned off all the lights, tested both doors to see if they were locked, and went out into the street. Walking home that last time was like no other time. Miss Laurie was with me! Louise Laurie! I was thinking how you could lose a ring, a locket, or a picture. But I couldn't lose the memory of Miss Laurie. I would carry it with me wherever I went, because it was inside me, in my mind and heart, and I could never, never lose it—even if I died.

THE TEACHER COMMENTS

ASSUMPTION

For several hundred years English literature has sustained itself primarily on the assumption that men and women find each other attractive.

I do not know who said that, but whoever it was adequately stated the case for the love story. The Hollywood formula—Boy Meets Girl, and so forth—though so hackneyed in expression that we laugh at it, is nevertheless a sound one. The writer who can turn a comic or a moving love story will lack neither fame nor cake, nor icing for his cake. At all levels the subject is good, from lightest absurdity to deepest tragedy, and the number of successful writers of fiction who have not dealt with the subject in one way or another can be counted, if at all, on the toes of the left foot. It is a safe assumption that people will go on reading, and hence writing, about love for at least a few more generations.

Fashions, of course, change, which is a condition of their being fashions. There was a time when public taste demanded that the subject be treated with periphrastic and antiseptic delicacy: when legs were limbs, eyes were orbs, hair was locks, and it was highly indecorous to suggest that women were bipeds, let alone mammals. The last twenty-five years have witnessed a savage reversal of that fashion, which in turn brought its own, now already dated, clichés—"the breasts and buttocks school" somebody called it. But steadily, through all vicissitudes of taste, morals, and modes of expression, it has remained, as a popular song recently reminded us, "the same old story."

Always, however, there is much more to a love story than the mere element of love itself. Boys have been meeting girls and getting them since the race started, and everybody knows it. Like other stories, the love story must show something greater than the events it relates, than the mere achievement or loss, as the case may be. It must express a theme that verifies or denies some fact of experience, belief, or hope common to a lot of people. *Why* does boy get girl? In life, it is enough to say: because they like each other. In a story, the questioning must go much deeper: *Why* do they like each other? In life, you are often nonplussed by that question; in a story you cannot be. Is it love at first sight, an experience quite common in life and often immediately acted upon? If so, in a story, what prevents boy from getting girl in the first paragraph and thus finishing the story before it was fairly begun? "They met, they loved, they married," is formula enough for life, where much is taken for granted, where similarity of background, or propinquity, or what Theodore Dreiser called "chemism" is sufficient to account for most of the love stories you see enacted. In fiction, nothing can be taken for granted except the general assumption that "men and women find each other attractive." Even that must be hedged about with questions before it is useful to the writer: *What* men and *what* women find each other attractive and under *what* circumstances and *why?*

"Miss Laurie Will Be Late Tonight" is a very simple love story. Yet it answers the questions all love stories must answer. It's theme, its verification of a fact of experience, hope, or belief, is that boy gets girl because he very well deserves to. It is not only the brave who deserve the fair. Although Tuck Roberts exemplifies the bravery of his time by his enlistment, the qualities which get him Miss Laurie are his shy modesty, his kindliness, his all-round decency and worth, qualities which, we hope, win the fair quite as much as the single, simple quality of bravery.

In Chapter VI, we discussed conflict. Notice that in this story the very traits that resolve the conflict are also those which furnish much of the obstacle. Miss Laurie likes Tuck and is all ready for him on page 265; within the limits of feminine modesty, she does her best to show him so, but against the obstacles of Tuck's own shyness and modesty, her attempts achieve nothing, save to heighten the conflict. Notice, also, that Tuck's traits work in conjunction with circumstance (his job) further to heighten the conflict, as well as to give substantial reason for his shyness in the presence of Miss Laurie. Finally, that very circumstance is made part of the conflict's resolution, when Miss Laurie contrasts her own life of study and loneliness with Tuck's. Incidentally, right there is a fact of belief common to many people—it doesn't make any difference what your job may be if you are a worthy person.

What makes a love story interesting, then, is not so much the fact of love, but what the success or failure of that love shows about people in general.

BACKGROUND

Mr. Ware speaks of fidelity to background in his preface, and in another chapter I call attention to his closing two sentences. I wish now to call attention to another kind of background and the manner in which Mr. Ware treats it. Consider the backgrounds of the two chief characters of this story, that is, their personal histories. What do you know of them? Very little of Miss Laurie and hardly more of Tuck. There is nothing of their families; nothing of their social life; of their possible previous loves, jobs, aspirations, and so forth. You know, to repeat, very little—and it is plenty. In Chapter III, I ask: "How much information about character and place and circumstance is necessary for the reader to understand the story?" "Miss Laurie Will Be Late Tonight" is a good example of my answer: "A whole lot less than the beginner believes." What we learn about Tuck and Miss Laurie we learn from their present and not their past. The point is worth emphasizing again and again. Wherever possible, always try to make your characters self-revealing in the story itself and not in disjointed flashbacks or long passages of "omniscient" (see Chapter X) descriptive observation.

Nevertheless, Mr. Ware's point of fidelity to background is not to be dismissed or taken for granted. This is particularly true where background is familiar to almost everyone. It is true even where background is remote. Readers have a kind of perverted delight in catching a writer off base. Probably it gives them a feeling of superiority. Anyway, as one who has from time to time, suffered from a slip here, an inaccuracy there, I can tell you that what Mr. Ware calls your "writer's conscience" will suffer acutely from anything that isn't exactly right. And probably more than your conscience will suffer if you get into print. Inaccuracy, lack of fidelity to background is an editor's nightmare. There is a classic and probably not apochryphal story concerning an editor of a "Western" magazine. One of his writers described some gunplay in a story, and equipped a character with a Colt Frontiersman-model revolver. The time of the story was 1843, the place Texas. According to my information, not less than seven thousand readers wrote in, complaining that the Frontiersman model didn't come out of Hartford, Connecticut until 1844, that it probably couldn't have got to Texas for another year, and that therefore the writer was two years out on his chronology and consequently didn't know what he was writing about and what did the editor mean by trying to hornswoggle the public with such palpable balderdash? Cancel my subscription!

Fidelity to background pays bigger dividends, however, than mere protection against carping readers. Consider the following sentences from page 274 of this story:

> I had never known it to be so still in the garage. The wind had died, and the ventilator didn't creak at all. You could just hear the time-clock, and then, when the motor in the Professor's car began to cool and contract, you could hear the sudden snap of a loose baffle-plate in the muffler.

Almost everyone has heard the ticking and snapping noises of a cooling motor, and when you rehear them in a story, part of your experience is invoked, the illusion of time and place is strengthened, and consequently your interest and faith in the story is greatly increased. The problem lies in the selection of details. A garage worker might be quite as interested in reading about "the beveling of valves, the fitting of bearings, and the caster and camber angles of front wheels, as adjusted by a device called the 'Bean Front End Machine,'" but as incidental background to you and to me, it would mean little, which is why the waste-basket, and not the story, became the repository for what Mr. Ware once thought was "wonderful atmosphere." It would be possible, of course, to write a whole story involving the workings of a front-end machine which *would* interest you and me, but it would be *another* story. Readers like to learn about all sorts of things of which they are ignorant, and they like to experience the long familiar as well. Because this is a story based on the familiar, it is no place to introduce mechanical marvels. Fidelity to background must underlie fidelity to story; it cannot be a substitute or a diluent of story. For another warning, even when your background is most important to the story and the reader's illusion, don't overdo it or be too self-conscious about it. A recent good undergraduate story about airplane pilots was marred by too much use of technical jargon, especially in the characters' conversation on the radio-telephone. The reader got the impression that every other word was "Roger" or "over."

In considering the background of "Miss Laurie Will Be Late Tonight," mark Mr. Ware's use of sensuous detail. He invokes not only visual imagery, but also auditory (as in the sentences just quoted) and tactile ("Her fingers touched my arm for a second. . . . She took them away, but I could still feel them there.") imagery as well. Visual imagery is of first importance, for other images are often implicit in it, but the writer should remember that taste, touch, sound, and smell all carry strong associations, and he should attempt to enrich his writing by appeals to other senses as well as to sight.

X

THE WRITER COMMENTS

STRICTLY PERSONAL

The inclusion of "An Underground Episode" in this volume is the result of an accidental conversation on whether or not stories ever really happen. That is to say, could you lift a relation of events from life, write them as they occurred, and show for your pains a work of art or a story? Conceivably, actual events could arrange themselves so that with very little addition or deletion you might get a story. But in general you run the same risks as you would in reproducing dialogue verbatim, for in general the story emerges only by distortion of the original happening which may have suggested it. This has been demonstrated and reiterated elsewhere. It is a rule, and therefore must have an exception. "An Underground Episode" is, in that respect, exceptional.

The title of this preface, "Strictly Personal," is Mr. Bailey's description of what follows: "An Underground Episode" is a true story, or perhaps it would be better to say a story which happened. It was lifted bodily from the writer's personal experience. On the other hand, the interpretation of the adventure or the writer's viewpoint on what happened to him, is not real. The viewpoint did not take shape in the writer's mind during the event itself and is merely an item of perspective. The dialogue is as close to verbatim as memory permits; but between the episode and the writing several years elapsed, so one cannot be too certain.

Yet "An Underground Episode" is so completely factual that it serves to violate the rule of distortion so carefully propounded in previous chapters. There are no distortions, but there are three exaggerations. The story is extremely simple, being the account of a boy's crawling through a sewer pipe in order to facilitate its cleaning, and thus save his construction company the expense of tearing out the new-laid pipe and re-laying it. The writer himself crawled through the pipe. The actual distance, unforgettably, was 154 feet. In the story, the distance was lengthened to three hundred feet.

The writer is his own chief character, but he revised his age downward from twenty (actual) to seventeen (fictional). The motive for the exaggeration is clear. To a younger boy, the greater distance is a greater obstacle, and the greater the obstacle the bigger the story.

The episode actually took place on Thanksgiving Day, 1921, in the town of Ecorse, Michigan, on the outskirts of Detroit. The weather that day was cool and windy, with scattered clouds; but in the story the weather was changed to sleet, and the time to night, in order to heighten effect.

To the best of my recollection, everything else in the written story is actual, including, to my uneasiness, the name of at least one character. Nick Christopher was, and is, Nick Christopher. Alamo Laska is a fiction name for Paddy Sheehan. Stender is fiction for Steve Healy, who was then foreman for a small sewer-construction company, and is now head of the fabulous S. A. Healy Company, whose feats of tunnel construction are renowned, and whose recent exploit of buying the Stevens Hotel in Chicago and installing some of the tunnel men as chambermaids during a labor shortage has been recorded in *The Saturday Evening Post*—with pictures.

Since this is strictly personal, the writer adds for further gossip interest that not long ago he and Steve Healy had a reunion after twenty years. It was a curious and exciting experience. The Delaware Acqueduct which Steve was boring under a portion of the State of New York was twenty feet in diameter. The sewer pipe through which the boy struggled in "An Underground Episode" was eighteen inches! This seemed like an eloquent and monumental change, yet Steve remembered the writer's foul and terrifying journey in all detail as one of those experiences that befall people who work underground. To the writer it was, and still is, a nightmare.

As for the story itself, there is little to say. It might be called a journey-story—a movement through space from the mouth of an open pipe to the manhole at the opposite terminal. The entrance to the pipe is the story's beginning; the sensations inside the pipe are the story's development; and the arrival in the manhole where light and human beings await is the ending, or the "wow." Or perhaps the story is of a boy ensnared in his desire to prove himself worthy not only to himself, but to men whom he admires. At any rate, this boy, through foolhardy volunteering, found himself embarked on an errand too large for him. Reduced to still simpler terms, "An Underground Episode" is a record, and a faithful one, of sensation actually experienced. It appeared first in *Story* magazine, again in an anthology called *Story in America,* and recently in Whit Burnett's *Time to Be Young.*

An Underground Episode

THREE figures leaned against the slanting rain—Alamo Laska, Nick Christopher, and the boy who had run away from home. They rested on their long-handled shovels and, as they gazed into the crater which by their brawn they had hollowed in the earth, the blue clay oozed back again, slowly devouring the fruits of their toil.

Laska, the nomad, thought of the wild geese winging southward to warm bayous. Nick's heart, under the bone and muscle of his great chest, swelled with sweet thoughts of his wife and child who lived in a foreign city across an ocean. The boy felt the sting of rain against his cheeks and dreamed of his mother who seemed lovely and far away.

It was Sunday. The regular deep-trench gang lounged in their warm boarding-house and drank dago red, while out on the job the three men toiled alone. They breathed heavily, and the gray steam crawled upon their backs, for it was cold.

"Look at 'er filling in," growled Laska, "faster than a man could dig."

"Mud's get inna pipe," said Nick. "The Inspector make us tear him out if she fill any more."

Backed close to the edge of the crater stood a giant trench-digging machine. In the dusk it appeared as a crouched and shadowy animal—silent, gloomy, capable. But a broken piston had crippled its engines, and they were swathed in tarpaulin.

A long gray mound stretched away from the crater opposite

the machine. Buried thirty feet below the mound was the new-laid sewer pipe. From the bottom of the pit at the machine, the pipe ran a hundred yards horizontally under the surface, opening in a manhole. This hundred yards of new-laid pipe was the reason for the three men digging in the rain. They had dug eleven hours trying to uncover the open end of the pipe in order to seal it against the mud. But rain and ooze and storm had bested them. The bank had caved, and the mud had crawled into the mouth of the pipe, obstructing it.

"It's getting dark fast," said Laska, "an' we're licked."

"We can't do nothing more," said the boy.

Nick Christopher scraped the mud from his shovel. He looked up into the whirlpools of the sky. "In a year I go old country. I see my wife. I see my kid."

"Nick," said Laska, "go over to the shanty and get a couple of lanterns and telephone Stender. Tell him if he don't want the Inspector on our tail to get out here quick with a gang."

Nick stuck his shovel in the mud and moved away across the plain toward the shanty.

The cold had crept into the boy. It frightened him, and in the darkness his eyes sought Laska's face. "How could we clean out the pipe, even when the gang got down to it?"

"Maybe we could flush her out with a fire hose," said Laska.

"There's no water plug within a mile."

Laska said nothing. The boy waited for him to reply, but he didn't. Picking up his damp shirt, the boy pulled it on over his head. He did not tuck in the tails, and they flapped in the wind slapping against him. He was bare-headed, and his yellow hair was matted and stringy with dampness. His face was thin, a little sunken, and fine drops of moisture clung to the fuzz on his cheeks. His lips were blue with cold. He was seventeen.

Laska stared into the pit. It was too dark to see bottom, but something in the black hole fascinated him. "If we could get a rope through the pipe we could drag sandbags through into the manhole. That would clean her out in good shape."

"How could we get a rope through?"

"I dunno. Stender'll know." Laska walked over to the digging machine and leaned against its towering side. The rain had turned to sleet. "It's cold," he said.

The boy followed Laska and went close to him for warmth and friendship. "How *could* we get a rope through?"

Laska's shoulders lifted slowly. "You'll see. You'll see when Stender gets here. Say, it's freezing."

After a long time of waiting, a yellow light flamed into being in the shanty, and they heard the muffled scraping of boots on the board floor. The shanty door opened. A rectangle of light stood out sharply.

Swart figures crossed and recrossed the lighted area, pouring out into the storm.

"Ho!" called Laska.

"Ho!" came the answer, galloping to them in the wind.

They heard the rasping of caked mud on dungarees, the clank of shovels, the voice of Stender, the foreman. Lanterns swung like yellow pendulums. Long-legged shadows reached and receded.

The diggers gathered about the rim of the pit, staring. Stender's face showed in the lantern light. His lips were wrinkled, as if constantly prepared for blasphemy. He was a tall, cursing conqueror. Orders shot from his throat, and noisily the men descended into the pit and began to dig. They drew huge, gasping breaths like mired beasts fighting for life.

The boy watched, his eyes bulging in the dark. Hitherto he had thought very briefly of sewers, regarding them as unlovely things. But Laska and Nick and Stender gave them splendor and importance. The deep-trench men were admirable monsters. They knew the clay, the feel and pattern of it, for it had long been heavy in their minds and muscles. They were big in three dimensions, and their eyes were black and barbarous. When they ate it was with rough and tumble relish, and as their bellies fattened, they spoke tolerantly of enemies. They played lustily with a view to satiation. They worked stupendously. They were diggers in clay, transformed by lantern light into a race of giants.

Through the rain came Stender, his black slicker crackling. "They're down," he said. "Angelo just struck the pipe."

Laska grunted.

Stender blew his nose with his fingers, walked away, and climbed down into the hole. They lost sight of him as he dropped over the rim. The sound of digging had ceased, and two or three men on the surface rested on their shovels, the light from below gleaming in their flat faces. Laska and the boy knew that Stender was examining the pipe. They heard him swearing at what he had found.

After a moment he clambered up over the rim and held up a lantern. His cuddy, gripped firmly between his teeth, was upside down to keep out the wet.

"Someone's got to go through the pipe," he said, raising his voice. "There's fifty bucks for the man that'll go through the pipe into the manhole with a line tied to his foot. Fifty bucks!"

There was a moment of quiet. The men thought of the fifty dollars and furtively measured themselves against the deed at hand. It seemed to the boy that he was the only one who feared the task. He did not think of the fifty dollars, but thought only of the fear. Three hundred feet through a rathole, eighteen inches in diameter. Three hundred feet of muck, of wet black dark, and no turning back. But, if he did not volunteer, they would know that he was afraid. The boy stepped from behind Laska and said uncertainly: "I'll go, Stender," and he wished he might snatch back the words; for, looking about him, he saw that not a man among those present could have wedged his shoulders into the mouth of an eighteen-inch pipe. He was the only volunteer. They had known he would be the only one.

Stender came striding over holding the lantern above his head. He peered into the boy's face. "Take off your clothes," he said.

"Take off my clothes?"

"That's what I said."

"You might get a buckle caught in a joint," said Laska. "See?"

The boy saw only that he had been trapped very cunningly. At home he could have been openly fearful, for at home everything about him was known. There, quite simply, he could have said: "I won't do it. I'm frightened. I'll be killed." But here the diggers in clay were lancing him with looks. And Laska was bringing a ball of line, one end of which would be fastened to his ankle.

"Just go in a sweater," said Laska. "A sweater an' boots over your woolens. We'll be waiting for you at the manhole."

He wanted so desperately to dive off into the night that he felt his legs bracing for a spring and a tight feeling in his throat. Then, mechanically, he began to take off his clothes. Nick had gone clumping off to the shanty, and shortly he returned with a pair of hip-boots. "Here, kid. I get 'em warm for you inna shanty."

He thrust his feet into the boots, and Laska knelt and tied the heavy line to his ankle. "Too tight?"

"No. It's all right, I guess."

"Well—come on."

They walked past Stender who was pacing up and down among the men. They slid down into the crater, deepened now by the diggers. They stood by the partly covered mouth of the pipe. They were thirty feet below the surface of the ground.

Laska reached down and tugged at the knot he had tied in the line; then he peered into the mouth of the tube. He peered cautiously, as if he thought it might be inhabited. The boy's glance wandered up the wet sides of the pit. Over the rim a circle of bland yellow faces peered at him. Sleet tinkled against lanterns, spattered down and stung his flesh.

"Go ahead in," said Laska.

The boy blanched.

"Just keep thinking of the manhole, where you'll come out," said Laska.

The boy's throat constricted. He seemed to be bursting with

a pressure from inside. He got down on his belly in the slush-ice and mud. It penetrated slowly to his skin and spread over him. He put his head inside the mouth of the pipe, drew back in horror. Some gibbering words flew from his lips. His voice sounded preposterously loud. Laska's voice was already shop-worn with distance. "You can make it! Go ahead."

He lay on his left side, and, reaching out with his left arm, caught a joint and drew himself in. The mud oozed up around him, finding its way upon him, welling up against the left side of his face. He pressed his right cheek against the ceiling of the pipe to keep the muck from covering his mouth and nose. Laska's voice was far and muffled. Laska was in another world—a sane world of night, of storm, and the mellow glow of lanterns.

"Are you makin' it all right, kid?"

The boy cried out, his ears ringing with his cry. It reëchoed from the sides of the pipe. The sides hemmed him, pinned him, closed him in on every side with their paralyzing circumference.

There is no darkness like the darkness underground that miners know. It borrows something from night, from tombs, from places used by bats. Such fluid black can terrify a flame, and suffocate, and drench a mind with madness. There is a fierce desire to struggle, to beat one's hands against the prison. The boy longed to lift his pitiful human strength against the walls. He longed to claw at his eyes in the mad certainty that more than darkness curtained them.

He had moved but a few feet on his journey when panic swept him. Ahead of him the mud had built into a stolid wave. Putting forth his left hand, he felt a scant two inches between the wave's crest and the ceiling of the pipe. There was nothing to do but go back. If he moved ahead, it meant death by suffocation. He tried to back away, but caught his toe in a joint of the pipe. He was entombed! In an hour he would be a body. The cold and dampness would kill him before they could dig down to him. Nick and Laska would pull him from the muck, and Laska would say: "Huh, his clock's stopped."

He thrashed with delirious strength against his prison. He felt the skin tearing from the backs of his hands as he flailed the rough walls. And some gods must have snickered, for above the walls of the pipe were thirty feet of unyielding clay, eight thousand miles of earth below. A strength, a weight, a night, each a thousand times his most revolting dream, leaned upon the boy, depressing, crushing, stamping him out. The ground gave no cry of battle. It did no bleeding, suffered no pain, uttered no groans. It flattened him silently. It swallowed him in its foul despotism. It dropped its merciless weight upon his mind. It was so inhuman, so horribly incognizant of the God men swore had made it.

In the midst of his frenzy, when he had beaten his face against the walls until it bled, he heard a ringing voice he knew was real, springing from human sympathy. It was Laska, calling: "Are you all right, kid?"

In that instant the boy loved Laska as he loved his life. Laska's voice sheered the weight from him, scattered the darkness, brought him new balance and a hope to live.

"Fine!" he answered in a cracking yell. He yelled again, loving the sound of his voice and thinking how foolish yelling was in such a place.

With his left hand he groped ahead and found that the wave of mud had settled, leveled off by its own weight. He drew his body together, pressing it against the pipe. He straightened, moved ahead six inches. His fingers found a loop of oakum dangling from a joint, and he pulled himself on, his left arm forward, his right arm behind over his hip, like a swimmer's.

He had vanquished panic, and he looked ahead to victory. Each joint brought him twenty inches nearer his goal. Each twenty inches was a plateau which enabled him to vision a new plateau—the next joint. The joints were like small deceitful rests upon a march.

He had been more than an hour on the way. He did not know

how far he had gone, a third, perhaps even a half of the distance. He forgot the present, forgot fear, wet, cold, blackness; he lost himself in dreaming of the world of men outside the prison. It was as if he were a small superb island in hell.

He did not know how long he had been counting the joints, but he found himself whispering good numbers: "Fifty-one, fifty-two, fifty-three . . ." Each joint, when he thought of it, appeared to take up a vast time of squirming in the muck, and the line dragged heavily behind his foot.

Suddenly, staring into the darkness so that it seemed to bring a pain to his eyes, he saw a pallid ray. He closed his eyes, opened them, and looked again. The ray was real, and he uttered a whimper of relief. He knew that the ray must come from Stender's lantern. He pictured Stender and a group of the diggers huddled in the manhole, waiting for him. The men and the manhole grew magnificent in his mind, and he thought of them worshipfully.

"Seventy-six, seventy-seven, seventy-eight . . ."

The ray grew slowly, like a worth-while thing. It took an oval shape, and the oval grew fat, like an egg, then round. It was a straight line to the manhole, and the mud had thinned.

Through the pipe, into the boy's ears, a voice rumbled like half-hearted thunder. It was Stender's voice: "How you makin' it?"

"Oh, just fine!" His cry came pricking back into his ears like a shower of needles.

There followed a long span of numbness. The cold and wet had dulled his senses, so that whenever the rough ceiling of the pipe ripped his face, he did not feel it; so that struggling in the muck became an almost pleasant and normal thing, since all elements of fear and pain and imagination had been removed. Warmth and dryness became alien to him. He was a creature native to darkness, foreign to light.

The round yellow disk before him gave him his only sense of

living. It was a sunlit landfall, luring him on. He would close his eyes and count five joints, then open them quickly, cheering himself at the perceptible stages of progress.

Then, abruptly, it seemed, he was close to the manhole. He could hear men moving. He could see the outline of Stender's head as Stender peered into the mouth of the pipe. Men kneeled, pushing each other's heads to one side, in order to watch him squirm toward them. They began to talk excitedly. He could hear them breathing, see details—and Stender and Laska reached in. They got their hands upon him. They hauled him to them, as if he were something they wanted to inspect scientifically. He felt as if they thought he was a rarity, a thing of great oddness. The light dazzled him. It began to move around and around and to dissolve into many lights, some of which danced locally on a bottle. He heard Stender's voice: "Well, he made it all right. What do you know?"

"Here, kid," said Laska, holding the bottle to his mouth. "Drink all of this that you can hold."

He could not stand up. He believed calmly that his flesh and bones were constructed of putty. He could hear no vestige of the song of victory he had dreamed of hearing. He looked stupidly at his hands, which bled painlessly. He could not feel his arms and legs at all. He was a vast sensation of lantern light and the steam of human beings breathing in a damp place.

Faces peered at him. The faces were curious and surprised. He felt a clouded, uncomprehending resentment against them. Stender held him up on one side, Laska on the other. They looked at each other across him. Suddenly Laska stooped and gathered him effortlessly into his arms.

"You'll get covered with mud," mumbled the boy.

"Damn if he didn't make it all right," said Stender. "Save us tearing out the pipe."

"Hell with the pipe," said Laska.

The boy's wet head fell against Laska's chest. He felt the rise and fall of Laska's muscles and knew that Laska was climbing with him up the iron steps inside the manhole. Night wind smote him. He buried his head deeper against Laska. Laska's body became a mountain of warmth. He felt a heavy sighing peace, like a soldier who has been comfortably wounded and knows that war for him is over.

TEACHING AND THE ABSOLUTE

For several reasons I wanted to include "An Underground Episode" in the book. First, I wanted to use it as an exercise in humility. After we had completed several chapters, and I had read them over, it seemed to me that I had failed sufficiently to emphasize the general nature of the principles I was trying to set forth; that I had posed as a sort of oracular authority on the immutable and absolute laws of fiction. Perhaps that is because of a flaw in the plan of the book. I have always conducted my classes as seminars, insisting on one requirement only: the strictest informality. In Chapter I, I wrote: "It is no exaggeration to say that you will find no stories in life." Now, toss that statement at a group of lively students, who have been told to challenge, argue, contradict, refute or deny anything said from the podium, and your class begins to sound, in Jacques Barzun's wonderful phrase, like an aviary on fire. This requires Teacher, when the shrill panic has subsided, to take a big breath and really get into the problem. Lacking, in this book, the astringent presence of the students, Teacher must himself raise objections.

"It is no exaggeration to say that you find no stories in life." Well, here's one and an extremely good one. Explain, please.

From Mr. Ware's more than three hundred published stories, it would have been easy to pick a dozen that exemplified cleavage to a set of rules. But to learn a craft is more than to learn a set of rules. It is to learn, among other things, that no formulas by themselves will guarantee success, and that no broken taboos will automatically result in failure. If general principles will work fifty-one per cent of the time, or even less, knowledge of them is indispensable to the apprentice. It is our belief that they work much more than fifty-one per cent of the time, though certainly short of a hundred. There are only two absolutes of which you may be sure: "That is right which succeeds; that is wrong which fails."

Success and failure, however, are themselves relative terms. I recall a lady in a summer-school class of mine who had, fifteen years earlier, contributed some stories to one of the "quality" magazines. Various cares had interrupted her literary work, and now she wished to take it up again, principally, she told me, in order to make some money. In a conference at the end of the session, I advised her to submit one of her stories, which seemed to me ingenious and salable, to a pulp magazine. She was affronted. She bridled. Snatching the manuscript from my hand, she walked, tight-lipped, out of the office. Almost a year later to a day she returned, bringing with her the current issue of *Love Story* magazine. It contained the disputed story. "I tried it on every quality magazine, then on every slick," she told me. "Then I swallowed my pride and took your advice. It sold the first time out." In its own humble way, therefore, that story was a success, though a failure in terms of its author's ambitions. And its value to the writer, it is worth pointing out, was much greater than the check it brought: it taught her something about the nature of magazine fiction that she had to learn, one way or another, if she wished to write magazine fiction.

My explanation of the success of "Underground Episode," therefore, is partially this: It is a "right" story, an exception, as Mr. Ware says, to the principle of distortion of fact.

On the other hand, as Mr. Ware also points out, it is not an absolute exception. I do not wish to quibble over words, but the "exaggerations," as Mr. Ware calls them, are very close to what we elsewhere mean by "distortions." First, there is the lengthening of the distance from one hundred fifty-four feet to three hundred. Second, there is the reduction in the boy's age. Third, there is the change in the weather. These changes were made for the same reason that Web River's age and relationship to the dead man were changed, namely, in Mr. Ware's words, "to heighten effect."

There is yet a fourth change. Suppose the experience had happened to you, and you were telling it, either vocally or in a letter, to a friend. What person would you use? You would use, naturally, the first person. Why does Mr. Ware, who frequently writes first-person stories, here change to the third?

PERSPECTIVE

A story, in order to be told, must be "seen" by the writer in a certain, predetermined perspective. If you take an event and a character, or groups of them, and try to fashion a story from them, the story will be very largely conditioned by the particular perspective in which you make the reader see them. There are many possible perspectives in which the characters and events of a story can be placed, but one must be chosen, and the choice of such placing depends entirely on the effects the writer wishes to gain and on the kind of writer he is. Send two untrained people to report a fire; one will return with a vivid description of the flames searing orange against the night sky, the hum of the engines, the pigmy, ghost-like figures of the firemen atop the extension ladders. The other, perhaps, will be unconcerned with the physical aspects of the event, but will concentrate on finding out what the fire means to the inhabitants of the building.

In "Underground Episode" an important effect in Mr. Ware's telling of the story is the communication of a harrowing experience. Suspense heightens that effect—did he, or didn't he make it? Did he suffocate in the mud, or did he live? If the story were in the first person, logic would destroy that suspense; obviously "I" must have made it, or "I" wouldn't have lived to report it.

There is another reason for the choice of the third person: The story is an account of simple courage, of the triumph of valor over fear. As readers, therefore ordinarily skeptical people, we do not like to have a character boast to us, and that is what a first-person account of courage amounts to. We will accept virtues if they are presented in proper humility: Tuck Roberts' triumph, for example, is acceptable because of his endearing modesty. Rush Atwood's story raises no distaste in the reader because Rush is admitting that he made a mistake in thinking he was tough enough to transcend the needs of human sympathy. It amounts to this: We will take vice in the first person (Ring Lardner's "Haircut"), or unconscious yet triumphant foolishness (Upson's Alexander Botts), or grief or satire, or emotional problems, but not unqualified virtue. That is to say, our generosity in fiction is just about what it is in life—are the people we think good those who go about telling us they are? If a friend were telling us this story vocally, we should be interested in it as a thrilling experience, but we should be annoyed if he did more than confess his fear. To be sure, Mr. Ware makes no explicit point of the boy's courage, but it is implicit in the boy's relation to the men, and why he goes through with the job. Although we might admire our friend for his courage, if he told the story modestly, yet we should resent his conceit if he told it as a fable of courage.

POINTS OF VIEW—THE THIRD PERSON

In order to place a story in perspective, it is necessary to establish a point of view, a coign of vantage, from which the events are to be seen, felt, and understood; from which, that is, they are to be told.

Probably nine writers out of ten choose for the point of view of a given story that taken by Mr. Ware in "An Underground Episode"; they chose the third person. Mr. Ware is himself the tenth writer; despite the high proportion of first-person stories in this book, he tells me that his overall proportion of third-person stories is five to one. We may say that third-person point of view is the normal one, the one the beginner will probably be wise to choose for his early stories.

There are, however, four distinct ways of presenting a story through the third person. First, the writer reports events with a flat objectivity, telling his story and explaining his characters only by what they say and do, not by what any one of them *thinks, feels, hopes, fears, interprets,* or *understands.* The writer shows us only the exterior manifestations of such mental and emotional activity, he does not report them directly. This book contains no example of the method; the reader is referred to Hemingway's "The Killers" as a famous illustration. The story is a vivid study of arrogance and fear reported solely through dialogue and action, but principally through dialogue. This is a difficult method for the beginner because it removes from his use the rich veins of direct emotion—it must all be translated through speech and action. For the same reason, however, it offers a most valuable exercise in the selection of telling details. Probably you have a friend or relative whose total personality you love, but who possesses irritating qualities and traits that sometimes exceed your endurance. You fight. What precipitates the fight? What specific words or actions, lifted out of the emotional context of your relationship, could you report to a stranger that would enlist his sympathies on your side? Or what gestures, looks, and words tell you that your instructor is angry or delighted with your work—or simply indifferent to it? In general, how do emotions manifest themselves? How do words intended to convey one emotion, betray its opposite?

These questions are worth long pondering and hours of exercise.

In the second method of third-person presentation, the writer tells everything from the limited point of view of one character's thoughts and soliloquies. This is the so-called "stream-of-consciousness" method, and it is one that must be presented to beginners with several warnings. Here is an excerpt, compounded to show a few of the pitfalls into which the beginner is likely to stumble:

> Good Heavens! she thought, she'd almost forgotten. Day George gets back. Looked a mess. Had to buy new hat. Ugh! Certainly didn't like *that* one! Did she have money? Yep. Lipstick? Yep. "Oh, hel-*lo* Mrs. Yorrell. I'm certainly glad to *see* you." (Lousy old sack. Always hated her. Hope she knows. God, would she, Mirabelle, ever grow to look like that? "For at my back. . . ." Ugh!) But now this hat she had to buy . . .

And so on. Where the idea came from that stream of consciousness should be written in pidgin English and what somebody has called the "non-sentence," I can't guess, but it seems to be a fixation with beginning writers. The stream of consciousness, as a technique in fiction, is neither very new (you find it in the eighteenth century), nor very daring. In unskilled hands it can become boring; often the writer, indulging in this free association of ideas, fails to corset them, and they bulge out into all kinds of irrelevances and sometimes just plain showing off, as in the next-to-last-sentence of the excerpt above. Nevertheless, for some kinds of stories the method is extremely effective, for it allows a more complete immediate presentation of total personality than any other third-person approach can achieve. It would, for example, be an effective point of view for telling the story sketched in Chapter II about the girl on the train. The danger would probably be temptation for the writer to tell us too much about the shopping expedition and the girl's friend, at the expense of the story proper. Often, the skilled writer puts the stream-of-consciousness story in the first person—excellent examples are Dorothy Parker's "The Telephone Call" and "The Waltz."

The third method of telling a story through the third person is exemplified by those stories in which the chief character is presented explicitly to the reader as something other than what he thinks he is.

> The interpretation that others put upon Caldwell Cadwallader's appearance and acts was not the interpretation he put upon them. That

gentleman, surveying himself in the mirror, adjusting his assertive tie, patting the thin hair that clung reluctantly to his pate, was pleased with what he saw. He smiled as he thought of the events on the day's calendar, events that, it seemed to him, must surely bring his life to a new apex of satisfaction. But if he could have known what was going on in the mind of a certain person who, on the other side of the city, was at the moment also looking into a mirror, he would have faced the day with very different emotions.

"If Caldwell Cadwallader shows up at this thing," Gwendolyn told herself, as she drew lipstick across her mouth, "I'll—I'll *kick* him!"

This method is often good for opening situations, after which the writer takes up with a protagonist and follows through with the rest of the story. It requires that the writer address the reader directly, in a tone which implies that he knows everything about the character he is describing—in fact, this method has been described by Miss Mirrieles as "omniscient." It allows the writer to do almost everything in the way of interpretation, explanation, and the giving of information, and therein lies its danger. It puts the writer too much into the story, forces him upon the reader, tempts him toward coyness, and causes irony and satire to have a heavy-handed, obvious quality. It is, however, sometimes useful for broad, comic effects.

We come, then, to the fourth method of third-person telling. Here, the author chooses one protagonist through whose eyes, emotions, thoughts, and experience the story's perspective will be established and maintained. It is the method used in all the third-person stories in this book and in the great majority of all stories whether they are written for the pulp or quality-group magazines. In short, it is the normal way to write a story, and the beginner is advised to use it most of the time. It is the freest method, allowing the writer to enter or withdraw at will from the mind of the chief character, to describe his actions objectively, to describe vividly scenes and events of which the chief character may be only dimly aware, and to use thinking and feeling without putting them into the stream-of-consciousness form. Study the third-person stories in this book, and note the flexibility of this point of view.

Note also, however, the limitation that is put upon the writer. Once you have chosen and introduced the person from whose point of view the story is to be told, you must not change it, save with rare exceptions, and then only at your peril. You will see professional writers occasionally changing point of view from one character to another, but not very often. In the Raleigh series, Mr. Ware indulges in one or two such changes. On page 168 of "In the Reign of Jeff Raleigh," for example, we enter Alice's mind for a paragraph or two, and at the end of "The Rampage of Baby Raleigh" we shift for a moment into Mr. Corfu's point of view with the first sentence of the last paragraph.

But the warning to stay with your chosen protagonist must be heavily emphasized. The logic of this limitation is largely the logic of life itself. If you are in a roomful of people, you don't really know what is going on in the mind of anybody but yourself. Speech and actions are indications, yes, but not—as both experience and stories are constantly demonstrating—conclusive proof. You may think you are pleasing somebody, but how do you know that the person's manifestations of pleasure are genuine? You don't know; you can only surmise. To preëmpt the contents of more than one mind, to see a given event through more than one pair of eyes simultaneously, is to violate this logic. The reader's "willing suspension of disbelief," which is as important to fiction as Coleridge said it was to poetry, is the writer's most precious asset. If you tell me one minute what Gregory is thinking, the next what Susan is thinking, and the next what Aunt Minnie is thinking, you are going to confuse me, irritate me, and make me skeptical. "How do you know?" I demand, and you haven't a logical answer. At that point the suspension of disbelief itself suspends. I have lost faith in the illusion your story is trying to maintain, and hence you no longer have a story, for it is a condition of a story that it be a piece of writing somebody wants to read.

One or two exceptions to this pretty hard and fast rule may be mentioned. A character, at the moment of his introduction, may be described objectively or omnisciently. In "The House That Jeff Built," for example, Alice's father is introduced in the following sentence: "At sixty-one, Cornelius Ross was a bald dynamo of information, vitality, and decision." But consider that Jeff knows this, and might himself have so described his father-in-law, and note that from then on Mr. Ross reveals himself entirely by what he says and does. Here is where the rules for revealing character, as given in Chapter II, apply. When you use the normal third-person point of view, your protagonist reveals himself by what he says, thinks, does, and by what other people say, think, and do about him. What other characters think must be revealed by what the protagonist thinks of them and by what they say and do—but not by what they think.

For another exception, there is the story whose theme is the varying reactions of a group of people to the same event. This kind of story is, in reality, a series of stories welded into a whole by the intensity of the author's purpose. For example, a number of small-town citizens portray, with ironic accuracy, the true character of a recently deceased and famous native son. But this is a difficult story form, because of its structural monotony.

On the whole, these and other exceptions he may see need not perturb the beginner. If his story demands that he transcend principles, then of course he must do so. Until he is confronted with such a story, however, let him remember that in normal third-person telling the point of view should almost never be shifted from one character to another.

POINTS OF VIEW—THE FIRST PERSON

Contrary to popular belief, there is no editorial prejudice against first-person stories. But there are many difficulties of technique, especially for the beginner. Two of them have already been mentioned with reference to "An Underground Episode": "I" must not tell fables about his own virtue. What "I" can do is tell fables about his mistakes, foolishness, nastiness, grief, and so on.

Stories in the fishing and shooting magazines, however, show notable exceptions to this limitation. Pick up any copy of *Woods and Rapids,* and you will see several first-person stories that recount, with a smug burp of self-satisfaction, how "I" finally outwitted the old lunker (buck) that for years had made fools of all other fishermen (hunters). Here, however, the use of "I" has specific function: It gives the reader the illusion, particularly if the story is accompanied by a photograph of warrior and defunct monarch, that somebody really did go fishing or shooting and bring back something, that it isn't all just a figment. Most people read the sporting magazines with more than simple amusement in mind. They want to know how the thing was done in order to gain useful information about their hobby. Although this is really getting into the field of pretty specialized writing, sometimes the same technique can be applied to stories for general magazines. I once read a hilarious story about some married people in an argument as to whether husbands or wives had the harder job. The husbands contended that the wives failed to use imagination in housekeeping, and to prove their point rigged up a sort of Rube Goldberg contraption for dishwashing that really worked! Any housewife—and nowadays when Daddy does his share of the housework, any husband as well—is going to have an already generated interest in such story material!

Another difficulty with first-person treatment is that, like the stream-of-consciousness method, it tempts the writer toward indulgence in irrelevancies. During composition, the writer's identification with "I" is so close that he finds it hard to keep the story properly focused. Mr. Ware makes this admission in the closing sentences of "Miss Laurie Will Be Late Tonight." It is a point to be emphasized, for the line between fidelity to background and irrelevance to story is often thin. When in doubt, sacrifice background.

Just as there is more than one way to present third-person point of view, so there is more than one way to use first. In this book there are five first-person stories, and they show three different uses of the first person.

In "Last Trip Together," "A Place to Cry," and "Miss Laurie Will Be Late Tonight," the narrator is the chief character. In "Some Have to Get Hurt," the narrator's part in the action is subsidiary to that of the boy, although by the story's end, we see that the narrator really carries the story's theme. In "Weather Prophet," the narrator is only an observer, totally unimportant to the action of the story, his only function being to report what occurs.

It is worth asking what effects a change from first person to third would have on any of these stories. I believe that "A Place to Cry" and "Miss Laurie Will Be Late Tonight" could be transposed to third person with very little change, save in the verb forms. Try it. What would be lost, what gained? It is my belief that a majority of professional writers would have told those two stories in the third person, and that the explanation for Mr. Ware's use of the first is purely personal—it's the way he happened to "feel" them. That is, of course, always a most important consideration; despite the fact that the comment in this book has emphasized technique, neither Mr. Ware nor I, as we have elsewhere said, believe that you can write stories simply by following a set of technical principles.

To consider the other three stories, however, is to see that a change in point of view would cause great differences in the telling. How else would you report Web River's stream of consciousness—or, perhaps more accurately, his stream of soliloquy? And how would you achieve the complexity of "Some Have to Get Hurt" if the story concerned only the boy himself? As for "Weather Prophet," the things Mr. Ware was trying to accomplish demand first-person presentation and no other: only the detached observer, who plays no important part in the story, could solve the problems posed by the off-stage happenings.

Choice of a point of view depends, then, on a number of factors: what you are trying to tell, how you want to tell it, and how and what you "feel" about your material. Let the writer be willing always to experiment; he may often find that problems that appear insoluble when told from a certain point of view will evaporate if the perspective is changed.

SPACE-FRAME

Before finishing with this story, I wish to point out a feature which adds to its compression and hence intensity. Not only has the story a time-frame—the time it will take the boy to go through the pipe—but a distance-frame as well. Those three hundred feet of pipe comprise almost the whole story. Frequently, the placing of a story within a distance-frame, as well as a time-frame, may prove of value to the writer in organizing events. "At five o'clock this afternoon, I have to meet a man four hundred miles away." Will I make it? What will happen on the way? Why must I see him at five, and not at quarter past five, or six? "Weather Prophet" is another story with a space-frame; it answers the questions posed above.

[illegible]

[illegible] the problems [illegible] [illegible] problems that arise [illegible]

[illegible]

[illegible] as well [illegible]

Index